# LOUISIANA NOTARY EXAM
# OUTLINE TO THE 2022 STUDY GUIDE

*A Simpler Summary of the Official Book*

Michele Childress

QUID PRO BOOKS
New Orleans, Louisiana

Copyright © 2022 by Michele Childress. All rights reserved. No part of this book may be reproduced or shared, in any form including copying of the digital files, without written permission by the author. No copyright is claimed in quotations from the state study guide, which is quoted in occasional portions, and summarized and paraphrased throughout, as a matter of fair use for academic purposes.

Published in 2022 by Quid Pro Books.

ISBN 978-1-61027-458-6 (trade paperback)
ISBN 978-1-61027-457-9 (ePUB)
ISBN 978-1-61027-456-2 (mass mkt. pbk.)

QUID PRO BOOKS
5860 Citrus Blvd., Suite D
New Orleans, Louisiana 70123
*www.quidprobooks.com*

This information is provided to aid comprehension of notary practice and procedure, and of the Louisiana notary examination and its official study guide, and should not be construed as legal advice or the practice of law. Please consult an attorney for inquiries regarding legal matters. For information on how to contact the author about this guide (corrections are welcome!), see the About the Author section at the end of the book.

Publisher's Cataloging-in-Publication

Childress, Michele.

Louisiana Notary Exam Outline to the 2022 Study Guide: A Simpler Summary of the Official Book  /  Michele Childress.

p.  cm. .

Series: *Self-Study Sherpa Series*, #8

ISBN 978-1-61027-458-6 (trade pbk.)

1. Notaries. 2. Notaries—United States. 3. Notaries—Louisiana. 4. Notaries—Louisiana—Handbooks, Manuals, etc.  I. Title. II. Series.

KF8797 .C56 2022                                                                                                                          2022538792

Cover design copyright © 2022 by Quid Pro, LLC. The Self-Study Sherpa Series image of the munching mountain goat, *Sherpa*, is a trademark of Quid Pro, LLC, with original artwork © by Mary Ruth Pruitt, used by permission and with the thanks of the author. The author also acknowledges the helpful editorial suggestions of Alan Childress.

Fourth trade paperback printing, September 2022.

# Contents

Notes of the Series Editor ................................................... i
1. The Role of the Notary in the Civil Law Tradition ......................... 1
2. The Civil Law in Louisiana .............................................. 3
3. The Notary's Role in Louisiana .......................................... 4
4. Louisiana's Court System ................................................ 5
5. Sources of Law and Legal Authority ...................................... 8
6. Registry and Recordation ............................................... 12
7. The Office of Notary Public in Louisiana ............................... 16
8. Things and Ownership ................................................... 26
9. Servitudes ............................................................. 32
10. Donations ............................................................. 42
11. Obligations and Contracts ............................................. 51
12. Persons, Family, and Marriage ......................................... 61
13. Sale .................................................................. 71
14. Lease ................................................................. 77
15. Mandate and Representation ............................................ 84
16. Suretyship ............................................................ 90
17. Security and Pledge ................................................... 95
18. Mortgage ............................................................. 100
19. Juridical Acts ....................................................... 110
20. Oaths ................................................................ 124
21. Forms of Conveyance and Mortgage ..................................... 125
22. Property Descriptions ................................................ 136
23. Titled Movables ...................................................... 140
24. Successions and Testaments ........................................... 147
25. Trusts ............................................................... 167
26. Public Inventory ..................................................... 173
27. Small Succession ..................................................... 175
28. Business Entities .................................................... 177
29. Miscellaneous Acts and Forms ......................................... 185
30. Caveat Notarius ...................................................... 191
About the Author ......................................................... 193

# MORE NOTARY EDUCATION RESOURCES FROM QUID PRO BOOKS

## Books

Sold online at Amazon, B&N, etc., and such eBook sites as Kindle, Nook, Apple, and Kobo.

*Louisiana Notary Exam Sidepiece to the 2022 Study Guide: Tips, Index, Forms—Essentials Missing in the Official Book*, by Steven Alan Childress (2022)

*Louisiana Notary Exam Sample Questions and Answers 2022: Explanations Keyed to the Official Study Guide*, by Steven Alan Childress (2022)

*Become a Notary Public in Louisiana: Process and Possibilities*, by Steven Alan Childress (2021)

*Louisiana Civil Law Dictionary*, by Gregory W. Rome and Stephan Kinsella (2011)

## Webinars

Remote education found at *www.notarysidepiece.com*, and registered with the Secretary of State

"The Big Picture" seminar

"The Final Lap" seminar and sample-exam workshop

"I Passed — Now What?" practical seminar

# Notes of the Series Editor

The Louisiana notary examination is famously difficult. Its pass rate averages about 20% each administration, including some as low as 6% (March 2021). Part of the difficulty is the required state "study guide," *Fundamentals of Louisiana Notarial Law and Practice*, currently in a 2022 purple edition. Even though the exam is open-book (allowing you to use only that study guide), most people find this 705-page text to be difficult to understand, navigate, and keep straight as they go. It's not well-organized, and even at the sentence level, it presents a challenge. It lacks an index. Of course, it has important and interesting information essential to passing the exam and becoming a notary public. But it's long, repetitive, legalistic, and—most of all—just plain hard to read. This is especially true today, as the study guide has expanded by leaps and bounds over the past few years.

Out of this tradition grew a need for other study resources, in addition to classes or webinars many candidates take. Books, including several also found in this *Self-Study Sherpa Series* (see the list of Quid Pro offerings on the previous page), share exam information, study tips, cross-references, index entries, examples of notarial acts, and practical advice. Classes, though not required to take the exam, are often helpful to explain notary law and exam info, too. (Michele and I offer shorter introductory and review seminars remotely at *notarysidepiece.com*, besides my full-length course at Tulane.) Certainly many people pass without taking a class, as there are many ways to prepare successfully. Study groups, in-person or on Facebook, provide helpful support as well.

So you may think it's a stretch to offer a new book into this mix. But when Michele and I were discussing what written materials would be really helpful to people preparing for the exam—but not already generally available—we kept coming back to one missing piece to the puzzle: an outline summarizing, as simply as possible, the study guide itself. We didn't perceive this need alone; we had heard from students and Facebook posters a consistent question: why isn't there a summary of this very long book? And many of the resources mentioned above have smaller portions of summaries of parts of the study guide. Probably some teachers of notary prep have given their students materials that summarized parts of it, too. But we couldn't find anything the public could purchase, certainly at an affordable price, that outlined the study guide comprehensively and as simply as possible, explaining concepts along the way.

So Michele took on this project and offers it with the hopes that it fills that need for you. She comes from a world where such outlines are a common and necessary part of exam prep. In law schools and before taking the bar exam, students use outlines all the time, starting from 1L year. Most of all, no one goes into the bar exam without reading commercial outlines from Bar-Bri, Kaplan, or another provider. We were very familiar with the format, organization, and even tone of these books. We wanted to bring that universe of help to the world of Louisiana notary prep.

Extending traditional *legal* study aids to *notary* prep makes particular sense in Louisiana. Unlike in common law states, where notaries have very limited duties, the civil law notary must know the *law* of property, sales, contracts, relationships, mortgages, trusts, and even estate planning. They write wills, small successions, leases, donations, and affidavits in a way that would be illegal for non-lawyers in any other state. That's part of the reason the study guide is so long, detailed, and difficult, to be fair.

As a result, the notary exam in this state—and no other—is considered to be a *mini-bar exam*. It just made sense to us that the typical bar exam materials that we (and everyone) used to pass the bar would come to the world of notary exam prep, too. And I personally considered Michele—with her two decades of experience in notary and legal practice, understanding of Louisiana substantive law, and gift for breaking down a hard concept into its most elemental form—to be the right person to write this outline.

# LOUISIANA NOTARY EXAM OUTLINE TO THE 2022 STUDY GUIDE

We hope you find this useful as you read and navigate the state study guide and prepare to pass the notary exam. Of course, it's not allowed during the exam (just as bar exam outlines aren't used the day of). So, it's still advisable to index, cross-reference, and mark up the study guide itself for exclusive use that day. But getting to that point, and making it over the line successfully, ought to be significantly aided by having a breakdown of the guide at your fingertips.

*Some notes on conventions:*

- The outline is presented as much as possible in bullet-point format.
- Page citations to the *Fundamentals* study guide are inserted in a lighter font so as not to distract too much but be handy to match up with the official text.
- References to Louisiana Civil Code articles and other statutes are provided in this font as well, and often assist the reader to locate the particular part of the page in *Fundamentals* to review.
- These lighter-font citations also serve as the appropriate punctuation for that passage, replacing either a period or a comma as needed. And generally throughout, punctuation and clutter is minimized, as long as the phrasing is clear.
- Cross-references to related passages or chapters are typically noted in parentheses.

Best of luck!

STEVEN ALAN CHILDRESS
Professor of Law, Tulane University
April 2022

# 1

# The Role of the Notary in the Civil Law Tradition

- There is an international organization of civil law notaries, the Union International du Notariat Latin, which includes notaries from France, Spain, Italy, and most Latin American countries p 3
- This organization is possible because most notary functions are the same in civil law countries p 3
- The duties of the notary in the civil law countries: p 5
    - Are lawyers who perform quasi-public functions with rigorous training
    - Authenticate declarations made by parties to legal transactions
    - Provide their documents with a fixed date; and keep the originals in their custody
    - Determine if title to land is marketable

## The concept of the notary as a public official

- Status as a public official flows from the notary's license/commission to practice as a notary, which is conferred by the state p 6
- Public character of the notary is reinforced by strict standards enacted by the state regarding record keeping p 6
- Concept of notary public as a public official exists in most civil law jurisdictions p 6
- "Public official" as applied to the notary is independent of any branch of government and unrelated to functions handled by public bureaucrats p 6
- The number of notaries is not fixed by law in Louisiana, but the governor may declare a moratorium on notarial appointments p 7

## The function of the notary as a multi-party counselor

- Not confined to preparing and authenticating documents.
- May act to seek to harmonize opposing interests, such as agree on the terms of a sale (while not practicing real estate if not a licensed real estate agent, because practicing real estate without a license is also against the law).
- May, very narrowly, perform any act necessary or incidental to the exercise the powers and functions of the office of notary public, while definitely not practicing law. The unauthorized practice of law is forbidden and may cost you your commission.
- His role is one of the highest degree of responsibility, but is different from that of attorney and client p 8
- In drafting documents, he must: p 8
    - Avoid possible future annulment of the act he is drafting

- o Advise the parties that there may be legal consequences to the act, including tax liabilities

## The Authentic Act

- A document which authenticates the signatures of a transaction p 8
- Considered full proof of the acts recited in the document p 8
- Authentic act is full proof of the existence of what the notary has seen or heard personally, which is that the parties appeared before him and swore before him that the statements were true p 8
- To rebut an authentic act, it must be impeached p 9
- Authentic act requires that the notary attests that he knows the parties, that the parties have legal capacity, that the parties and the witnesses have read the act and had any consequences explained to them, and that the parties manifested their consent and accepted the transaction p 9
- It is so full of redundant authentications that it is difficult to disprove its validity
- In some civil law countries, the notary has the duty to keep and maintain the original authentic act p 9
- A copy of every act involving the transfer of real property is filed in a central office so they may be examined p 9

## The role of the notary as conveyancer

- In civil law jurisdictions, a notary can act as a title agent, preparing the closing documents and sale documents for immovable property p 9
- Property must be meticulously described, along with price, encumbrances, and ensuring that taxes have been paid
- In some civil law countries, notaries can act as an escrow agent, holding monies pending the search of the title records p 10

## The notary and the registry system

- Notaries have to be familiar with the different registry systems: p 11
  - o Land/title registry
  - o Court registry for authentic acts, marriage contracts
  - o Corporate filings
  - o Testamentary filings

Note: The introduction to the definition and rules for the Authentic Act is useful because it foreshadows more detailed discussions in Chapters 11 and 19. Much of the rest of this chapter is about civil law notaries in other countries, but does not apply to non-attorney notaries in Louisiana. For example, such Louisiana notaries may not give legal or title opinions.

# 2

# The Civil Law in Louisiana

## Other systems of law p 13

- Islamic law – quasi-religious system based on the Koran
- Socialist law – legal system that incorporates socialist beliefs into a legal system
- Common law – system of law derived from England, used in most of the English-speaking world and all of the other states in the United States, based on judge-made law, or jurisprudence.
- Civil law – system of law derived from Roman law, most famously from the Napoleonic code, used in most of Europe and South America, Central America, and some of Africa

## Common law and civil law, compared and contrasted

### Role of judges

- Common law – judges make law: they rely on previous cases as guidance and make decisions that will, in part, control future decisions. Prior case law is of the utmost importance in common law p 14
- Civil law – judges interpret the law: they rely on the code as the source of law and use prior case law to interpret ambiguous provisions of the law p 15

### The Louisiana Civil Code

- Our comprehensive system of laws governing most private conduct p 15
- It is our framework for society p 16

### Origins of our Civil Code

- Napoleon wanted a code of law so universal it would be in everyone's home p 16
- Napoleon gave the code to Crozat, who made an edict that the law would be in effect for the territories which included Louisiana. When Jefferson purchased Louisiana, Claiborne, our first governor, made an act that the laws in effect would continue and that was ok fine p 16-17
- Then there was a digest, which forms the basis of Louisiana civil law p 17
- *We do not have a "Napoleonic code"*: our digest of laws was interpreted in light of Spanish laws in effect when Louisiana was ceded to the United States p 17
- If there is an error in translation of the code from French to English, the French is deemed to control p 17

# 3

# The Notary's Role in Louisiana

### An uncommon heritage

- Under Roman law, where the office of notary has its origin, notary was just a secretary or scribe, only writing contracts p 19

### Broad powers in Louisiana

- Notaries can make inventories, appraisements, partitions, wills, protests, matrimonial contracts, conveyances, and almost all contracts and instruments in writing p 19
- Empowered to execute authentic acts, receive acknowledgments of acts under private signature, officiate at family and creditors meetings p 19

In Texas, for example, a notary can only take acknowledgements and proof of written instruments, protest instruments, administer oaths, and very few other limited duties p 19

# 4

# Louisiana's Court System

## The relationship between the notary and the court

- Courts play an integral role in fulfillment of notary's obligation to the public p 23
- Courts hear cases and rely on attestations and oaths contained in notarial documents p 23
- Notary could be called to court to testify in court regarding the acts, declarations, and oaths he has passed p 23

## The court's role in appointment of the notary

- Office of notary public is for a specific parish (although the jurisdiction may be statewide), as explained in Chapter 7 p 23
- Although you may have passed the notary exam or have a license to practice law, the *district court* decides if the notary public has good moral character and fitness to be a notary p 23

## The court's role in suspension or revocation

- Once commissioned, the *district court* decides if a notary should be suspended or have his commission revoked p 24
- This revocation action is filed in the district court in the parish where the notary holds his commission *or* the parish where the alleged misconduct took place p 24
- If revoked, the district court may issue an order barring recommissioning p 24

## Types of courts and jurisdictions

### Courts of limited and general jurisdiction

- Limited jurisdiction – limited to adjudicate certain matters, such as small claims courts or juvenile courts p 24
- General jurisdiction – state district courts can hear all civil and criminal cases and conduct jury trials, except those they aren't authorized to hear, such as worker compensation cases or bankruptcy.

### Justice of the peace courts

- Handle minor money disputes for small amounts, issue some arrest warrants, set bail obligations, and hold preliminary hearings in minor criminal cases p 25
- Justices of the peace are magistrates (do not need to be lawyers), not judges, but should be addressed as Judge p 25

- There may be more than one in a municipality because they are local within a parish p 25

### *Mayor's courts*

- Handle minor traffic matters and petty ordinances p 25
- Cannot exist within the jurisdictional limits of a city court p 25
- Mayor's court magistrates are magistrates (do not need to be lawyers), not judges, but should be addressed as Judge p 25
- There may only be one in a municipality, because it is local to a municipality p 25

### *City courts, parish courts*

- These are courts of limited jurisdiction p 25
- Handle money matters up to $15,000 or $20,000 p 25
- Misdemeanor criminal jurisdiction, not felonies p 25
- Full juvenile jurisdiction if there is no juvenile court in the parish p 25
- City and parish court judges must be lawyers p 25
- Parish courts are the same as city courts; only two parishes (Jefferson and Ascension) have parish courts p 25

### *District Courts*

- Courts of general jurisdiction, handling both criminal and civil matters; can hold jury trials p 25
- 41 numbered district courts cover 63 parishes p 25
- The 64th parish is Orleans, which has separate criminal and civil district courts. These courts are not numbered p 25
- District courts have general original jurisdiction, and limited appellate jurisdiction p 25
  - Appeals from the justice of the peace or mayor's court come before the district court as new trials p 25
  - Appeals from certain administrative courts, like zoning boards, come to the district court as appeals p 26
  - Appeals from criminal convictions in justice of the peace, city, or mayor's courts under parish or city ordinances are reviewed for trial error p 26

### *Courts of Appeal*

- There are 5 state courts of appeal p 26
- They hear appeals of civil and criminal cases, except death penalty and cases involving constitutionality of laws p 26
- They can hear appeals directly from administrative courts like worker's compensation courts, and civil service commissions p 26
- They exercise supervisory jurisdiction, at their discretion, which means that they can intervene in a lower court matter to correct a matter of law before an appeal is lodged p 26

### *Louisiana Supreme Court*

- Exercises original jurisdiction in cases involving discipline of lawyers and judges p 27

- Exercises appellate jurisdiction without the case first having gone to a court of appeal in death penalty cases, or any case where a statute or municipal ordinance has been declared unconstitutional p 27
- In all other cases, the Louisiana supreme court has *discretionary* appellate review. Cases get to the court by two paths:
  - Supervisory jurisdiction
  - Writ of certiorari, where the justices decide if a case should be heard in one of the following usual cases p 27
    - Conflicting decisions among courts of appeal
    - Significant unresolved issue of law has arisen that need to be decided immediately
    - Justice requires that a previous decision of the supreme court be overruled
    - Court of appeal has erroneously applied the law
    - Lower court has grossly departed from proper judicial proceedings that result in an abuse of power

# 5

# Sources of Law and Legal Authority

The non-attorney notary must not practice law or give legal advice, but must have sufficient knowledge of the laws which govern his office and which help him exercise his notarial powers, which is the purpose of the notary applicant exam p 28

## Sources of law

- Legislation - the solemn expression of legislative will p 28 LA CC art 1
- Custom – practice repeated for a long time and generally accepted as having acquired the force of law p 28 LA CC art 2
- Law and legislation always trump custom p 28

## Legislation

In civil law, the supreme lawmaking authority is given to the citizens in the following way:

- The citizens make a constitution p 28
- The constitution gives the authority to make laws to a legislature
- The role of the notary is created by the legislature and legislative branch and that role is to give legal effect to acts made in conformity with civil and commercial law p 29

But, in common law states, judges, as well as legislators, have the role of lawmakers p 28

## Books containing Louisiana law

- Civil Code
- Revised Statutes
- Code of Civil Procedure
- Children's Code
- Code of Evidence
- Code of Criminal Procedure
- Constitutional Ancillaries

## Louisiana Civil Code (cited as La. C.C. art. xxx)

- The current Louisiana civil code is the Civil Code of 1974, as revised and amended by legislation
- The civil code is a compilation of private law (governing relations between private individuals) regulat-

ing almost everything from interpersonal relationships, to property matters, to contracts, etc. p 29
- Many of the civil code articles are supplemented by the revised statutes p 29

## Books in the Civil Code p 30

I. *Of Persons* – covers persons, absent persons, husbands and wives, marriage and divorce, minors, emancipation, etc.

II. *Of Things and the Different Modifications of Ownership* – covers ownership of property, servitudes, boundaries, etc.

III. *Of the Different Modes of Acquiring the Ownership of Things* – covers donations, obligations, contracts, leases, rents, mortgages, etc.

IV. *Of the Conflict of Laws* – covers situations where different laws apply when persons or property are subject to the laws of more than one state

## Revised Statutes Title 9 (cited as La. R.S. 9:xxx)

- The Civil Code Ancillaries in Title 9 are the main other source for Louisiana law for notaries. This title covers subjects from marriage and divorce, paternity proceedings, adult adoptions, immobilization and deimmobilization of mobile homes, and the trust code, among many other laws p 30

## Revised Statutes Title 10 (cited as La. R.S. 10:xxx)

- Louisiana Commercial Law: this covers negotiable instruments and security instruments on movables, among many others p 31

## Revised Statutes Title 12 (cited as La. R.S. 12:xxx)

- Louisiana Corporate Law: this covers articles of incorporation, laws governing naming of corporations, and limited liability corporations, among many other commercial laws p 31

## Revised Statutes Title 13 (cited as La. R.S. 13:xxx)

- Louisiana Courts and Judicial Procedure: this article covers witness acknowledgment, along with the relationship between the notary and the court p 31

## Revised Statutes Title 14 (cited as La. R.S. 14:xxx)

- Louisiana Criminal Law: this covers crimes of which the notary can be culpable, such as bribery, corrupt influencing, and malfeasance in office p 31

## Revised Statutes Title 31 (cited as La. R.S. 31:xxx)

- Louisiana Mineral Code: this is useful to notaries in preparation of real estate documents p 31

## Revised Statutes Title 32 (cited as La. R.S. 32:xxx)

- Louisiana Motor Vehicle and Traffic Regulation: this title contains the vehicle certificate of title law and contains the Office of Motor Vehicle policies and procedures p 32

## Revised Statutes Title 35 (cited as La. R.S. 35:xxx)

- Louisiana Notaries Public and Commissioners: this *important and tested* title governs the behavior and discipline of notaries public p 32

## Revised Statutes Title 42 (cited as La. R.S. 42:xxx)

- Louisiana Public Officers Law: this covers all laws regarding behavior of public officers. Notaries are public officers, so this applies to notaries as well p 32

## Revised Statutes Title 44 (cited as La. R.S. 44:xxx)

- Louisiana Public Records and Recorders Law: this is important to notaries because notaries affix their seals and their records become a permanent record p 32

## Code of Civil Procedure (cited as La. C.C.P. art. xxx)

- Contains procedural laws and rules regarding civil actions, such as how proceedings are held, where an action can be brought, how to electronically file certain documents, and captions and forms of documents. The law governing small succession is found here, not in the Civil Code p 32

## Code of Criminal Procedure (cited as La. C. Cr. P. art. xxx)

- Contains procedural laws applicable to criminal proceedings against adults p 33

## Children's Code (cited as La. Ch. C. art. xxx)

- Contains laws affecting juveniles, adoptions, and rights of parents and minors p 32

## Code of Evidence (cited as La. C. E. art. xxx)

- Provides the rules of evidence for determining questions of fact in all judicial proceedings, and determining the scope of testimonial privileges p 32

## Constitutional Ancillaries

- Sections of the Louisiana constitution of 1921 that were continued as statutes by the present constitution of 1974, but have not been incorporated into the Louisiana Revised Statutes, nor have they been repealed by the legislature.
- Despite the name, they do not have constitutional status, but are considered *statutory* law p 33

## Jurisprudence

- Court decisions (jurisprudence) are not sources of law, but are guidance to interpret and apply the law p 33
- Louisiana Supreme Court decisions are binding on courts under its jurisdiction p 33
- United States Supreme Court decisions are binding on all courts p 33
- United States Courts of Appeals decisions at the federal level are persuasive on all federal and state courts within its circuit p 33  Louisiana is in the Fifth Circuit in the federal court system p 33
- Courts can look to other states for guidance on unique questions of law p 34

- Louisiana does not recognize the legal principle of *stare decisis*, the doctrine that courts stand by their precedent in making decisions p 34
- If no law or authority exists to aid a court in making a decision, the court can decide according to equity – which is justice, reason, and prevailing usage p 34 LA CC art 4

## Attorney General Opinions

- These are a source of legal authority but are not law p 34
- They reflect the opinion of the state's chief legal officer p 34

# 6

# Registry and Recordation

**Public Records Doctrine** p 38

- Set of principles regarding acquiring and proving title to Louisiana immovables
- Public records doctrine is strictly adhered to
- Founded upon public policy and purpose of assuring stability of land titles
- Does not create rights in land itself, but can deny the effectiveness of rights if property transactions are not properly recorded
- If something that should be recorded is not recorded, third persons (those not parties to the instrument, discussed below) can rely on an assumption that it does not exist p 38
- Public records come from many sources

**Recording transfers of immovable property (see chapter 21) helps create the public record** p 38 LA CC art 1839

- Must be made by authentic act or by act under private signature (so must be in writing), unless an oral transfer is made, property is delivered, and transferor testifies under oath
- Transfer of immovable property is only effective against third parties when filed in the registry in the parish where the property is located p 38
- Act of conveyance must designate name of person responsible for all property taxes and assessments p 39 LA RS 9:2721
- If the property is bought subject to a prior recorded lease, that lease remains in effect p 39

**For the following instruments creating real rights in immovable property to be effective against a third party, they must be recorded:** p 39 art 3338

- An instrument that transfers an immovable
- An instrument that establishes a real right in an immovable
- The lease of an immovable
- An option or right of first refusal
- A contract to buy, sell, or lease an immovable, or a contract to create a real right in an immovable
- An instrument that modifies, terminates, or transfers the rights crested or evidenced by any of the above

# 6 • REGISTRY AND RECORDATION

## Some things are effective against third parties even if they are not recorded p 39 art 3339

- Matters of capacity or authority (such as a power of attorney, chapter 15)
- Occurrence of suspensive or resolutory condition
- Exercise of an option or right of first refusal
- A tacit acceptance
- A termination of rights that depends upon the occurrence of a condition

## Effect of recording other documents p 39 art 3340

- If the law makes the recording of an instrument a necessary condition to the rights of that instrument, that instrument is not effective against third persons until it is recorded
- Recording a document only has the effect that lawmakers intend it to have once it is recorded

## Limits on the effects of recordation p 40 art 3341

- Does not create a presumption that the instrument is valid or genuine
- Does not create a presumption of capacity or status of the parties
- Has no effect unless the law expressly provides for its recordation
- Is effective only with respect to immovables located in the parish where the immovable is recorded

## Who is a third person or third party? p 40 art 3343

- A person who is not a party to or personally bound by an instrument is a third person
- A witness to an act is a third person with respect to it
- A person who assumes or is bound by a contract is *not* a third person

## Ancient documents; presumptions p 40 art 3351

- If the document has been recorded for 10 years, it is presumed to have been signed by all parties whose signatures are affixed (time settles controversies)
- The recording of the document has effect from the time when the act is deposited in the proper office and endorsed by the proper officer

## Parish recorders

- Notaries used to keep originals of all their authentic acts p 40
- In 1810, immovable property had to be recorded in the office of the judge of the parish where immovable property was situated p 41
- Now, the *clerks of the district courts* are parish registers of conveyances and recorders of mortgages, and are notaries public, ex-officio p 41 LA RS 13:751
- The clerk records every mortgage, conveyance, or instrument of any kind submitted for recordation in the public record p 41

## Facts about recording

- Instruments regarding mortgage or privilege in immovable, or pledge of lessor's rights in lease of immovable and its rents, are recorded in the mortgage record of the parish where the immovable is situated p 41 art 3346
- Recording is effective when it is filed with the recorder; if there are errors or omissions, this doesn't change the effective date p 41 art 3347
- The instrument will be time- and date-stamped when it is filed/recorded p 41 art 3348
- The recorder can issue certified copies upon request, which shows the original filing time and date, and has the full effect of the original p 41 LA RS 13:103
- A notary who received the original (or his successor) may certify a copy of an authentic act as best evidence where the original is lost p 42 LA RS 9:2758 (see also Chapter 29 on "Certified True Copy" and its limits for recorded instruments)

## Notarial documents which are recorded p 42

- Acts involving movable and immovable property
- Conveyances, sales, exchanges, and donations
- Mortgages
- Acts of cancellation of mortgage
- Business organization charter (after filing with Secretary of State)
- Bonds
- Oaths of office

## State agencies

### *Secretary of State* p 43

- Chief elections officer – qualifies people for office, oversees elections
- Official registry of public officials – maintains official database of elected and appointed public state officials, and issues Apostilles, which are certificates attached to notarial acts intended registry in foreign countries
- Commercial division – receives and processes all commercial documents for all private corporations in the state
- Also maintains the state archives among other duties

### *Department of Public Safety* p 43

- Office of Motor Vehicles
- Office of State Fire Marshal
- State Police
- The study guide notes that it is of the utmost importance to be cautious and take the notarial commission seriously. The Department of Public Safety exists to keep us safe. The book reminds us that a notary "helped out" a friend and a terrorist got a driver's license with that notarization which was connected to 9/11.

**Office of Motor Vehicles** p 44
- Official registry of vehicle ownership for Louisiana-titled vehicles
- Issues drivers' licenses

**Louisiana State Police** p 44
- Criminal background checks
- Concealed handgun permits
- Gaming enforcement administrative forms

*Department of Health and Hospitals – Vital Records registry* p 44
- Birth, death, and marriage records

*Department of Social Services – Support Enforcement Services (SES)* p 44
- Paternity establishment, among many other duties

# 7

# The Office of Notary Public in Louisiana

### The office generally

- The notary is a public official in and for a parish, commissioned in a parish, but generally with state-wide jurisdiction
- Appointed by the Governor with the advice and consent of the Louisiana senate
- Must meet the requirements set forth in R.S. Title 35 (a statute found in study guide Appendix A)

### Public office defined p 45 LA RS 42:1

- Any state, district, parish, or municipal office, elective or appointed; or
- Any position as a member on a board or commission, elective or appointed when the office or position is established by the constitution or laws of this state

### Oath of Office

- Every official shall take an oath under the constitution of Louisiana p 45
- A notary public is required to take and file an oath of office with the Secretary of State *and* in the clerk of court in the parish of commission p 45

### Term of office

- Issued without expiration date (unlike other states) p 45
- Continues in effect as long as the notary maintains his qualifications for the office p 45
- Notary may exercise his power in the parish of appointment and any other parish in which he is authorized, except when he is under suspension by the court or by operation of law p 45

### Independent public function

- Powers are enumerated by statute p 46
- Exercise of powers are a public function p 46
- Duties of the notary are public but do not make him an agent of the state; he operates independently, not subject to direct supervision of the state p 46

### *Notary fees are not public funds*

- Notary fees are exempt from LA R.S. 42:282 which requires public officers to maintain records of their

fees for official duties p 46
- Notaries are not subject to audit by the legislative auditor p 46

## *Taxes and licenses*

- Notary commission is *not* a license (despite use of term *license* in other parts of study guide) p 46
- Office of notary is not a trade or profession p 46
- Notarial office is not subject to occupational licensure p 46
- Notarial fees are not subject to occupational license tax p 46

## *Occupational license not required*

- Because the office of notary is not a trade *per se*, the notary is not subject to further licensing by local governments p 46
- If the notary practices other functions in the office (like accounting, lawyering, auto title, public stenography, etc.), those may require occupational licensing p 47
- Notary fees are exempt from self-employment tax under IRS regulations, but are reportable as income p 47

# Official misconduct p 47 LA RS 14:134

- The notary is subject to *criminal* prosecution for official misconduct if he does any of the following:
  o Intentionally refuses to or fails to perform any duty lawfully required of him; or
  o Intentionally performs his duties in an unlawful manner; or
  o Knowingly permits any other officer or public employee to intentionally fail or refuse to perform any duty legally required of him
- Any duty is a lawful duty required of a public officer if it is delegated to him by a public officer or public employee. The delegation by another does not relieve him of duty.
- The crime of malfeasance is punishable as a felony, by up to 5 years in prison and a fine of up to $5000 p 47
- In addition to the prison time and fine, malfeasance may require paying restitution to the state p 47

# Bribery and corrupt influencing

- These crimes apply to notaries in their public capacity p 47
- These crimes are when the notary "looks the other way" for a price p 47
- ***Public Bribery*** is covered under LA R.S. 14:118 p 48
  o Giving or offering to give anything of value in exchange for influencing any public official (including notaries); or
  o The acceptance of anything of value in exchange from someone for the purpose of influencing a public official (including notaries).
  o The crime of public bribery is punishable as a felony, by up to 5 years in prison and a fine of up to $1000.
  o Public bribery may also require paying restitution to the state p 48

- Property given to public officials in commission of public bribery is considered contraband and is seized and forfeited p 48
- *Corrupt Influencing* is covered under LA R.S. 14:120 p 49
    - The giving or offering to give, or accepting or offering to accept, anything of apparent present or prospective value to someone with the intention that that person will corrupt the influence of a public official (including notaries) p. 49 So, it is not direct public bribery, but bribery by proxy, or influence-peddling.
    - The crime of corrupt influencing is punishable as a felony, by up to 10 years in prison and a fine of up to $10,000.
    - Corrupt influencing may also require paying restitution to the state p 48

## Unauthorized exercise of notarial powers

- If someone has never had the power to be a notary or who has had their commission judicially revoked, and practices under these conditions, they are subject to penalties laid out by LA R.S. 35:601 p 49
    - Convicted of the unauthorized practice of notarial powers
    - Subject of a fine of up to $1000; and/or
    - Subject to imprisonment for up to two years
- If a duly commissioned notary has had their commission suspended for failing to maintain a current bond or insurance, or failure to file annual reports, but continues to act as a notary during their suspension, they are subject to penalties laid out by LA RS 35:602 p 49
    - Subject to a fine of up to $1000
    - Judge may further suspend or permanently bar the notary from being a notary
- Attorney-notaries are disciplined by the Louisiana Attorney Disciplinary Board LA RS 35:604 p 49

## Other crimes: Injuring public records

- Falsely declaring something in a record that the notary makes, that is untrue, is punishable under LA R.S. 14:132 p 50
    - The intentional removal, mutilation, destruction, alteration, falsification, or concealment of any record, document, or other filing in any public office
    - This crime is punishable as a felony, by a prison term of up to 5 years and a fine of up to $5000 for first degree injuring; and punishable as a felony, by a prison term of up to 1 year and a fine of up to $1000 for second degree injuring

## Other crimes: Filing false records

- Filing a forged or altered document violates LA R.S. 14:133 p 50
    - Filing in any public office or maintaining as required by law, with knowledge of its falsity:
    - Any forged document, any wrongfully altered document, or any document containing a false statement or false representation of a material fact
    - The crime of filing or maintaining false records is punishable as a felony, by up to 5 years in prison and a fine of up to $5000
    - In addition to the prison time and fine, filing a forged or altered document may require the notary to pay restitution to the state

## Other crimes: Forgery

- Forgery violates LA R.S. 14:72 p 51
    - Unlawful to forge, with intent to defraud, any signature purporting to have legal effect
    - Forgery includes altering, making, completing, or authenticating a document so it purports to be that of someone else; to be a copy of something that does not exist; to be the act of someone who did not authorize that act
    - The crime of forgery is punishable as a felony, by up to 10 years in prison and a fine of up to $5000

## Commission suspension

- Suspension is not a revocation or removal from office p 52
- Non-attorney notaries can be suspended for a variety of reasons under LA R.S. 35:16 p 52
- Automatic suspension occurs by law if a notary:
    - Is an attorney-notary and is suspended from the practice of law for disciplinary reasons p 52 LA RS 35:14
    - Stops being a registered voter in the parish where he is commissioned and fails to register to vote in his commission parish after notice p 52 LA RS 35:16
    - Is convicted of a felony p 52 35:16
    - Fails to maintain the required bond or insurance coverage p 52 LA RS 35:71
    - Fails to timely file an annual report with the Secretary of State p 52 LA RS 35:202
- Court-ordered suspension for cause occurs if a notary:
    - Engaged in dishonesty, fraud, deceit, or misrepresentation p 52 LA RS 35:15
    - Certified as true what he knows or should have known was false p 52 LA RS 35:15
    - Violated any provision of any law governing the office of notary p 52 LA RS 35:15
    - Abandoned his commission p 52 LA RS 35:15
    - Failed to pay over money due to others from an escrow account p 53 LA RS 35:71
    - Failed to satisfy any final judgment rendered against him in his capacity as a notary p 53 LA RS 35:71

## Removal from office

- Can be removed by the Governor, the courts, or the legislature p 53
- The Governor may remove anyone he appoints to be a notary, and removal by the Governor does not require cause p 53
- The legislature may remove a notary in 1 of 2 ways:
    - If the notary is impeached by the Louisiana House of Representatives and convicted by the Louisiana Senate for commission or conviction of a felony or gross misconduct while in office; or
    - The Louisiana Senate declines or fails to confirm the appointment of the notary p 53
- A judicial revocation can occur under 4 provisions of law:
    - A registered voter in the parish where the notary holds his commission complains to the DA that he believes the notary no longer resides in that parish p 54 LA RS 18:671-674

- o A notary convicted of a felony can be removed if the DA wins a removal suit in the parish where the notary is commissioned p 54 LA RS 42:1411-12
- o If the district court finds out a notary is practicing during a period when he is suspended, the court *may* remove a notary p 54 LA RS 35:602
- o The district court *must* revoke a notary's commission if the notary has committed a felony for which he has not been pardoned; or committed gross malfeasance; or ceased to be qualified for the office p 54 LA RS 35:15-16 This revocation is discretionary (may) only when the court has found that the notary has
  - Engaged in dishonesty, fraud, deceit or misrepresentation
  - Certified as true what he knows or should have known was false
  - Violated any provision of law governing the office of notary or exercise of notarial authority
  - Abandoned his commission

# Notarial powers

### *What Louisiana notaries may do — General powers:* p 55 LA RS 35:2

1. To make inventories, appraisements, and partitions
2. To receive wills, make protests, matrimonial contracts, conveyances, and generally, all contracts and instruments of writing
3. To hold family meetings and meetings of creditors
4. To receive acknowledgments of instruments under private signature
5. To make affidavits of correction
6. To affix the seals upon the effects of deceased persons, and to raise the same
7. To make authentic acts in accordance with LA C.C. art. 1833
8. To swear in persons to give testimony at a deposition before a general reporter or a freelance reporter under LA R.S. 37:2551
9. To verify interrogatories and other pleadings
10. To certify true copies of originals passed before him

### *Notary who is an agent for a party*

- A notary who is an agent for a person can be a notary for that person, as long as that notary does not have a beneficial interest in that particular instrument p 56

### *Notary who is connected with a bank or corporation*

- A notary who is a stockholder for a bank or corporation can notarize for people within the corporation as long as the notary is not a party or does not have an interest or have a conflict in that particular instrument, either individually or as a representative of the corporation p 56 (discussed further in chapter 30)

### *Jurisdictional limits*

- Notaries may administer oaths in any parish for depositions or to verify interrogatories, otherwise they must execute acts only within their jurisdiction p 56
- But notaries who have taken and passed the statewide exam on or after June 13, 2005 have *statewide* jurisdiction p 58 (are commissioned in one parish but may do notary work in all of them)

## 7 ▪ OFFICE OF NOTARY PUBLIC

# Duties of office

- Comply with the constitution of the state of Louisiana and the Constitution of the United States of America, act with honesty and integrity, and comply with all laws

## *Recordation and registry*

- Failure to follow recordation laws can result in a $200 fine for each violation p 59
- Duty to timely record all acts affecting immovable property in the office of the recorder for the parish where the property is located p 59 LA RS 35:199
- All sales, exchanges, donations, and mortgages of immovable property must be recorded; if made through a power of attorney, that must be recorded with it
- The instrument can pass this duty along to someone other than the notary if all of the parties agree (such as to the non-notary party or a real estate broker)
- In Orleans Parish, it must be recorded within 48 hours in an office called the Land Records Division p 60 LA RS 35:199c
- But in all other parishes, it must be recorded within 15 days (the difference between Orleans and other parishes is often tested)
- Recordation requirements do not apply to cemetery plots

## *Certificates, research, and taxes*

- Notaries used to have to get mortgage and tax certificates from parish recorders p 61
- Now mortgage and tax certificates do not have to be annexed to acts of conveyance, outside of Orleans Parish p 61
- Any party can get a certificate to show that applicable taxes have been paid except for the current year, and annexing this certificate to the mortgage or conveyance is conclusive evidence of the payment p 61
- Common practice is for the notary to obtain the tax certificates and annex them, or to have the parties (in the instrument) waive the need for them and hold the notary harmless p 61
- Orleans Parish has some other special rules:
  - No public official shall transfer any property within the city limits of New Orleans unless all state, parish, and city taxes have been paid LA RS 9:2921
  - Proof of payment will be evidenced by a tax certificate LA RS 9:2922, 2924
  - Buyer may assume the taxes for the current year because they are due and payable the next year p 62 LA RS 9:2925
  - Special assessments may pass on to future buyers in an act conveying real property p 62
  - Any public officer (notary) who transfers property in the city of New Orleans without having ensured all taxes are paid in violation of LA R.S. 9:2921 shall be fined between $100 and $200 p 62 LA RS 9:2927
  - A notary effecting any transfer of property in New Orleans must make sure the seller has not sold it first. He shall get a certificate, whicj shall have a description of the property and be annexed to the act. If this is violated, the notary is subject to a fine of between $250 and $500 p 62 LA RS 9:2928

## *Other directives the notary must do*

- Notify the Secretary of State within 60 days of any change of mailing address, residential address, or both p 62 LA RS 35:191

- Include all required information in notarial acts p 62
- Include all required information in acts which affect real rights in immovable property p 63

# Appointment

- Governor appoints an individual to be a notary in and for a particular parish after an applicant meets the requirements p 64
- Appointment is in and for the *one* parish of the commission (though those who pass the state exam now have statewide *jurisdiction*, above); but some earlier-commissioned notaries could be appointed in two parishes by "dual commission" p 68
    - Can have dual commission if the notary has only a parish-wide jurisdiction (commissioned before June 13, 2005), with a residence in his home parish *and* an office in an adjoining parish.
- The appointment process involves all 3 branches of government:
    - Executive – Secretary of State handles all of the applications; Governor submits all names to the Secretary of State for advice and consent p 64 LA RS 35:191
    - Judicial – character and fitness are decided by the courts if the issue arises during the application process p 64 LA RS 35:191
    - Legislative – Senate consents and confirms appointments at the end of the first regular legislative session p 64 LA RS 35:191

## *Qualifications to be a notary*

- Must be a resident of the state of Louisiana (citizen or alien) p 64 LA RS 35:191
- Be at least 18 years old p 65
- Be able to read, write, speak, and be sufficiently knowledgeable of the English language
- Have a high school diploma or equivalent
- Not be under interdiction or incapable of serving because of a mental infirmity
- Not have been convicted of a felony, unless they have been pardoned
- Must be a registered voter in the parish of their residence, unless a resident alien

## *Procedures for appointment*

- Submit an application provided by the Secretary of State to the Secretary of State p 65
- Take and pass an exam given by the Secretary of State, unless you are one of the following:
    - Attorney licensed to practice law in the state of Louisiana
    - Notary changing residence to another parish who has already passed the statewide exam after June 13, 2005 (don't have to take the exam again)
    - Currently commissioned notary obtaining a dual commission (applies to those commissioned before June 13, 2005 who have not since passed the state exam)
    - Notaries who are changing their residence to another parish and who have held a commission for more than 5 years (also those commissioned before June 13, 2005)

## *Bond or insurance*

- Non-attorney notaries must furnish and maintain either a surety bond in the amount of at least $10,000, or maintain Errors & Omissions insurance of at least $10,000 p 65 LA RS 35:71, 72

- A notary bond is a financial guarantee you typically purchase from a surety company. The bond ensures that, as a notary, you will fulfill all your obligations and protect the public from financial harm resulting from any wrongdoing on your part when performing notarial duties p 65
- The bond is not given as a cash deposit, but it is usually a contract of suretyship or special mortgage like a property bond p 65
- All public officers are required to give a bond secured by reputable surety company doing business in the state p 66 LA RS 42:181 (or an acceptable alternative suretyship, such as a personal bond)
- Bonds of state officers are made payable to the Governor p 66 LA RS 42:183
- Special mortgage on property they have situated in the parish where they regularly do business may be substituted for a bond p 66 LA RS 42:199

## *Operation of bond as mortgage*

- The bond does not automatically act as a mortgage against the notary's property, and is not included on a mortgage certificate unless the notary is sued and a notice of litigation (*lis pendens*) has been filed in the mortgage records p 66 LA RS 35:73

## *Acceptable bonds* p 67

- Commercial surety bond – underwritten by a surety company authorized to do business in this state
- Personal surety bond – underwritten by an individual
- Property bond – special mortgage on immovable property in the parish of the notary's commission

## *Approval and recordation of bond* p 67

- Bond must be submitted to, and approved by, the clerk of court in the parish of commission (unless notary gets an Errors & Omissions policy, which is statewide)
- Must be made payable (subscribed) to the Governor
- Must be filed with the Secretary of State (either bond or E&O policy) p 67 LA RS 35:192
- Must be secured by a person who resides in the parish of the notary's commission or, more commonly, by a commercial surety company doing business in this state p 67 LA RS 42:181
- Personal surety bonds must be acceptable to the presiding judge in the parish of the notary's commission, then filed with the Secretary of State p 67 LA RS 35:75
- A property bond can be secured by a special mortgage on property situated in the parish of the notary's commission, and that bond must be recorded p 67 LA RS 42:198, 186
- Commercial surety bonds need not be recorded, but are approved by clerk p 67 LA RS 35:193

## *Dual commission: need for second bond*

- As noted above, a notary with a restricted parish commission (issued prior to June 13, 2005) may apply for one concurrent dual commission in and for a parish where he maintains an office p 68
- A separate bond must be posted for each parish unless the parish has fewer than 40,000 residents. p 68 LA RS 35:191

## *Commission issuance* p 67

- Exam is taken and passed unless exempt (see exemptions above, like being an attorney)
- Oath of office is taken before a notary or other state officer and filed with Secretary of State

- Bond (or alternative, such as the declarations page of an Errors & Omissions policy), properly executed, and approved, is filed with the Secretary of State
- Official signature is on file with Secretary of State

## Commission status

### *Maintaining current bond* p 68

- You have to post bond (file with the Secretary of State) and update it upon its renewal or you cannot practice as a notary
- Commercial surety bonds are generally good for 5 years
- Personal surety bonds are good for the life of the surety
- Errors & Omissions liability policies are written for 1 year or 5 years, depending on what is purchased, but 5 years is necessary to gain your commission

### *Maintaining qualifications for office* p 68

- Live in the parish in which the notary holds a commission p 68
- Be registered to vote in the parish of your commission (unless you are a resident alien)
- Be currently bonded or insured (unless you are an attorney-notary)
- For dual commissioned notaries, live in one of the parishes you are commissioned in, and maintain an office in one or both of the parishes, and be bonded or insured in both, unless the parish is under 40,000 residents

### *The de facto doctrine* p 70

- A *de jure* public officer (notary) is one who is validly commissioned to practice as a notary because they meet all of the qualifications
- A *de facto* notary is one who has been a notary but for some reason is not qualified, but who has passed a notarial act
- The *de facto* doctrine is that courts may hold the notarial acts of *de facto* notaries as valid. But it is not a given that they will; it depends on the good faith of the person exercising the notarial power
- If you are *de facto* suspended or not able to act as a notary, acts passed by you may be declared invalid, and you may be liable for damages

### *Annual reports* p 72 LA RS 35:202

- All active notaries are required to file an annual report with the Secretary of State confirming their qualification for office, their mailing address, and the status of their bond
- Annual report is available 60 days before your commission anniversary
- Annual report is due on your commission anniversary
- If you don't file it timely, financial penalties and commission suspension may occur. But:
  - Attorney-notaries are not required to file
  - Notaries on leave of absence are not required to file – can be on leave of absence for up to 36 months; or if in the military, after a request in writing, for 60 days after his discharge from the military p 73 LA RS 9:131-133
  - Notaries electing retired status are not required to file

## 7 ▪ OFFICE OF NOTARY PUBLIC

## Miscellaneous information p 74

- Notary fees are not fixed by statute
- A notary's *signature* is his "seal" (though out-of-state documents may require a stamp)
- The notary must exercise reasonable prudence in ascertaining the identity of the affiant or party executing documents p 74
    - Acceptable ID: state-issued driver's license, state-issued ID, U.S. passport, or U.S. military ID
    - Need not verify ID through documentation if you personally know the signing party
    - Need not verify ID through documentation if someone you personally know vouches for the identity of the signing party. But the book warns of a case imposing fraud liability on a notary who verified the identity of one signator just on the say-so of another, who herself was only identified by the notary through documentation (not personal knowledge)

## *Liability* p 75-76

- The notary is personally liable for damages
- The surety is bound to the limit of the bond
- Liability arises when the notary:
    - commits malfeasance
    - acts in dereliction (negligent disregard for proper performance) of his official duty
    - defrauds persons who act by relying on the genuineness of instruments he created in his official capacity

## *No duty to inspect documents or guarantee validity*

- If a notary does not create a document, he just authenticates or attests to the validity of the signature and does not inspect the document for legal flaws or guarantee the document for validity p 76
- Notary *does* have to ensure the truthfulness of the recitations and statements he signs, like the attestations and signatures p 76

## *Limits of liability; prescription*

- The notary can have unlimited liability for damages p 76
- The prescriptive period ("statute of limitations" in common law states) is
    - 1 year from the date of the alleged act, omission, or neglect; or
    - 1 year from the date the alleged act, omission, or neglect is discovered or should have been discovered; and
    - No more than 3 years after the date of the alleged act, omission, or neglect
    - There is no peremptive period (period of time fixed by law for the existence of a right) in the case of fraud p 77

## Notaries and the Unauthorized Practice of Law

- Do not offer opinions or advice on the meaning of the law, even if asked p 78
- Do not prepare legal documents

Violators are subject to up to 2 years in prison, and/or a $1000 fine p 79 LA RS 37:213

# 8

# Things and Ownership

## Things

- Ownership is the right that gives a person direct, immediate, and exclusive authority over a thing p 82 cc art 477

### *Division of things: Common things, public things, and private things*

- Things are divided into common, public, and private things p 82 art 448
- *Common things* are not owned by anyone, such as the air and the high seas p 82 art 449
- *Public things* are vested in the state in its public capacity and are owned by the state or its political subdivisions, like public streets, running waters (streams), parks, wild animals.
    - The seashore is public to the extent of the highest water of high tide p 82 art 450, 451
    - Public things are never in commerce
        - The public is entitled to fish in the public waters (may need a license), land on the seashore, moor ships, etc., provided they do not harm neighboring property p 83 art 452
- *Private things* are owned by private persons, natural or juridical, or by the state or its political subdivisions, acting as private persons in the way that they own them
    - cars, buildings, and office equipment are examples of privately things owned by the state (so, a fire engine is a private thing) p 83 art 453
    - Anything that is not common or public is private
    - Owners of private things may dispose of them as they want to, unless limited by law p 83 art 454
    - Banks of navigable rivers and levees are private things subject to public use p 84 art 456
- Roads are either public or private. Public roads are for public use, private roads are for private use p 84 art 457
- If something for the public use is unlawfully obstructed, the obstruction may be removed p 84 art 458
- If a private building just encroaches on a public right of way without preventing the use of the right of way, and the building can't be moved without substantial damage to the owner of the building, the building can remain p 84 art 459

### *Corporeal and incorporeal things, immovables and movables*

All things are classified as either corporeal or incorporeal (either with or without "a body"), *and* movable or immovable

- Movables can move or be moved from place to place p 85 art 471

- Immovables are defined by the Civil Code as land and its component parts, and rights associated with tracts of land
    - land and its component parts p 85 art 462, p 87
        - component parts are usually movables but deemed immovable by law because they are attached to an immovable or serve to complete an immovable p 85 art 466, 467
        - things hardwired into a building or which would cause destruction if removed are usually considered component parts, like hvac, doors, staircases
        - buildings, other constructions, standing timber, and unharvested crops are components when they are owned by the same person who owns the land p 85 art 463, p 87
        - if the building and standing timber are owned by someone other than the person who owns the land, they are separate *corporeal immovables* p 85 art 464
        - if there are other constructions (not buildings) and unharvested crops owned by someone other than the owner of the land, they are considered separate *corporeal movables* p 85 art 464, p 88
        - things incorporated into an immovable like gutters and cabinetry are component parts p 88 art 466
    - rights and obligations associated with tracts of land are immovables p 85 art 470, p 88
- Whatever the law doesn't consider an immovable is a movable p 85 art 475, p 89

## *Corporeal and incorporeal things*

- Corporeal things are tangible; they can be touched or felt p 84 art 461, p 87
- Incorporeal things are comprehended by the understanding, such as rights of inheritance, servitudes, and obligations p 85 art 461
    - Incorporeal immovables – rights and actions that apply to immovables, such as mineral leases p 85 art 473
    - Incorporeal movables – rights and actions that apply to movables, such as an interest in a juridical person like a corporation or partnership (even if that corporation owns immovable property)
    - Cash is a corporeal movable p 87
    - A check is an incorporeal movable p 87

## *Immovable by declaration* p 86 art 467, p 88

- Movable component parts placed on an immovable like machinery and appliances that are made part of the immovable, not by physically being joined to it, but by owner "declaring" and registering things as component parts of an immovable by filing a writing in the conveyance records in the parish where the movable is situated p 86 art 467, p 88
- Commonly, trailer homes will be made immobile by declaration in an authentic act, but this is done under an article other than LA CC art. 467, which applies to non-residential buildings p 86
- Trailer homes are made immobile under LA RS 9:1149.4
- If the owner of the land wants to deimmobilize a component part, they can do so by an act translative of ownership p 87 art 468 (see Chapter 13 on sale)

There used to be *immovable by destination* and *immovable by nature*:

- Immovable by destination – a movable placed on an immovable for its service and improvement, like mini-blinds in a mobile home
- Immovable by nature – a movable placed on an immovable for the use or convenience of the building, like conduit pipes

These are outdated terms that have been replaced by immovable by declaration p 86

## Ownership and possession

- Ownership and possession are two different things p 89 art 481
- Ownership is the right that gives a person direct, immediate, and exclusive authority over a thing  p 82 LA CC art 477, p 89
- Possession is the detention or enjoyment of a corporeal thing p 89 art 3421
- A person who is not the owner but who has possessed the thing for over a year acquires a right to possess it (but ownership remains with the owner). This is called an *adverse possession* p 89 art 3422

### *The 3 parts of ownership in Louisiana*

- Ownership is composed of 3 parts: the usus, fructus, and abusus
    - Usus = use of the thing
    - Fructus = fruits from the thing
    - Abusus = right to dispose of the thing

These 3 parts can be separated and parceled out. If someone has all 3 of these things, they have complete ownership. If they have only the right to dispose of the thing, they have naked ownership. If they have the right to the fruits and the right to use the thing, they have a usufruct. This will be discussed in detail in the next chapter.

- Ownership may be subject to a resolutory condition. A resolutory condition is an agreement that exists between the parties but will end if a certain event occurs. An example: a sale with the right of redemption, which is a sale where I can get the property back if the person to whom I sell the property dies p 90 art 478
- Ownership may be vested in more than 1 person, each having an equal share, called ownership in indivision (discussed below) p 90 art 480
- A possessor is presumptively considered the owner until the true owner can be discovered p 90 art 3423
- A possessor must
    - Intend to possess as owner
    - Take corporeal possession of the thing p 90 art 3424, 3425
- Exercising a real right, such as a servitude, is considered quasi-possession p 90 art 3421

### *Ownership of fruits*

- The owner of a thing acquires the ownership of its natural fruits (produced by the earth) and civil fruits (things like rents) in the absence of the rights of other persons. Fruits are things created without lessening the original thing, so fruits are different from products p 91 art 483, 551
- Civil fruits are created by operation of law or by juridical act p 91

If one person has the legal right to use and enjoy the fruits or profits of something belonging to another, they have a usufruct over the property of another p 91

### *Accession*

Ownership of a thing includes by accession everything it produces or is united with, subject to certain exceptions.

- Accession is the addition to or increase in value of property by growth or improvement p 90 art 482
- Owner owns growth or increase by accession unless someone else has these rights p 91 art 483

- The owner of the land owns everything directly above and below it, unless otherwise provided by law. The owner may make works/additions on or below the land unless prohibited by law (for example, you may own airspace above your home, and build upwards, subject to building codes) p 91 art 490
- Accretion formed by land building up on a bank of a river or stream is called *alluvion* and is owned by the owner of the river or stream bank. The land gained by the river or stream removing water and leaving the river or stream bed dry is called *dereliction*, and belongs to the owner of the owner of the bank p 91 art 499

**Accession in relation to immovables**

- Component parts, such as buildings and unharvested crops, generally belong to the land p 92 art 490, but may be owned by another p 92 art 468
- Buildings and standing timber owned by someone who does not own the land are corporeal immovables p 92 art 464
- Mineral rights are incorporeal immovables p 92 LA RS 31:18
- Unharvested crops and ungathered fruits of trees are movables by anticipation p 92 art 474
    - Movable by anticipation – unharvested crops or ungathered fruits of trees when they belong to a person other than the landowner p 92 art 474
- Accession of property normally subject to accession may be avoided if ownership of this property is evidenced by a written act translative of ownership filed in the conveyance records in the parish where the immovable to which they are attached is situated p 92 art 491-493
- If crops or other items are attached to an immovable without the consent of the owner, they become attached to the immovable by accession p 92 art 493

**Accession in relation to movables**

- Movables are divided into principal and accessory things for the purpose of accession
    - Accessory thing is the corporeal movable that serves the use, ornaments, or complements the principal thing p 94 art 508
    - Principal thing is generally the most valuable or, if close in value, that which is bulkier p 94 art 509
- If an accessory thing is incorporated into a principal thing to form a whole thing, the owner of the whole thing will own the accessory thing, but may have to reimburse the owner of the accessory thing p 94 art 510

## *Transfer of ownership*

- Ownership can be transferred by succession, either testate or intestate (see Chapter 10 on donations and Chapter 24 on successions)
- Ownership can be transferred by the effect of obligations or contract (see Chapter 11 on obligations, Chapter 13 on sale, and Chapter 21 on transfer of immovables)
- Ownership can be transferred by operation of law p 95 arts 517, 518, 870

## *Protection of ownership*

- Rights of a possessor are subordinate to the rights of an owner p 95
- If someone is adversely possessing a thing that does not belong to him, the owner can recover it up to the point of acquisitive prescription (see below) p 95 art 526
- The possessor of a movable is presumed to be the owner p 95 art 530

- For an immovable, a person who is not in possession of an immovable who claims ownership against someone who is in possession of the immovable must prove that he got title either from a previous owner or by acquisitive prescription. If neither party is in possession, the one with the better title will prevail p 95 art 531

## *Acquisitive prescription*

- The acquisition of ownership or other real rights through possession or use for a certain period of time p 95 art 3446
- Acquisitive prescription is interrupted when possession is lost p 95 art 3465
- If possession is recovered within 1 year, the interruption is considered to have never happened p 95 art 3465

### Acquisitive prescription of immovables

- All private things are susceptible to prescription unless provided for by law
- The person must intend to possess the thing as an owner for a period of either 10 or 30 years p 95 art 3473, 3486
- 10-year acquisitive prescription is possession for 10 years in good faith with just title of a thing that is susceptible of being acquired by prescription p 96 art 3473
    - Just title doesn't have to be a good title, only a juridical act that is sufficient to transfer ownership or other real rights, filed in the conveyance records of the parish where the immovable is situated p 96
    - Just title of an undivided interest only operates for acquisitive prescription for the undivided interest p 96
- 30-year acquisitive prescription is possession for 30 years with or without good faith, with or without just title of a thing that is susceptible of being acquired by prescription p 96 art 3486
- The possessor has to believe that they are the owner of the thing being possessed p 96 art 3480

### Acquisitive prescription for movables

- Ownership and other real rights in movables can be acquired through 3 or 10 year acquisitive prescription p 96 art 3489
- 3 year acquisitive prescription is possession for 3 years in good faith under an act sufficient to transfer ownership p 96 art 3490
- 10 year acquisitive prescription is possession for 10 years without good faith and without any act sufficient to transfer ownership p 96 art 3491

## Ownership in indivision

- When a thing is owned by more than one person, it is owned in indivision: all owners share equally unless law or juridical act states otherwise p 97 art 797
- Co-owners share the fruits and products in proportion to their ownership (which is presumed to be equal) p 97 art 798
- Co-owners may use and manage the co-owned thing by agreement p 97 art 801
- Co-owner may lease, alienate (sell), or encumber (mortgage, etc.) his share of the co-owned thing p 97 art 805

## 8 • THINGS AND OWNERSHIP

- All of the co-owners must consent to a lease, alienation, or encumbrance of the entire co-owned thing p 97 art 805
- A co-owner in indivision may demand the *partition* (sale or division) of the property unless prohibited by law or juridical act p 97 art 807
- Co-owners may agree to not partition for up to 15 years by contract, unless it is a nuclear power plant, then it can be 99 years because we all need to know this p 98 art 808
- Partition can be:
    - Voluntary and extrajudicial – on their own, they can create a juridical act
    - Judicial – they can request the court to partition the property p 98 art 809
- Partition can be:
    - in kind, which is preferred if the property in question can be split evenly and fairly. This is where the court will split the property into similar and even physical lots and each co-owner is given a similarly valued lot p 98 art 810
    - by licitation (sale), which happens if partition in kind is not possible: the sale proceeds are split between co-owners in proportion to their share p 98 art 811
- Action for partition never prescribes – it never stops being available to the co-owners p 99 art 817
- If the parties do an extrajudicial partition (outside the court, like before a notary), and one of them receives a value that is less by more than ¼ the fair market value of the portion they should have received, they can bring a lawsuit or an action for lesion beyond moiety.

# 9
# Servitudes

## Definition

- A servitude is a charge or burden on a thing, usually an immovable, for the benefit of another person or another estate p 100

## *Kinds of servitudes*

- Personal servitude – a charge on a thing (movables or immovables) for the benefit of a person. There are 3: usufruct, right of habitation, and right of use p 100 art 534
- Predial servitude (formerly called "landed" servitudes because they run with the land) – a charge on a servient estate for the benefit of a dominant estate, with the two estates belonging to different owners p 100 art 646
  - If an estate (an immovable piece of property) has a right granted to it which gives the estate an advantage, it is considered to be a predial servitude p 100 art 733
  - If the right granted is only for a person, it is not a predial servitude, unless it is heritable for himself, his heirs, and assigns p 100 art 734
  - The difference is basically that a predial servitude "runs with the land," while a personal servitude benefits a specific person. Even though there are a lot more details in the study guide on predial servitudes, usually the examiners focus more on personal ones, especially usufructs.

## Personal Servitudes

### Usufruct

- A real right of limited duration on the property of another p 101 art 535
- Is incorporeal, but can be movable or immovable, depending on what thing is burdened with the usufruct p 101
- Person for whom the usufruct is granted is called the usufructuary p 101
- A usufructuary can be a natural or a juridical person p 107 art 549

### *General rules about usufruct*

- The usufructuary can sell, donate, lease, or encumber his right, but all this terminates at the end of the usufruct, and the usufructuary may be liable to the naked owner for any abuse to the thing p 101 art 567
- Naked owner cannot interfere with the rights of the usufruct p 101 art 605
- Naked owner can sell his ownership, but the sale cannot affect the usufruct p 101 art 603

- Naked owner can establish servitudes and real rights on the property but cannot interfere with the usufruct p 101 art 604

- The usufruct terminates under many circumstances, one of which is if there was a lien/encumbrance on the property prior to the usufruct being placed on the property, and the lien has to be enforced. In this case, the usufruct terminates, but the usufructuary may have a right to sue the naked owner p 102 art 620

- If the property is sold at a judicial sale, for example a foreclosure, the properly recorded usufruct is not affected p 102 art 620

- If the usufructuary (who by some agreement has the power to dispose of nonconsumable property) sells, disposes of, or destroys the property, the usufructuary then has a usufruct on the proceeds of the original sold property or insurance claim p 102 art 616, 617

- The usufructuary takes the things subject to usufruct in the state in which they are at the commencement of the usufruct p 103 art 557

## *General rules about fruits of the usufruct*

- Right of usufruct extends to accessories of the thing at the beginning of the usufruct p 103 art 559

- Rights to fruits commences at the effective date of the usufruct p 103 art 554

- If the usufructuary hasn't used all the *natural* fruits at the end of the usufruct (e.g. unpicked apples), the unsevered or remaining fruits belong to the naked owner p 103 art 555

- If the usufructuary hasn't used all the *civil* fruits at the end of the usufruct (e.g. uncollected rents), the unsevered or remaining fruits still belong to the usufructuary p 104 art 556

- Usufructuary may cut trees and remove stones on the land on which they have a usufruct, but only for improvement of the land (i.e., they cannot clear a forest and make the land something different fom what it was before) p 104 art 560

- Usufructs of mines and quarries are governed in the mineral code p 104 art 561

- Usufructuary of timberland may retain proceeds of timber operations as long as he manages the timberlands as a prudent administrator p 104 art 562

- Cash dividends belong to usufructuary p 104 art 552

- Liquidation dividend or stock redemption belongs to naked owner, subject to the usufruct p 104 art 552

- Usufructuary has the right to vote shares of stock or exercise similar rights in corporations unless otherwise provided p 104 art 553

## *Usufruct over consumable things*

- Consumable things are things that cannot be used without their substance being changed, like food, money, and stocks of merchandise p 102 art 536

- The usufructuary becomes the owner of the consumable BUT at the end of the usufruct, he must
  - pay the naked owner the value that the consumable had at the beginning of the usufruct; or
  - replace the consumable with things of the same kind and quantity p 103 art 538

## *Usufruct over nonconsumable things*

- Nonconsumables are things that can be used without their substance being altered (even though natural deterioration may gradually occur), such as shares of stock, land, houses, vehicles, animals or furniture p 103 art 537

- The usufructuary of nonconsumables has the right to possess them and to derive the utility, profits, and advantage that they may produce, under the obligation of preserving their substance p 103 art 539
- The usufructuary of nonconsumables is entitled to possess and enjoy the thing to the exclusion of the naked owner p 103 art 539
- He may enjoy the natural and civil fruits it may produce p 103 art 550, 556

## *Divisibility of usufruct*

- Usufruct can be divided, or partitioned p 104 art 541
- Naked ownership can be divided or partitioned, subject to the usufruct p 105 art 542
- A usufructuary having a share in indivision alone cannot request partition in kind or by licitation, nor can a naked owner having a share in indivision alone request partition in kind or by licitation. But if the usufructuary and naked owner come together and jointly seek partition in kind or by licitation, then they can make that happen p 105 art 543

## *Methods of establishing a usufruct*

- Juridical act during the lifetime of the grantor: this is called a *conventional* usufruct p 105
- Grantor's express statement in his last will and testament p 105
- By operation of law: this is called a *legal* usufruct p 105 art 544
    - Usufruct of surviving spouse: generally, in an intestate situation, a spouse may have a usufruct over some portion of a spouse's share of community property p 105 art 890 (see Chapter 24 on successions for a detailed discussion)

## *Termination of the usufruct*

- Usufruct of a natural person terminates at the death of that natural person p 106 art 607
- Usufruct of a juridical person terminates at either 30 years or the end of the juridical person, whichever happens first (unless the juridical person is the trustee of a trust) p 106 art 608
- Legal usufruct of surviving spouse terminates at death of usufructuary or at remarriage p 105 art 890
- Usufruct may be created for shorter term (so the above are the outer limits, which the grantor can change) p 106 art 610
- Usufruct may be modified in any manner consistent with usufructs p 106 art 545

## *Usufruct in favor of several usufructuaries*

- Usufruct can be created in favor of consecutive usufructuaries p 107 art 547
- As soon as one usufruct ends, it inures to the next usufructuary p 107 art 547
- The usufruct must be alive or conceived (or in existence if a juridical person) at the time the usufruct is granted p 107 art 548

## *Responsibilities of the usufructuary*

- Make an inventory of the property subject to the usufruct; if not, the naked owner can prevent the usufruct from possessing the property p 107 art 570
- The usufructuary can file a sworn detailed descriptive list instead of an inventory in certain succession proceedings p 108 La CCP art 3136
- Usufructuary shall give security that he will use the property as a good and prudent administrator and

fulfill all obligations imposed on him by law; security may be dispensed with unless required  p 108 art 572

- Usufructuary may be required to give security in an amount of the value of the property subject to the usufruct  p 108 art 573
- Security can be dispensed with in the following circumstances: p 108 art 573
    - A person has a legal usufruct under article 223 (parental usufruct on minor child's property) or 3252 (special indigent surviving spouse usufruct of up to $1000)
    - An 890 (surviving spouse) usufruct unless the naked owner is not a child of the usufructuary *and* is a forced heir of the decedent
    - A parent has a legal usufruct under article 891 (where the brothers and sisters inherit from the dead sibling but the parents get usufruct over the property) unless the naked owner (brother/sister of the deceased) is not a child of the usufructuary
    - Surviving spouse has a legal usufruct under article 2434 (the marital portion) unless the naked owner is a child of the decedent but not a child of the usufructuary
- Usufructuary is always charged with being a prudent administrator and delivering the property to the naked owner when the usufruct terminates  p 109 art 539
- If the thing is damaged because of fraud, default, or neglect, the usufructuary is liable for losses  p 109 art 576
- The usufructuary must make all "ordinary" repairs and the naked owner may compel him to make those repairs  p 109 art 577
- The naked owner must make all "extraordinary" repairs (reconstruction of the whole or substantial part of the property is extraordinary, everything else is ordinary)  p 109 art 578
- Usufructuary must pay annual and periodic charges like taxes and condo fees during the usufruct  p 109 art 584

## Right of Habitation

- Nontransferable, nonheritable strictly personal servitude that allows a natural person to dwell in the house of another  p 109 art 630
- The right of habitation is created and extinguished in the same manner as usufructs, except it never arises by operation of law  p 109 art 631
- It can last until the death of the person with the right unless a shorter period is stipulated in the act creating it  p 109 art 638
- If the person with the right was unmarried at the time the right arose, the right extends to his family  p 110 art 633
- The person with the right of habitation may have guests  p 110 art 634

## Right of Use

- A heritable, transferrable right in favor of a natural person or juridical person over a specified use of an estate that is less than full enjoyment, more limited than habitation  p 111 art 639
- It can also be a personal right granted in a predial servitude in favor of a natural person or juridical person  p 111 art 640
- Right of use can be in favor of a natural or juridical person  p 111 art 641
- The right of use can include future rights that may be contemplated to become necessary  p 111 art 642

- The right of use is transferrable p 111 art 643
- The right of use is heritable p 111 art 644
- The right of use is otherwise governed by the same rules as usufructs and predial servitudes p 111 art 645

# Predial Servitudes

- Predial servitude is a charge or burden on a *servient* estate for the benefit of a *dominant* estate, belonging to two different owners p 112 art 646
- Predial servitude is an incorporeal immovable p 112 art 649
- An estate is a distinct corporeal immovable
- There must be a benefit to the dominant estate; a future benefit will suffice p 112 art 647
- The two estates don't have to touch or abut each other, but must be near enough so that one can derive a benefit from the other p 112 art 648
- Predial servitude cannot be separated from the dominant estate; it cannot be leased, alienated, or encumbered p 112 art 650
- Predial servitude may be limited to certain days, or hours p 112 art 652
- If the dominant estate is partitioned, the servitude runs in favor of each estate subdivided from the original subdivided estate but cannot place an additional burden on the servient estate p 112 art 747
- Servient estate owner only has to maintain his estate in a suitable condition to allow for the exercise of the servitude p 113 art 651
- Servient estate cannot interfere or make inconvenient the enjoyment of the servitude p 113 art 748

## *Kinds of predial servitudes*

- Natural, legal, and conventional p 113 art 654

### Natural servitude

- These servitudes arise from where estates are naturally situated, like if one estate is higher than another so drainage occurs between the different elevations p 114 art 655
- May only be altered by agreement of the parties if the public interest is not adversely affected p 113 art 729
- These servitudes are not created by law but are recognized by law p 114 art 655
- The servient estate may not impede the flow of water p 114 art 656

### Legal servitude

- May only be altered by agreement of the parties if the public interest is not adversely affected p 113 art 729
- These servitudes arise by operation of law for the benefit of the general public or for particular people p 114 art 659
- One legal servitude example is that people must keep their buildings in proper repair so that pieces don't fall down on passersby p 114 art 660
- Building owners may generally do what they want with their buildings, but cannot deprive neighbors of enjoyment of their estates, like building such that it blocks a neighbor's sunlight or view p 115 art 667

## 9 • SERVITUDES

Other legal servitudes relate to common enclosures, common walls, and rights of passage p 115 art 672

### *Types of legal servitudes – Common walls and enclosures*

- The landowner who builds first can rest ½ of a partition wall on the land of his neighbor, with restrictions p 115 art 673
- A boundary fence is presumed to be common unless there is evidence to the contrary (like a survey) p 115 art 685
- If there is no enclosure on adjoining lands, a landowner may force his neighbor to help pay for a fence p 115 art 685
- A ditch between 2 estates is presumed to be common unless proved otherwise p 115 art 686

### *Types of legal servitudes – Rights of passage*

- The dominant estate is the enclosed estate, the servient estate is the estate over which the right of passage runs
- The owner of an estate with no public road access may claim a right of passage over neighboring property to the nearest public road or utility p 115 art 689
- The extent of the right of passage must be suitable for the kind of traffic reasonably necessary for that kind of estate p 115 art 690
- The owner of the enclosed estate may construct a road in compliance with state and local standards on the right of way so they can use their right of passage p 116 art 691
- The right of passage can't be just anywhere the enclosed estate wants it; it must be the shortest route to the public road where it is the least injurious to the servient estate p 116 art 692
- If an estate becomes enclosed because of a voluntary act of its owner, like donating away the pieces around actual passage, neighbors are not bound to furnish him passage p 116 art 693
- If a piece of property is partitioned, and a part of that property is now enclosed, the owner of the land on which the passage was previously exercised shall grant a right of passage to the enclosed estate, even if it is not the shortest route. So, if a subdivision splits up lots, and one is left in the middle, that one in the middle gets a gratuitous right of passage where it has always had a right of passage p 116 art 694
- The owner of the enclosed estate cannot relocate the right of passage, but the owner of the servient estate can relocate it at his own expense p 116 art 695

### Conventional or voluntary servitudes

- These are entered into by contract, juridical acts, or by acquisitive prescription p 117 art 697, 740
- They can only be on distinct (owned by different owners) corporeal immovables p 117 art 698
- If a right is granted that confers an advantage on an estate, it is presumed that this right is a predial servitude. If the right is granted to a person as the owner of an estate and is for himself, his heirs, and assigns, the right is also presumed to be a predial servitude p 117 art 733, 734
- Conventional servitudes are either affirmative (giving the owner of the dominant estate the right to do something) or negative (restricting the owner of the servient estate from doing something) p 117 art 706
    - Affirmative servitudes – right of passage, drainage rights
    - Negative servitudes – prohibition of building, prohibition of use of an estate as a commercial or industrial establishment, prohibit building a wall blocking a neighbor's view
- Conventional servitudes are also either apparent (perceived by exterior works) or nonapparent (no exterior signs) p 118 art 739

- Apparent servitudes are evidenced by, for example, a roadway, a window in a common wall, or an aqueduct p 118 art 707
- Apparent servitudes may be created by contract, by juridical act, or by acquisitive prescription p 118
- Nonapparent servitudes include building restrictions, utility servitudes, rights of passage
- Nonapparent servitudes can be acquired by title only p 118 art 739

Examples of predial servitudes can be found in article 699, but are not limited to those listed therein: rights of view, light, passage, etc. p 119 articles 700-705

## *Establishing a predial servitude*

- Predial servitudes can be established by title, by destination of the owner, or by acquisitive prescription p 119 art 740

### Predial servitude by title

- This is done by a sale or a donation, either of which must be through a properly confected juridical act; a predial servitude by title is an alienation (sale or donation) of a part of property to which laws of alienation of immovables apply p 119 art 708, 722 So for example, you sell a piece of your property by subdividing it, and when you transfer the title to the new, adjacent landowner, you reserve or give a servitude on one of the pieces of property that is transferred. This is one of the ways that an apparent servitude can be done, and is the only way a nonapparent servitude can be done. It must meet all of the requirements for transfer of immovables.

### Predial servitude by "destination of the owner"

- When there exists between two estates now owned by the same person a relationship that, had the two pieces of land or estates been owned by two different people, would have resulted in the formation of a servitude, then an *apparent, conventional* servitude is formed when the one owner no longer continues to own both of the estates – unless there is a provision to the contrary p 120 art 741 (common law *implied easement by prior use*). So, for example, if I owned two tracts of land, one of which had a water well on one of the pieces of land that both lots used for water, and I sold one of the pieces of land, then the other piece of land would still have a servitude for the water well, unless there was a provision to the contrary in the act of sale.
- A nonapparent servitude will arise only if the owner has previously recorded a written act in the registry of the court in the parish where the estate is located p 120 art 741

### Predial servitude by acquisitive prescription

- An apparent servitude may be acquired by acquisitive prescription of either 10 years (with good faith and just title) or 30 years (in the absence of good faith and just title) p 120 art 742

## *Who can create a predial servitude?*

- An owner or naked owner can create a predial servitude by title p 120 art 708, 710
- The predial servitude cannot infringe on the rights of the usufructuary p 121 art 710
- A usufructuary cannot create a predial servitude p 121 art 711
- A mandatary may establish a predial servitude if he has an express and special power to do so p 121 art 709
- A mandatary can accept a servitude on behalf of the owner of the dominant estate, and acceptance does not need to be in writing p 121

## 9 • SERVITUDES

- A minor or interdict may accept a servitude in his benefit without the assistance of his tutor or curator p 121 art 736

### *Predial servitude for a term or with a condition*

- A person having ownership for a term may create a predial servitude, but the servitude ceases with his ownership p 121 art 712
- If a predial servitude exists on an estate with a right of redemption, the servitude will cease if the right of redemption is exercised p 121 art 713

### *Predial servitude with co-owners in indivision*

- Need consent of all co-owners p 122 art 714
- If a sole co-owner attempts to grant a servitude, it is not null, but its execution is suspended until consent of all of the co-owners is obtained p 122 art 714
- If the property is partitioned by licitation (sale) and the co-owner who created the servitude buys the whole property, the servitude operates against the whole estate p 122 art 718
- If the property is partitioned by licitation (sale) and a third party buys the whole property, the servitude is extinguished p 122 art 718
- If a servitude is agreed to in a contract or juridical act, but the person creating does not yet own the property, the servitude will exist when the person who created it buys the property p 122 art 726

### *Multiple servitudes*

- The owner of the estate may create multiple servitudes, as long as they don't conflict with each other or with earlier-created servitudes p 123 art 720
- A predial servitude may be established on more than one estate for the benefit of just one estate, or one estate may have a servitude for the benefit of multiple estates. It's a mess out there, really servitude-wise p 123 art 724
- You can have a servitude on just part of an estate p 123 art 727 … or just part of the time art 728
- You can have a servitude on mortgaged property p 123 art 721
- You can have (rarely) a servitude on a public thing but this cannot be through acquisitive prescription p 124

### *Extinction of predial servitudes*

- Can happen in 1 of 5 ways: through destruction of the dominant or servient estate, prescription of nonuse, confusion, expiration of term, or renunciation

#### Extinction of predial servitude through destruction of an estate

- The total destruction of either of the estates, dominant or servient, extinguishes the servitude. For example, a property being permanently flooded. The destruction must be of the part that includes the servitude p 124 art 751

#### Extinction of predial servitude through nonuse

- Nonuse for 10 years p 124 art 753
- Nonuse begins from either last use (for affirmative servitudes) or the occurrence of an event contrary to the servitude (for a negative servitude) p 124 art 754

- If the owner of the dominant estate is prevented from using the servitude by an obstacle which he is powerless to remove, then prescription is suspended for up to 10 years p 125 art 755
- Prescription is not suspended if the servitude cannot be exercised because a building or other construction owned by the owner of the dominant estate is destroyed p 125 art 756
- Anyone using the servitude is okay to interrupt nonuse p 125 art 757
- A partial use of the servitude is okay to interrupt nonuse and constitutes use of the whole servitude p 125 art 759
- Use by a co-owner of the servitude prevents the running of prescription as to all co-owners p 126 art 762

**Extinction of predial servitude by confusion**

- When the same person owns the dominant and servient estate (called "confusion"), the servitude becomes extinguished p 126 art 765
- When the ownership of either the dominant and servient estates is retained by one person, and one of the properties is subject to a resolutory condition, the servitude is extinct by confusion until the occurrence of that resolutory condition. For example, if the dominant estate has a right of passage over a servient estate until a public road is built, the servitude exists until the resolutory condition (the building of the public road) occurs.
- Confusion does not occur between separate and community property. Separate property is always separate property, so a servitude on the servient estate is the separate property of a spouse even though the dominant property is community; the servitude will be separate and the servient property will be separate (unless they make it community; see Chapter 12 on matrimonial regimes) p 126 art 768
- Once extinguished by confusion, a servitude cannot be merely reestablished by separating ownership of the two estates p 126 art 769
- The owner of the servient estate can abandon the servient estate, or the portion burdened by the servitude, to the owner of the dominant estate p 126 art 770

**Extinction of predial servitude by renunciation**

- A servitude may be extinguished by the express and written renunciation of the dominant estate p 127 art 771
- A renunciation by a co-owner does not extinguish the servitude, just the right for that co-owner to use the servitude p 127 art 772

**Extinction of predial servitude by expiration of term or condition**

- If the servitude is established for a term or under a resolutory condition, it is extinguished when that term expires or the event happens p 127 art 773

# Building Restrictions

- Building restrictions are a limitation on the use of property imposed by an ancestor in title (like a subdivision, or a condo building) in accordance with a general plan where the purpose is to maintain certain building standards and uniformity in improvements p 127 art 775
- They may only be established by juridical act executed by the owner of an immovable or a group consisting of all of the owners of the affected immovables p 127 art 776
- Building restrictions are incorporeal immovables p 128 art 777
- Building improvements may impose affirmative duties on owners for upkeep and general maintenance,

## 9 • SERVITUDES

but can't impose fees for alienation, lease, or encumbrance of the immovable p 128 art 778
- They may be amended or terminated by agreement of the owners p 128 art 780
- If there is a noticeable violation of a building restriction, a lawsuit for violation must be brought within 2 years, or the immovable on which the violation is freed of the restriction p 128 art 781

Building restriction can be abandoned if there are a great number of violations of all or most restrictions p 128 art 782

# 10
# Donations

Donations are the only way property may be given or received gratuitously (freely) in Louisiana  p 129 art 1467
- *Inter vivos* donation is made during the life of the donor and is intended to have immediate and irrevocable effect  p 129 art 1468 (this chapter is mainly about such donations made by the living)
- *Mortis causa* donation is made to take effect after the death of the donor (via a will)  p 129 art 1469
    - Both natural and juridical persons can make and receive donations inter vivos
    - Only natural persons can make donations mortis causa
    - Both natural persons and juridical persons can receive donations mortis causa.

## Donations inter vivos

- Is a contract  p 129 art 1468
- Made by a person (natural or juridical)  p 129
- The person divests themselves of property they currently own  p 129 art 1529
- The person receiving the property accepts in writing or by required formality  p 129
- The donation is irrevocable  p 129 art 1468 (subject to some narrow exceptions discussed below)

Person who donates is called the *donor*.

Person who receives the donation is called the *donee*.

## Capacity to donate inter vivos

- All persons, natural and juridical, have capacity to donate except as prohibited by law  p 130 art 1470
- Generally, capacity is the same as for making contracts (see Chapter 11 on obligations), but there are a few special rules
- Donors of proper capacity must be capable of understanding that they are disposing of their property gratuitously and irrevocably  p 131 art 1477

## Capacity to receive

- All persons, natural and juridical, are capable of receiving.
- For minors, a parent or tutor has the ability to accept the donation on the child's behalf  p 130
- There is a difference between contractual capacity for a minor to accept a donation and capacity for a minor to legally receive a donation. All minors can legally receive a donation, but do not have the contractual capacity to accept a donation  p 130

10 ▪ DONATIONS

## GUIDE TO CAPACITY

| Make inter vivos donation | Determined at time donation is made | p 130 | art 1471 |
|---|---|---|---|
| Make mortis causa donation | Determined at time testator executes donation (testament) | p 130 | art 1471 |
| Receive inter vivos donation | Determined at time donee accepts donation | p 131 | art 1472 |
| Receive mortis causa donation | Determined at time of death of testator; donee cannot accept until donor dies | p 131 | art 1472 |
| Receive donation subject to suspensive condition | Capacity to accept is determined when condition if fulfilled | p 131 | art 1473 |
| Make donation inter vivos or mortis causa by minor donor under 16 | No capacity unless donation is to his spouse or children | p 130 | art 1476 |
| Make donation mortis causa by minor donor over the age of 16 | Has capacity | p 130 | art 1476 |
| Make donation inter vivos by minor over the age of 16 | No capacity unless donation is to his spouse or children | p 130 | art 1476 |
| Receive donation, minors generally | All persons, even minors have capacity | p 130 | |
| Receive donation inter vivos, fetus | Child must be in utero at the time the donation is made & later born alive | p 131 | art 1476 |
| Receive donation mortis causa, fetus | Child must be in utero at time of death of testator and later born alive | p 131 | art 1476 |

## Donative intent

- There must be a clear donative expression that the property is given gratuitously by the donor and that the donor is divesting himself without any compensation or benefit p 131
- Language must be clear and unambiguous: "I donate to" or "I give," *not* "I want them to" p 131
- Manual gifts must be done with clear intent to divest the donor of property and clear intent to donate with no expectation of return p. 131 art 1543

## Present and immediate transfer of ownership

- The donor gratuitously divests themselves
- At present and irrevocably
- Of the thing in favor of another p 132 art 1468

- Cannot donate future property, and donation is effective immediately upon acceptance p 132 art 1551

## Irrevocability

- A true donation must be irrevocable once it is donated to donee p 132 art 1468, 1551
- The donor must relinquish complete control over the donated property to the donee; if not, the donation fails p 132 art 1468
- It is allowable to donate the naked ownership of a thing and the usufruct to another, although reserving the usufruct for the donor may be problematic. Previously, one donating property to another but reserving a usufruct for himself was not considered a true donation, but LA C.C. art 1522 states that a donation of naked ownership to one and usufruct to another is permissible – but this does not address the question of reserving the usufruct to the donor himself. It is unsettled.

## Donations of community property

- For community property to be donated to a third party, it requires the *concurrence* of the other spouse p 133 art 2349
- Usual or customary gifts – like a birthday gift or an anniversary gift, modest in nature relative to the income of the spouses – do not require concurrence of the other spouse p 133 art 2349
- Spouses may donate unlimited amounts to each other p 133 art 2343
- One spouse may donate their interest in community property to the other, converting that property to the other spouse's separate property p 133 art 2343.1
- One spouse may donate their separate property to the community, making it community property p 133 art 2343.1
- There is an important difference between community property and property owned in indivision. If a spouse donates property to another spouse, it should be donated *to the community* to ensure that it is community property. There are different rules for community property and property owned in indivision (see Chapter 12). The way property is owned can affect everything from the way it can be sold to the way it is distributed through death.

## Acceptance

- Donations are only effective if accepted *during the lifetime of the donor*. If the donor dies before the donation is accepted, the donation fails p 134 art 1544
- Acceptance must be in writing unless it is a manual gift (corporeal movable) accompanied by actual delivery p 135 art 1543
- Acceptance must be express and unconditional by donee (e.g., a mere signature on a document is not enough to signify acceptance) p 135
- Ownership transfers at the time the donation is accepted p 134 art 1544, 1551
- The date of the donation is the date of the acceptance, not the date the donation was written or made; it is not retroactive p 134 art 1544
- A manual gift is accepted when the donor receives the gift p 134 art 1544
- The donation can be accepted by the donee or by a mandatary having power of attorney to receive donations p 134 art 1545 and 2997
- If the donee dies before accepting, successors may not accept for him p 134 art 1546
- A creditor may not accept for a donee p 134 art 1547

- A parent, other ascendant, or tutor of an unemancipated minor may accept on behalf of the minor even if that person is the donor p 135 art 1548
- Acceptance must be in writing unless it is a manual gift, then it must be by delivery p 148 art 1543
- Exceptions to the rule that acceptance must be express and unconditional: p 135
    - For immovable property: by LA R.S. 9:2371, alienating (selling or donating) or encumbering (mortgaging) a property is an act which constitutes acceptance under article 1544
    - For incorporeals: authentic acts which transfer ownership, or transfer by rules for that type of instrument (including those subject to UCC rules and regulations), indicate acceptance under article 1544

## Charges or conditions

- The donor may impose charges or conditions on the donee providing that they're not contrary to good morals or law p 136 art 1528
    - *Suspensive conditions* are ones that withhold the donation until the condition is fulfilled p 136 This means the donation cannot happen until the charge or condition happens and the donor accepts. An example of a suspensive condition in general is in real estate, a purchase of a home predicated on the sale of another home. If this were a donation, the donation would fail if the first home did not sell.
    - *Resolutory conditions* are ones that stop the donation once the condition occurs p 136 This means that the donation is effective for the reason the donation is made, and should the charge or condition fail, then the donation will also fail. For example, if the donor donates land for a road the donation is valid, but if the donee changes the use to a fenced yard, then the donation is null because the resolutory donation has failed and the property is returned to the donor.
- A *prohibited substitution* p 136 involves two or more successive donees, where the donor first gives the thing to one donee, but requires that the donee in turn gives it to a second donee. This is only permissible through a trust or other instrument. For example, if I want to give my diamond ring to my oldest daughter, then make her give it to her daughter, it is a prohibited substitution.

## Right of return

- The donor may, in the body of the donation, stipulate the right of return of the donated thing if the donee dies before the donor p 137 art 1532, 1533
- Only the original donor can reserve this right of return p 136 art 1532
- If the thing has passed to the donee's heirs, the thing is returned to the donor
- If the thing has been transferred for value to a third party, the donee's successors owe the donor the loss incurred as a result of the transfer p 136 art 1532, 1533

## Prohibited dispositions p 137

- Entirety of one's estate art 1497-1498
- Donations with immoral or impossible conditions art 1519
- Donations with prohibited substitutions art 1520
- Donations of future property art 1529
- Donations depending on the will or whim of the donor art 1530
- Donations paying future unspecified debts art 1531

## *Prohibitions against donation of all property*

- You cannot donate yourself into poverty. If the donor doesn't keep enough for their subsistence, the donations will be null.
- This donation will be set aside p 138 art 1498
- Only the donor's circumstances *at the time of the donation* will be considered, and they must reserve enough for their subsistence at this time p 137
- If the donation is onerous, for example a donation for future caretaking of the donor, this prohibition will not apply p 138
- Forced heirship considerations apply even if it is onerous or remunerative p 138
- If the donor does donate all their patrimony, a donation for a movable is null for the whole p 137
- If the donor does donate the entirety of their patrimony, a donation for an immovable is null for the whole, subject to these qualifications:
  - The donor can receive it back if it has not been alienated
  - If the donee has alienated (sold, donated, etc.) the immovable, by onerous title, then the donee has to return the value that the immovable had at the time of the initial donation
  - If the donee of the immovable now has the immovable and the immovable has a real right in it, the donor can get the immovable back, subject to the real right; and the donee owes the donor the diminution in value of the immovable

There is no set value as to what constitutes "subsistence"; it varies based on location and circumstance. Donors often try to donate away all of their possessions for medical purposes.

## *Prohibitions against donations containing impossible conditions contrary to law or morals*

- Cannot make a donation inter vivos which contains conditions contrary to law or morals p 140 art 1519
- The unlawful or immoral condition is stricken, but the remainder of the donation is enforced as written p 140

### Impossible conditions contrary to law

- When a law prohibits an action and the donation requires it, or when a law permits an action and a donation forbids it p. 139 art 1519
- Language is important in law. "Shall" means it is mandatory; "may" means it is permissible.
- The example in the book is that people may contract out of guarantees such as warranty against redhibitory (hidden) defects in immovable property between the buyer and seller, because this is "suppletive," or permissive p 139 But parties may never contract out of the right to rescind a sale for lesion beyond moiety (when the sale price is less than half of the fair market value) because this is never waivable, even if the parties agree to it. This is called "imperative" p 139

### Impossible conditions against public policy

- Example in the book is the restraint on the sale of immovable property (unless it is in a trust). It is in the public interest to keep property in commerce p 139

### Immoral conditions

- Requiring donee to engage in activities against the good moral conduct of the community, or their own moral or religious conduct p 140

## 10 • DONATIONS

### *Prohibited substitutions*

- Donor gives full ownership to a first donee who must preserve the thing donated p 140 art 1520 The first donee must then give the donated thing to a second donee not of their own choice p 140
- Both donations are invalid p 140
- This is prohibited, but may be accomplished by putting the thing in a trust or by giving naked ownership to one donee and usufruct to another see art 1522

### *Prohibitions against donations of future property*

- Donations inter vivos can only be of property the donor presently owns p 141 art 1529
- Future property donations are null p 141

### *Prohibitions against donations inter vivos that impose conditions that depend solely on the will or whim of the donor*

- Donor who makes a *potestative* donation (a donation that is fulfilled only if the donor chooses to do so), and has no measurable guidelines, makes the donation null p. 141 art 1530
- Example is if the donor has the right to revoke the donation at any time
- This only applies inter vivos, because in donations mortis causa, the testator can no longer exercise his will p 141

### *Prohibitions against donations conditioned on donee paying future and unspecified debts and charges*

- Donation is null if it makes donee pay debts or charges not existing at the time of donation unless they are certain or ascertainable p 142 art 1531
- Can be future debts if they are described with particularity in the donation p 141
- If they are unspecified, the donation will fail
- An acceptable unspecified amount may be "all bills related to college education" or "all tax bills related to immovable property for five years," because this is ascertainable

## Revocation and dissolution

Donation may be: p 142 art 1556

- Revoked for ingratitude of donee
- Dissolved for nonfulfillment of suspensive condition
- Dissolved for occurrence of resolutory condition
- Dissolved for nonperformance of other conditions and charges

### *Revocation of donation inter vivos*

- Donation inter vivos may only be revoked for *ingratitude* of done, by:
  - Attempting to take the life of the donor; p 142 or
  - Being guilty of (similar to the right to disinherit; see later discussion in successions Chapter 24): p. 142
    - Cruel treatment

- Crimes
- Grievous injury

## *Dissolution of inter vivos donation*

- If the donation inter vivos is conditioned on a suspensive condition, the donation is dissolved when the condition can no longer be fulfilled p 143 art 1562
- If the donation inter vivos is conditioned on a resolutory condition, the donation may be dissolved only by the parties or by judicial decree, if the resolutory condition is satisfied p 143 art 1562

## *Donor's rights and donee's liabilities upon revocation or dissolution*

Donor has the right to full restoration of the thing donated or the value of the thing if it cannot be restored p. 143

- Upon *dissolution* of a donation inter vivos, the donor is entitled to return of the thing free from alienations, leases, or encumbrances (liens, etc.) created by the donee or his successors. If this is not possible, the donor is entitled to the value of the property or value in diminution of the property p 143 art 1565
- Upon *revocation* of a donation inter vivos, the donor is entitled to return of the thing if the donee is able to. If the donee is unable to return the thing donated, he is liable to the donor for the value of the thing p 144 art 1560
- Upon dissolution *or* revocation, the donee must restore or repay the value of the fruits p 144 art 1566
- If the donor is entitled to receive the thing in the same condition because of revocation or dissolution, but the thing is unable to be restored to the original condition, the donor may opt to receive the thing in its current condition and receive compensation for any loss of value p 145 art 1567

## Form of donations

- Form includes the document itself as well as ritual p 145
- Authentic act must be perfected in prescribed order with all parties present, or it will fail as an act p 145
- Failure to follow statutory requirement of form for donations can be fatal to donation p 145
- Donation of property in Louisiana must follow Louisiana law, even if donation takes place outside of Louisiana. This requires an authentic act even if the state the act is perfected in does not require one p 145

## *Form requirements*

- An act of donation must be an authentic act, unless it is a manual gift of a movable (as discussed below) p 146 art 1541, 1543
- An act of donation for an immovable must be an authentic act p 146 (not by manual gift)
- Donations required to be in writing also require acceptance to be express and in writing.
  - The acceptance may be in the donation
  - The acceptance may be in a subsequent writing unless prohibited by law
  - The acceptance does not need to be in an authentic act p 146
- Authentic act must identify the donor, the donee, and the thing donated. If not identified sufficiently, it must be identifiable p 146 art 1542
- If the authentic act is not in proper form, it can be confirmed by an authentic act that would be retroactive to the date of the original donation p 146 art 1845, 1846

## 10 · DONATIONS

## Simulated donations or donations in disguise

- This is a sale or transaction that is actually a donation but that skirts the rules and formality of donation rules. It may be a valid contract of a different nature, but will fail as a donation. The most often repeated example is that you cannot sell your farm for a dollar. This is not a true sale, but is actually a donation. For the transfer to have effect, it must be in the form for gratuitous donations, an authentic act p 147

- A *relative simulation* is one where the contract has an effect, for example to actually transfer the property but for a different price than stated p 147 art 2027

- This violates the basic contractual idea that there must be a price in a contract, either fixed or determinable and must not be out of proportion of the thing sold p 147 art 2464

## Four exceptions to authentic act requirement for donations

- Manual gift p 148 art 1543
- Certain incorporeal movables transferable by endorsement or delivery p 148 art 1550
- Onerous donation p 148 art 1526
- Remunerative donation p 148 art 1527

### *Manual Gifts*

- A corporeal movable may be delivered to the donee with no other formality p 148 art 1543
- Donee taking possession constitutes acceptance p 148
- Donation is valid and effective at the time of delivery p 148
- A titled motor vehicle can be a manual gift even though title still must be recorded with the OMV. p 148 Manual delivery of a pickup, for example, transfers ownership, but OMV requires more
- For the title of the motor vehicle to transfer with the OMV to the donee, an authentic act of donation must accompany the title (unless it is part of a licensed car dealer transaction, then the parties can use a statement that a manual gift occurred) p 148

### *Other incorporeal movable property: promissory notes and other negotiable instruments*

- These may be donated by authentic act *or* in compliance with the requirements for that particular instrument p 149 art 1550 For example, checks can be signed over by the usual bank process
- Investment property controlled by UCC rules may be donated by a writing that evidences donative intent and directs the transfer to the donee to his account or for his benefit p 149
- Promissory notes and other negotiable instruments are generally transferred by change of possession and/or endorsement, or by authentic act (though not necessary) p 149
- Donations of insurance policies and beneficiaries are governed by the provisions of the policies and not the laws of this state p 149
- Interests in business cannot be transferred this way; they are not evidenced by certificates, so an authentic act is necessary p 149

### *Onerous and Remunerative Donations*

- These donations have charges or conditions, or are made for serviced rendered, and are not subject to ordinary donations rules (including the requirement of an authentic act) p 150
- These donations follow the rules of ordinary contracts, p 150 but out of caution should be made in au-

thentic act in case the 2/3 value (below) is found to be lacking p 151
- If an onerous or remunerative donation transfers title to immovable property, it must be in an authentic act *or* an act under private signature (it must still meet the form for any such transfer) p 152

**Onerous donations**

- A donation that is made with an obligation imposed on the donee that results in an advantage to the donor art 1526
- This is a *future* charge, burden, or condition
- Example: I will donate a car to you if you drive my child to school every day for the next year
- Regular donations formalities do not apply unless *at the time of the donation,* the cost of performing the obligation is less than 2/3 of the value of the thing donated

**Remunerative donations**

- A donation that is made to repay someone for services rendered that are capable of being measured in money (unless at the time of the donation, the value of the services is less than 2/3 the value of the thing) p 150 art 1527
- This is compensation for *past* services rather than a gratuitous gift
- Example: I am donating a car to you for *having driven* my child to school for the past year

**Dation En Paiement compared**

- Not a remunerative donation, but more like an offer in compromise art 2657 (see Chapter 21)
- There must be a debt of a certain sum in money p 151 (not services rendered)
- The debt must exist at the time of the execution of the dation instrument p 151

# Recordation

- To be effective against third persons, immovable property donations must be properly recorded in the parish where the property is situated p 152 art 3338
- Notary is obligated to record unless this is waived by the parties in writing p 152 LA RS 35:199
- Donations of titled movables may be subject to OMV registration requirements p 152

# 11

# Obligations and Contracts

Every juridical act that a notary prepares is an *obligation*, a legal relationship between 2 or more persons (or a person and the state).

An obligation exists when p 153 LA CC art 1756

- a person is bound to take or not take an action (*the obligor*) in favor of another (*the obligee*) – the obligation may be created voluntarily or may be imposed by law
- the performance or duty is legally enforceable

An obligation can arise from p 153 art 1757

- contracts
- law (such as a vendor's lien)
- wrongful acts (such as a judgment lien)
- the management of affairs of another (such as tutorship)
- unjust enrichment
- other acts or facts

If a person has a simultaneous right to take (or not take) an action and simultaneous right to enforce obligations against the other party, the parties are called *mutual obligors* and *mutual obligees*, or *co-relative obligations*.

A *contract* is an agreement between 2 or more parties where obligations are created, modified, or extinguished p 154 art 1906

## Real obligation

- Describes the relationship between a person and a thing (as opposed to a personal right which is described as the relationship between two persons)
- A real right is a right in a thing that is good against the world. A real obligation is an obligation incurred as a result of a real right p 154 art 1763
- A real obligation: p 154
    - creates rights in immovable property
    - owner of that property may assert that right against other persons
    - may also be understood as ownership and its dismemberments
- An example is a servitude or a mortgage

## Heritable obligations

An obligation is *heritable* if it may be transferred by:

- Donation
- Sale
- Assignment
- Another means (example: testamentary donation)

It is presumed that obligations are heritable unless shown to be otherwise, for example in the language that creates the obligation p 154

There is a rebuttable presumption (it is taken to be true unless someone can prove otherwise) that an obligation is heritable, unless prohibited by law or contrary to the nature of the obligation. For example, old real estate covenants that prohibited groups of people from living in certain subdivisions: these have been found to not be heritable even though they were at one time real rights attached to the property p 154

Heritable means transferrable between *living persons*, not **in**heritable, and enforceable against the successors of the original obligors and obligees p 155 art 1756

## Strictly personal obligations

A strictly personal obligation is only enforceable by the original obligee or against the original obligor   p 155 art 1766

- The obligation is strictly personal on the part of the obligor if it requires the special skill of the obligor
- The obligation is strictly personal on the part of the obligee if it is intended for the exclusive benefit of that obligee

## Conditional obligations

A conditional obligation is one whose occurrence depends on an uncertain event p 156 art 1767, 1778 The uncertain event can be suspensive or resolutory:

- Suspensive condition (condition precedent) is not enforceable unless and until that uncertain event occurs p 156 art 1767 For example, a father may obligate himself to employee his child once the child has graduated from college. Graduation from college is the key uncertain ingredient for the obligation to be conditional, and graduation from college suspends the fulfillment until that has happened, if it does
- Resolutory condition is an obligation that is immediately enforceable but comes to an end if an uncertain event occurs p 156 art 1767 For example, a mother gives a son a vehicle unless he moves to a foreign country.

Conditions in conditional obligations may be: p 156

- Expressly defined by the parties, set forth in the contract
- Implicit in the nature of the contract, anticipated by an ordinary person
- Implicit by the intent of the parties
- Determined by law

Suspensive conditions must not be unlawful or impossible; this makes the entire obligation unenforceable, unless the parties agree that the unlawful or impossible portion would just be stricken and the rest of the obligation will remain p 156 This happens in real estate contracts: often there is a clause that will state that should any part of this contract be found invalid, the invalid portion be stricken as if not written…

Suspensive conditions that depend on the will or whim of the obligor are unenforceable as a potestative condition p

157 art 1770 (example in the book is: I will buy your car *if I like it* – this is not a real obligation).

Suspensive conditions that are unlawful or impossible make the obligation null p 157 art 1769

Resolutory conditions must not be unlawful or immoral, but if they are found to be so, the obligation may be enforced without the resolutory condition p 156 For example, in the case of restrictive covenants, the covenants were removed from the sale of properties

Resolutory conditions that depend on the will or whim of the obligor: p 157 art 1770

- The obligation is enforceable
- Resolutory condition must be exercised in good faith (example in book: at-will employment contracts, firing must be exercised in good faith)

An obligation for an output contract without a definitive amount is a valid contract: p 157 art 1975

- Quantity may be determined by output of one party or requirements of the other
- Requirements must be measured in good faith

For example, the obligation to buy all the oranges from a crop or all the crabs from a crabbing trip is valid

### *Express or implied conditions*

Conditions may be expressed in a stipulation; or implied by law, contract, or intent of the parties p 157 art 1768

### *Express or implied term*

Performance may be expressly stated or implied from the nature of the contract. Performance not subject to a term is due immediately p 157 art 1777 A term may be certain or fixed, or it may be uncertain, either when it is determinable but not fixed or when it is not determinable. If it is not determinable, the obligation must be performed with a reasonable time p 158 art 1778

Performance of the term of the obligation must be in accordance with the intention of the parties or by established usage when intent cannot be determined p 158 art 1785

## Transfer of obligations

Unless an obligation is strictly personal, it may be transferrable to another by operation of law or by consent p 158

- The original obligor remains bound to the obligation p 158 art 1821 (unless the obligee releases the original obligor)
- To be enforceable against third persons, assumption must be in writing
- Assumption is always voluntary
- Assumption does not occur by operation of law

## Subrogation

Subrogation is where a third person is substituted in place of another person for their rights and duties p 159 This happens a lot for insurance purposes.

- Subrogor – the person whose rights and duties are transferred
- Subrogee – the person to whom the rights and duties are transferred

When subrogation occurs, the obligation is extinguished for the original obligee. The right to enforce the obligation now belongs to the subragee unless provided for by law or contract p 159 art 1826

Subrogation can occur:

- by consent (by contract, like when you take out an insurance policy, it is included in that contract). This contract must expressly be made in writing p 159 art 1828
- by operation of law; there are 5 ways legal subrogation can take place p 160 art 1829
    - In favor of an oblige, who pays another obligee whose right is preferred to his because of a privilege, pledge, mortgage, or security interest
    - In favor of a purchaser of movable or immovable property who uses the purchase money to pay creditors holding any privilege, pledge, mortgage, or security interest on the property
    - In favor of an obligor who pays a debt he owes with others (or for others) and who has recourse against those others as a result of the payment
    - In favor of a successor who pays estate debts with his own funds
    - In the other cases provided by law

Subrogation performance may be accomplished by a third person unless the original obligor or obligee has an interest in performance only by the obligor p 160 art 1855

## Proof of obligations

- The person seeking to enforce the obligation has the burden of proving it exists; the person claiming that the obligation has been satisfied bears the burden of proving that p 160 art 1831
- If the obligation was required to be in a particular form, such as a written authentic act, the obligation must be proved by that act unless provided for by law p 160 art 1832
- If the original is lost or destroyed, its existence may be proven in another manner, perhaps by testimony p 160 art 1832
- If the lost juridical act is not a contract, like an Act of Adult Adoption, special rules apply, not Civil Code art 1832 p 318
- If your contract is valued under $500 and it is a type of contract that does not need to be in writing, it *may* be proved by what is considered to be competent evidence (maybe just testimony if it is believable); if your contract is valued at over $500 and is not the kind that needs to be in writing, it *must* be proved by at least one witness and corroborating circumstances p 161 art 1846

## Proof of obligations: types of acts

### *Authentic act* p 161 art 1833

- An act or instrument
- Executed before a notary public
- In the presence of two competent witnesses
- Signed by each party who executed it, by each witness, and by each notary public before whom it was executed
- Typed or handwritten printed name of each person *shall* be placed in a legible form immediately beneath the signature of each person signing
- The authentic act can be executed by the parties separately, but each party must complete their portion completely as the authentic act requires (e.g. each with two witnesses)
- Failure to include typed or printed names will not invalidate authenticity of act, but clerks may reject the act for filing
- If the party is unable to or does not know how to sign their name, they may make a mark

A validly confected authentic act constitutes full proof of the agreement it contains as between the parties, heirs, and successors by universal or particular title p 161 art 1835 So, testimonial evidence cannot be used to negate the contents p 162 art 1848

If a party states that the act was the product of forgery, fraud, or lack of capacity, then they may use extrinsic evidence (e.g. testimony) to prove that the authentic act was not validly confected p 162 art 1848

An act that fails to be authentic at the time it was confected may still be valid as an act under private signature p 162 But testimonial evidence cannot be used to prove the contents of an act under private signature either, unless there was a vice of consent like fraud, duress, or lack of capacity p 162 art 1848

### *Act under private signature (also called a private act)*

- An act in writing signed by the parties p 163 art 1837 is an act under private signature
- It is signed by, but does not necessarily have to be written by, the parties; and does not have to be signed in front of a notary

### *Act under private signature, duly acknowledged (also called acknowledged act)* p 163 art 1836

Act under private signature duly acknowledged (by a party) is an act under private signature that

- Is originally executed without a notary present
- A party thereafter acknowledges the signature
- Before a court, or
- Before a notary and two witnesses
- An act under private signature duly acknowledged cannot substitute for an authentic act when an authentic act is required (e.g. gratuitous donation of immovable)

Chapter 19 discusses other versions of acknowledgment (e.g. witness acknowledgment), and acts generally

## Contracts

An agreement where at least two people create, modify, or extinguish an obligation or mutual obligations p 164 art 1906

Contracts are mini laws that the parties create between themselves p 164 and may only be dissolved through the consent of the parties or on grounds created by the state; and must be performed in good faith p 164 art 1983

There are *unilateral* contracts, like donations inter vivos where the donor has an obligation to convey and the donee merely accepts p 164 art 1907 Contracts may also be *bilateral*, having mutual obligations.

## General principles

Parties have the broad freedom to contract for any purpose that is: p 164 art 1971

- Lawful
- Possible
- Determined or determinable

The only exception is if the law has restricted the parties' right to contract because the proposed agreement is illegal or has a detrimental effect on the public or otherwise p 164 art 7

### *Contracts provide evidence of intent of parties*

- Purpose of special forms for certain contracts is to provide evidence for the intent of that contract, such as a Sale Contract shows evidence that the parties intended to buy and sell a thing p 165

- Purpose of passing a contract before a notary is to provide evidence for the intent of that contract; the act of going to a notary is evidence that the parties intended to enter into the contract that was passed before the notary p 165
- Unambiguous contracts will be interpreted using the plain language of the contract p 165 art 2046 with words given their generally prevailing meaning or technical meaning if one exists p 165 art 2047 If words are susceptible of more than one meaning, the meaning that conforms to the contract will prevail
- Provisions in the contract are interpreted as a whole p 165 art 2050

## Types of contracts

Nominate and innominate contracts: p 165 art 1914

- Nominate contracts have a special name, like lien release or sale; they may have special forms or requirements
- Innominate contracts are not named p 166 art 1916

## Classes of contracts

I have separated these into 4 groups, because contracts may fall into one or more of these groups. For example, a contract may be an onerous and aleatory contract, and all onerous contracts are bilateral contracts, etc.

1. Unilateral contract p 166 art 1907
   - one party incurs an obligation

   Bilateral or synallagmatic contract p 166 art 1908
   - two or more parties are involved
   - the parties obligate themselves reciprocally
   - the obligation of each party is correlative to the obligation of the other
   - the reason that the parties obligated themselves is in return for the obligation of the other

2. Onerous contract p 166 art 1909
   - a contract where the obligor and obligee bound themselves for a benefit

   Gratuitous contract p 166 art 1910
   - a contract where the obligor binds himself to benefit the obligee or some other person

3. Commutative contract p 166 art 1911
   - When the performance by one party is correlative to the performance by the other party, like I will babysit your child Thursday if you babysit mine on Tuesday

   Aleatory contract p 166 art 1912
   - When some or all of one party's performance depends on an uncertain event, like I will buy all of the beads you catch at this parade, or I will buy all of the pearls from the oysters harvested from this oyster bed

4. Principal and accessory Contracts p 166 art 1913
   - A principal contract is a contract whose obligation is secured by an accessory contract. The accessory contract is entered into to provide security for the principal contract, like a sale with a mortgage. The sale is the principal contract, the mortgage is the accessory contract. The accessory cannot exist without the principal.

## 11 • OBLIGATIONS AND CONTRACTS

# Requirements for formation for contracts

Louisiana has the **4 C's** that every valid contract requires:
- Capacity
- Consent
- Cause
- Certain legal object

## *Capacity*

All persons are presumed to have contractual capacity except for: p 167 art 1918, art 27
- Unemancipated minors
- Interdicts
- Persons deprived of reason at the time of contracting

Minors do have some contractual capacity:
- Fully emancipated minors have full contractual capacity p 167 art 1922
- Unemancipated minor may contract for necessities for his support, education, or business; any other contracts made by unemancipated minors may be rescinded p 168 art 1923

## *Consent*

Is the voluntary agreement to assume obligations made through offer and acceptance p 168 art 1927

The book states that there is error when the parties think they are agreeing to something but each has a different thing in mind. Generally, this is stated as the parties must have a *"meeting of the minds"* to have a contract p 168

Capacity and consent often get confused. A person can consent all they want but they cannot have capacity to buy liquor if they are under the age of 21 in the United States. Likewise, a person with complete capacity (age, mental capacity, etc.) can never consent to selling a child or an organ because those contracts are void as against public policy.

### Vices of consent p 168 art 1948

- Error – there is no meeting of the minds, if one or both parties are in error – but only when it concerns a *cause* that was known or should have been known to the other party p 168 art 1949 For example, if I want to buy a house and use it as a dance studio, and subsequently the city denies me a permit for that use, the error only exists if I told the realtor that my intended use was for a dance studio and the realtor sold me the house based on that cause.

- Duress – physical, financial, or emotionally, consent is not freely given if the duress is directed at the person making the contract or the spouse, parent, or child of that person p 1968 art 1959, 1960 Threats of legal action are not considered duress. The act must threaten injury of considerable magnitude and must be accompanied by the apparent ability to bring about that injury causing fear in the reasonable person.

- Fraud – is the misrepresentation or suppression of the truth to make the contract happen p 169 art 1953 Fraud does not exist if a person could easily have found out the truth.

## *Cause*

An obligation or contract cannot exist without a lawful cause p 170 art 1966 Cause is the reason why someone obligates themselves p 170 art 1967 Don't Don't Don't use the term "consideration."

- Cause should be expressed in any contract but is not required p 170 art 1969
- The contract should adhere to the form required for the actual cause, no matter the cause stated in the contract. For example, if there is a donation in disguise, the form for a sale of an immovable should be adhered to in case the donation in disguise is discovered and litigated.
- The cause must be legal and moral p 171 art 1968

A party may be obligated by a promise that he knew or should have known would cause reliance on it to their detriment and the other party was reasonable in so relying. Recovery may be limited to expenses incurred as a result of reliance p 171 art 1967 For example, you contract verbally with a Scottish terrier breeder to buy a puppy in two weeks and have all of the paperwork, so you go and buy a kennel and leash, but then when you go to pick up the puppy, the breeder tells you that she inadvertently sold it to someone else that morning. You may be entitled to recoup some expenses for your detrimental reliance.

## *Object (certain object)*

The action or the thing which is the subject of the contract or obligation (e.g. the Scotty) p 171 art 1971

- Any object as long as it is legal, possible and determined or determinable p 171 art 1971
- Possibility or impossibility of an object is based on the object itself, it has nothing to do with the parties' ability to perform p 171 art 1972
- Future things may be the objects of contracts p 172 art 1976 (unlike donations inter vivos)

## Additional considerations

- Contracts have the effect of law between the parties p 172 art 1983
- Parties must perform in good faith
- Unless otherwise prohibited, rights and obligations are heritable p 173 art 1984
- Unless prohibited by law, contracts are dissolvable only by consent of the parties
- Contracts may have effects for third parties p 173 art 1985
- Contracts necessary to be in a certain form will be "absolutely null" unless in that form

## *Absolutely null contract*

- An absolutely null contract or act may not be confirmed p 172 art 2030
- An absolutely null contract is deemed never to have existed p 174 art 2033
- An absolutely null contract being declared null must restore parties to the position they were in before the contract was made p 174 art 2033 If restoration is impossible (for example, the house in the contract was sold or destroyed) the court may award damages
- You cannot benefit from your own turpitude, though; so a party performing under an absolutely null contract, who knew or should have known its cause was illegal/immoral, can't recover p 174 art 2033
- The action (time to file a lawsuit) for absolute nullity of contract never expires p 174 art 2032

## *Relatively null contract*

- A relatively null contract or act is null but may be confirmed or reformed p 172 art 2031
- Relative nullity may only be invoked by the person for whom the nullity exists; the court cannot invoke the nullity
- Relative nullity can be cured through confirmation p 175 art 1842 It must be express, identify the sub-

stance of the obligation, and intention to cure nullity; or performance is a tacit cure of relative nullity

- The action for relative nullity of a contract must be brought within 5 years from the time that the ground for the nullity ceased or was discovered p 174 art 2032

## Performance of the contract

- Parties must perform in good faith; failure to perform may result in specific damages, specific performance, or both p 173
- Performance by the obligor extinguishes the obligation p 173 art 1854
- If the contract requires valid transfer of an object, the contract is not extinguished unless the thing is validly transferred to the obligee p 173 art 1856
- Performance must be rendered to the obligee or to someone authorized by him p 173 art 1857
- Nullity of a provision does not render the entire contract null p 174 art 2034
- Nullity of a contract does not impair the rights of third parties acting in good faith p 175 art 2035

### *Ratification and confirmation*

- Ratification is where there is an obligation entered into *on an obligor's behalf* by another person, and the obligor accepts his obligation p 175 art 1843
- Confirmation and ratification are retroactive to the date of the confirmed or ratified obligation p 175 art 1844

## Dissolution of a contract

- Fortuitous event – one that was not foreseen at the time of the contract, like a hurricane p 175 art 1875 The other party may recover any performance he has already rendered p 175 art 1876
- Obligee's right to dissolution – when the obligor fails to perform, the obligee has a right to make the court dissolve the contract, or just regard the contract as dissolved, *and* the obligee may recover damages. The obligor may be given additional time to perform if the judge wants to p 176 art 2013 The contract may not be dissolved when there has been *substantial performance* and the part completed does not substantially impair the interest of the obligee
- Dissolution after notice to perform – if a party fails to perform, he may be served with a warning that he must complete performance within a time or the contract will be dissolved. The time must be reasonable for the contracted service. The notice is to put the non-performing party in default p 176 art 2015
- Dissolution without notice to perform – if the performance has been delayed and is no longer useful, the obligee may regard the contract as dissolved (like a photographer not showing up until after the wedding) p 176 art 2016
- Express dissolution clause – parties may expressly agree upon terms for dissolution in their contract p 176 art 2017

Effects of dissolution – the parties shall be restored to their position as before the contract p 176 art 2018 If partial performance was done, partial payment should be made.

A good faith third party who relied on the contract will not have his rights impaired p 176 art 2021

If the contract is one for an unspecified time, it may be terminated by either party by giving notice to the other party, reasonable in time and form p 177 art 2024

## Rules of interpretation

See also *General Principles* section (in this chapter) for articles 2045-2050; this section largely repeats.

- Contracts should be worded in general terms and interpreted to cover only things the parties intend it to cover p 177 art 2051
- A general contract which covers a specific situation should address that situation specifically and the contract should not be restricted to interpreting that way, both to the general and to the specific p 177 art 2052
- Doubtful or unclear clauses are interpreted in the light of the nature of the contract as a whole p 178 art 2053
- If there is no provision for a particular situation, it is assumed the parties want to bind themselves to whatever is necessary for the contract to achieve its purpose p 178 art 2054
- No one is allowed to take unfair advantage of another or enrich themselves unjustly at the expense of another p 178 art 2055
- Ambiguities are interpreted against the writer of the contract p 178 art 2056
- In the case where there is no possible other way to interpret a contract, it is written in favor of the obligor p 178 art 2057

# 12

# Persons, Family, and Marriage

There are 2 kinds of *persons*: natural persons and juridical persons p 179 art 24

- A natural person is a human being
- A juridical person is a corporation, LLC, unincorporated association, or a partnership: an entity to which the law gives personality. The juridical person is an entity which is separate from its members.

## Natural persons

- Natural persons commence upon their birth and end upon their death p 179 art 25
- One must be born alive, even for an instant, to ever be a natural person p 180 LA RS 40:32
- Fertilized human ovum, not implanted, is considered to be a *juridical person* p 179 LA RS 9:124
- A natural person who has reached majority may make all sorts of juridical acts unless prohibited by law p 180 art 28
- Right of ownership may exist in natural or juridical persons p 180 art 479

## Juridical persons

- Corporation, LLC, partnership, unincorporated association, among other entities, that are created by an act or instrument p 180 (see Chapter 28 on Business Entities for further discussion)
- The date of existence begins when the members or parties execute the instrument, or legislation creates them; and end with the same instrument, or as provided by law p 180
- Ordinary partnerships with no written agreement begin from the time the contract is formed p 180
- Unincorporated associations without written organizing documents begin from the time the parties agree to undertake the association p 180
- Fertilized human ovum, not implanted, is considered as a *juridical person* p 179 LA RS 9:124

## Domicile

- Domicile of a natural person is his habitual place of residence, which consists of residence and intent to remain p 180 art 38
- A person can have many residences, but only one domicile p 180 art 39
- Spouses can have separate domiciles p 180 art 40
- Domicile is generally where a person sleeps, votes, pays taxes, banks, registers a vehicle
- Domicile of an unemancipated minor is the same as his parents; or the parent with whom he primarily

resides, unless a court directs otherwise; or of his tutor if he is under a tutorship p 180 art 41

- Domicile of a juridical person is either: the state of its formation, or the state of its principal place of business, whichever is most pertinent to the particular issue p 181
- Natural persons are domiciled in a parish, juridical persons are domiciled in a state p 181
- A person can change domicile by moving to a new domicile p 181 art 44
- You can file an affidavit of domicile in the old and new parishes of domicile, but that alone does not change your domicile. You must have *intent* to change domicile. The affidavit may show evidence of intent, but is insufficient by itself to prove intent p 181 art 45

# Filiation

- Filiation is the legal relationship between parent and child, either legal (birth or adoption) or by acknowledgment p 182 art 178, 179
- Filiation is important for inheritance rights, government programs, and citizenship, among other rights p 182
- Filiation by the mother:
  - child born to the mother p 182 art 184
  - child adopted by the mother p 182 art 184
  - in the case of a surrogate birth parent, the woman who donated the ovum is considered the legal mother of the child p 182 LA RS 40:32.1
- Adoption gives the child all the same legal rights as if the child had been born to the parent; and the relationship between the adopted child and his natural parents is severed, except for certain inheritance rights p 183 art 199

## *Who is the father?*

- The legal husband of the mother is presumed to be the father, if the child is born or conceived during the marriage p 182 art 185
- A child born less than 300 days after the dissolution of the marriage is presumed to be a child of the marriage p 182 art 185 An ex-husband can disavow paternity in a case brought in civil district court in this instance.
- If the child is not the biological child of the husband, and there is no disagreement between the two men and the mother, a "three-party acknowledgment" authentic act can *disavow* the former spouse as the father and simultaneously establish paternity for the biological father p 182 art 190.1 For this particular disavowal action, a DNA report must be attached and filed with the Office of Vital Records. *This 190.1 action is a disavowal action, with a concurrent establishment of paternity.*
- Filiation can be accomplished through an act of acknowledgment.
  - If a man marries the mother of a child, with her consent, he may execute an authentic act establishing filiation/paternity and file with the Office of Vital Records p 183 art 195
  - If a man is not married to the mother of a child, he may execute an authentic act establishing filiation/paternity and file with the Office of Vital records p 183 art 196
  - Why would these actions be taken? In the first instance, the article 195 action, this may happen, for example, when a man marries a woman who has biological children who have no filiation, and wishes them to be filiated for emotional or legal reasons. In the second instance, a man may, for example, want to filiate a child he has had out of wedlock for inheritance reasons. There are many reasons why these actions are taken, but these two examples are the most common.

- Informal acknowledgment used to be recognized, but it has not been in the Civil Code since 2005, although courts may still allow a child to bring an action to filiate to a parent p 184 art 197

## Adult adoption

- Governed by the Children's Code p 185
- Adult adoption must be in an authentic act p 185 art 213
- Notarial Act of Adult Adoption may be accomplished (without judicial approval) if
    - The person has obtained the age of majority
    - The adoptive parent is the spouse or surviving spouse of the parent of the person to be adopted p 185 art 212
    - Spouses of the adoptive parent and adoptive child must appear and concur p 185
    - If the parent of the person to be adopted is alive, that parent must concur (in person, not through a mandatary p 185 art 213) in the act of adoption by the step-parent p 185
    - Name of the adopted person may be changed in the authentic act of adoption, but this does not automatically change the birth certificate; you must go through the Office of Vital Records with an affidavit of no objection from the District Attorney's office p 185 LA RS 9:465
- If the adopting person is not the spouse or surviving spouse of the parent of the person to be adopted, judicial approval is required to prevent undue influence over either party. It is not done by notarial act in this instance.
- There is no time limit for adult adoption p 186
- The act of adult adoption must be filed in the registry of any parish, and is effective from that date, but no requirement exists for the notary to file the copy of the act of adoption with Office of Vital Records unless a name change is requested p 186 art 214, LA RS 9:463
- Reasons? Tort cases when plaintiff is dying and has no heirs, reconnection with a birth parent, ease of inheritance, etc.
- Note: cannot adopt a spouse.

## Parental authority

- Right and obligation of parents (or those having legal parental authority) are: to provide for physical care, supervision, protection, discipline, and instruction of a minor child p 187 art 223
- Technically, both parents have equal parental authority over the child p 187 art 221
- Parental authority over the child exists until:
    - The child reaches the age of majority
    - The child becomes emancipated
    - The marriage terminates and a judicial determination of parental authority is issued p 187 art 234, 235
    - The child marries
- So, technically, you can think of the rules governing children in two different ways. The "regime" of parental authority is for parents and children in the traditional valid marriage under Louisiana law, while the "regime" of tutorship (guardianship) is for parents and children after dissolution of the traditional marriage; such a regime also exists where the child is illegitimate, or one parent dies.
- Other people can have custody and authority over the child, including ascendants (grandparents), other

collaterals (aunts, uncles, etc.), or tutors. If they are under the care of a tutor, the authority is governed by the rules of tutorship p 187

## *Parental rights and obligations*

- Represent the child, and if necessary, designate a tutor for the child p 188 art 222
- Physically care for the child, supervise him, protect him, discipline him, and provide him with instruction p 188 art 223
- Administer the property of the child as a prudent administrator p 188 art 229
    - In administering the child's property, the parent can use the fruits for the benefit of the family, but cannot sell, encumber, or lease the child's property without court approval p 188 art 230
    - This does not extend to the case where the minor may be sued and his assets must be sold to satisfy a judgment against the minor p 192 art 336

# Tutorship

- There is occasion for tutorship whenever parental authority does not exist as to an unemancipated minor child. Whenever a child is not under parental authority, he must be under tutorship, otherwise the child would be in legal limbo p 189 art 246

## *Tutorship by nature (also called "natural tutorship")*

- Parents are the natural tutors of their children. If one of them dies, the other becomes the child's tutor p 189 art 250
- Upon divorce, the tutor is the parent with custody; if they have joint custody, they have joint tutorship p 189 art 250
- If a child is not filiated to a man, the mother is the exclusive tutor to her child p 189 art 256

## *Tutorship by will*

- This is where a parent designates in a testament, or in an authentic act, who they want to raise their children in the event of the parent's death p 189 art 257
- If the parents are divorced or judicially separated (only available in covenant marriages), the custodial parent has the right to appoint a tutor upon that parent's death p 189 art 258
- If the parents are divorced or judicially separated and have joint custody, only the parent dying last may designate a tutor p 189 art 258
- Either parent may appoint a separate tutor to administer property in the event of their death p 189 art 258
- If the parent who died last has appointed several tutors, the person listed first shall be the tutor; if they cannot or will not be a tutor, the next on the list will be a tutor p 189 art 262

If a tutor is appointed, there will be Letters of Tutorship issued which confirm that the tutor has the ability to act on behalf of the child p 191 CCP art 4172

In addition to tutorship by nature and tutorship by will, this status can also be created by the effect of law (legal tutorship) or by appointment of a court (judicial tutorship).

## *Tutorship by the effect of the law* LA CC art 263

- When a tutor has not been appointed by parent dying last or when a new tutor is necessary, the court selects a tutor from the following:

- o The child's qualified direct ascendants
- o The child's qualified collaterals by blood within the third degree
- o The child's step-parent, keeping in mind the best interest of the child

### *Tutorship by the appointment of the judge* art 270

- When a minor child is an orphan whose parents have appointed no tutor by will or authentic act, and the child has no relations to be tutors by effect of law, the court shall appoint a tutor

## Emancipation

- This is how a minor (under the age of 18) can gain the legal capacity to make acts that persons over the age of 18 can. *Full judicial emancipation* confers majority status on the minor with some exceptions p 192 art 366
    - o Effective when judgment is signed p 193 art 369
    - o Full power of administration, pass all acts, grant leases, receive revenues and monies due to him, etc.
- *Limited judicial emancipation* confers some specific effects of majority on the minor p 192 art 366
    - o Effective when judgment is signed p 193 art 369
- *Limited emancipation by authentic act* confers specific effects of majority on the minor p 192 art 368 (the form of emancipation involving notaries, and most tested)
    - o Can only be used by minors over the age of 16
    - o Must be in an authentic act
    - o Must be executed by the minor and his parents or a tutor effectively having parental authority p 192 art 368
    - o Effective from the moment of execution whether recorded or not p 192 art 369
- *Emancipation by marriage* confers almost all of the effects of majority p 192 art 36
    - o Effective from moment of marriage
    - o Later termination of the marriage does not terminate the emancipation

### *Modification or termination of an act of emancipation*

- A notarial act of emancipation may be subsequently modified or terminated by an authentic act p 193 art 371
- A court may terminate or modify a notarial act of emancipation for good cause p 193 art 371
- An authentic act or judgment that modifies or terminates an emancipation is effective towards third persons as to *immovable* property from the moment the modification or termination is filed in the conveyance records where the immovable is situated p 193 art 371
- An authentic act or judgment that modifies or terminates an emancipation is effective towards third persons as to *movable* property from the moment the modification or termination is filed in the conveyance records where the minor is domiciled p 193 art 371
- Modification or termination of an emancipation does not affect any acts that happened before the modification or termination; those acts are still valid p 193 art 371

# Interdiction

- Notaries are not involved in interdiction but do need to know if a person is represented by someone
- Persons over the age of majority are put under interdiction when they are incapable of administering their estates, after a determination by a judge that there are no less restrictive means of being protected p 193 art 389
- *Full interdiction* is a natural person over the age of majority or an emancipated minor who is consistently unable to make *reasoned* decisions regarding his care and the care of his property, or to communicate those decisions, and whose interests cannot be protected by any less restrictive means p 193 art 389
- *Limited interdiction* is a natural person over the age of majority or and emancipated minor who is consistently unable to make reasoned decisions regarding the care of his person or property, *or any aspect of either*, or communicate those decisions, and whose interests cannot be protected by any less restrictive means p 193 art 390
- An example of the difference between the full and limited interdiction: A person who suffers from dementia may need to have a full interdiction, because they are completely incapable of taking care of themselves and there may be no less restrictive means of protecting their interests. A quadriplegic who is completely coherent may need a limited interdiction, because they are unable to physically take care of their person or property and there are no less restrictive means of protecting them, but the *curator* (similar to a tutor) will have only those powers absolutely necessary to meet their demonstrated needs.

If a curator is appointed, there will be Letters of Curatorship issued which confirm that the curator has the ability to act on behalf of the interdict p 194 CCP art 4564

# Marriage

- A legal relationship between two natural persons created by a consensual civil contract p 195 art 86
- Married persons owe each other fidelity, support, and assistance p 195 art 98
- Spouses are the moral compass of the family p 195 art 99

## *Requirements for a marriage*

- Absence of a legal impediment
  - Impediment of existing marriage: bigamy is a crime, so the new marriage would be absolutely null p 197 art 88
  - Impediment of same sex: mentioned in the book, but is unenforceable p 197 art 90
  - Impediment of relationship: one cannot marry certain blood relatives because incest is illegal. Ascendants may not marry descendants, siblings may not marry each other, nor may collaterals within the fourth degree, aunt-nephew, uncle-niece, etc. Courts can authorize a marriage if the collateral relationship is by adoption only and not by blood. Being a step-sibling is not an impediment p 197 art 90
  - Impediment of age: minors under the age of 16 cannot contract marriage at all; a minor age 16 or 17 cannot marry someone more than 3 years older than they are and requires parental consent p 197 art 90.1, LA CH C art 1545
- Marriage ceremony
  - Marriage license is part of the ceremony, and a ceremony cannot be conducted by an authorized officiant until that officiant has received a marriage license
  - An officiant is able to perform a ceremony once he has received a license authorizing him to do so p 197 LA RS 9:205

## 12 • FAMILY AND MARRIAGE

- o Marriage license may be sworn before a notary LA RS 9:224
- Free consent of the parties is required to enter into marriage expressed at the ceremony art 87
  - o Marriage must be entered into by the parties themselves, not by procuration or an agent art 92
  - o Must be physically present at the ceremony; cannot have a marriage over the internet art 91
- Marriage does not change the surname of either party. However, a spouse may, if they choose, use the surname of the other spouse (or of both spouses, like a hyphenated-name) p 197 art 100

### *Covenant marriage*

- Entered into by a man and a woman declaring their intent p 198 LA RS 9:224, 9:272
- Must receive premarital counseling p 198 LA RS 9:272
- Covenant commitment is a written declaration before a notary public and two witnesses and filed with the marriage license p 198 LA RS 9:273
- Divorce is only allowable if there is a total breach of the marital contract, and it is not an easy divorce. There are strict rules for divorcing under a covenant marriage, and divorce is only allowed under a specified list of reasons p 198 LA RS 9:272, 9:307

## Matrimonial regimes

- There are 3 kinds of matrimonial regimes in Louisiana: legal (community property), contractual (separate property), and mixed (partly legal and partly contractual) p 199 art 2325, 2326
- *Community of acquets and gains* is what we call community property. Acquets means property that has been acquired, usually through some means other than inheritance or otherwise separate in nature.
- The legal regime, or community property regime, is the default regime in Louisiana. See detailed discussion later in this chapter.
  - o If you are domiciled in Louisiana and get married, either in Louisiana or elsewhere (like a destination wedding, perhaps), you must enter into a separation of property agreement prior to marriage, or else you are presumed to have accepted the default community property regime p 200 art 2329
  - o If you are not domiciled in Louisiana, but move to Louisiana and become domiciled here, you have 1 year to enter into a separate property agreement. If not, after the 1 year is up, you are considered to have tacitly accepted the community property regime p 200 art 2329
  - o If, during the marriage, the spouses wish to enter into a separate property agreement, they may require judicial approval p 200 art 2329
- All property of married people is classified either as community or separate, except very limited certain undivided interests which are statutorily defined p 200 art 2335

### *Commonly misunderstood facts about community property*

- The way an asset is titled does not always control whether property is separate or community. It is necessary to look at the source of the funds used to purchase the asset. If community funds were used, it is usually community property, even if titled in only one spouse's name.
- Marriage alone does not automatically convert existing separate property into community property.
- It is possible for separate property to lose its identity as separate property by commingling that property with community property.

## Community property assets: what is community property?

- Property acquired during the legal/community property regime
- Property acquired with community things (like salary earned during a legal regime, or proceeds from sale of a community asset), or acquired with community and separate things (like if you have a separate piece of property with a community property house on it, and you sell that, the proceeds from that may possibly become community)
- Property donated to the spouses jointly
- Natural and civil fruits of community property, so the rents from a piece of community property would be community property
- Damages awarded for loss or injury to community things; for example, if the community property car is damaged in an accident, the proceeds from any lawsuit for property damages would be community
- All other property not classified as separate
- Fruits of separate property are community property (a rule often tested), unless reserved as separate property by the spouse who owns them p 200 art 2339 For example, if a spouse owns an apartment building as separate property, the rents from that building would be community property – unless that spouse specifically, in a declaration in an authentic act or act under private signature duly acknowledged, reserved those fruits to remain his separate property.

## Community property miscellaneous

- The community is not a separate juridical person, even though it is talked about in the third person p 201
- Each spouse owns an undivided ½ interest in the community, but this, unlike ownership in indivision, cannot be judicially partitioned prior to the termination of the regime (which is the termination of the marriage or entering into a new regime, a separate property regime) p 201 art 2336 But, during the community property regime, the spouses can voluntarily partition any community property in whole or in part
- A spouse cannot alienate, lease, or encumber to a third person his undivided interest in community property (also a difference between community property and ownership in indivision) p 201 art 2337

## Management of community property

- Either spouse, acting alone, can manage community property p 201 art 2346
- Both spouses have to agree before they can alienate, lease, or encumber community property p 201 art 2347
- If one spouse alone alienates, leases, or encumbers community property, the alienation, lease, or encumbrance is relatively null (it can be made valid by the concurrence of the other spouse), unless the other spouse has renounced the right to concur (then it is a valid transaction) p 202 art 2343
- A spouse can renounce their right to concur in acts concerning community property. If they do, their renunciation of a right to concur must be in writing, and can be valid for up to until revoked or up to 3 years p 202 art 2348
- Some situations do not require concurrence:
  - Certain donations to third persons: usual and customary gifts, like birthday gifts, commensurate with the economic position of the spouses p 203 art 2349
  - The spouse who is the sole manager of a community business has the exclusive right to alienate, encumber, or lease its movables, unless the movables are in the name of the other spouse p 203 art 2350

- Titled movables (such as a car), stock certificates, and other registered movables are transferrable by the registered-owner spouse p 203 art 2351
- The named member or partner of an LLC or LLP does not need concurrence to transfer their interest in that entity p 203 art 2352

### *Separate property assets: what is separate property?*

- Property that is acquired by one spouse with his separate property or funds p 204 art 2341
- Property owned before the establishment of a community p 204 art 2341
- Property acquired by inheritance p 204 art 2341
- Property donated to an individual spouse alone p 204 art 2341
- If a spouse acquires something during the marriage and declares it, in a juridical act, to be his separate thing, that declaration can be controverted by the spouse, unless the spouse concurred that it was his separate thing p 204 art 2342
- One spouse can donate his interest in a community thing to the other spouse and have it become that other spouse's separate property (must follow the rules of donation) p 205 art 2343
- One spouse can donate his separate property to the other spouse, stipulating that it becomes part of the community, and it will become community property p 205 art 2343.1 This must follow the rules of donation, such as that it be in an authentic act if it is gratuitous (or in writing if it is onerous).

## Termination of the community

- Death
- Divorce
- Matrimonial agreement that terminates the community p 205 art 2356
    - Notaries can do a prenuptial (antenuptial) agreement
    - But a postnuptial agreement requires judicial approval (unless the couple has moved into Louisiana within the last year)

### *Management and disposition of assets after termination of community*

- When a community property regime terminates for a reason other than the death of a spouse, rules governing co-ownership in indivision apply p 205 art 2369.1
- Each spouse/ex-spouse now has a duty to preserve and prudently manage the property until partitioned p 205 art 2369.3
- Neither spouse/ex-spouse acting alone can alienate, lease, or encumber the former community property p 205 art 2369.4-2369.7
- Either spouse/ex-spouse may demand that the property be partitioned p 206 art 2369.8

## Separate property regime (contractual regime)

- Spouses or potential spouses are free to enter into a contractual regime or opt out of the default community property rules p 206 art 2328, 2370
- Entering into a separate property regime must be done:
    - Before you enter into marriage, if you are domiciled in Louisiana p 206 art 2329

- o If you are already married, and move into Louisiana from another state, you have 1 year from the time you begin domicile in Louisiana to enter into a separate property regime (without needing judicial approval) p 206 art 2329
- o If you are married in Louisiana under the community property regime (or have moved here from out of state and lived here for more than 1 year), and you want to change from community property to separate property, you must petition the court to have a judicial declaration of a separate property regime. The court will want to examine the circumstances and make sure the separation of property isn't for any fraudulent reasons, and that it benefits both spouses p 206 art 2329
- Spouses are able to make individual purchases under a community property regime as separate property, as long as the other spouse concurs. This then becomes a "mixed" regime. These separate property and purchases do not need court approval, as they do not change the nature of the regime as a whole.

## *Management of assets under a separate property regime*

- Each spouse acting alone uses, enjoys, and manages his property without the consent or concurrence of the other spouse p 207 art 2371
- Each spouse is solidarily liable with the other spouse for obligations for necessities p 207 art 2372
- Each spouse contributes to the marriage/household expenses either according to the matrimonial agreement or, if none, then to his means p 207 art 2373

## Matrimonial agreements

- Must be an authentic act, or act under private signature duly acknowledged. All must be executed at the same time prior to the marriage. (If it is to be done before marriage, it can't be signed by prospective spouses but acknowledged *after* the wedding.) p 208
- Must be filed in the conveyance records of the parish where the parties have their matrimonial domicile, *and* in the parish(es) where the parties own immovable property p 209
- You can only include management of property in the matrimonial agreement; issues of fidelity, support, and assistance are not contractable p 208
- Spouses cannot contract away their marital portion, or order of succession p 208 art 2330

# 13
# Sale

A sale is a contract where a person transfers ownership of a thing for a price in money p 210 art 2439

- Must have thing
- Must have price
- Must have consent of parties

Sale is a nominate contract (one that has a name: its name is *sale*) which give the buyer and seller special rules for their type of contract p 210

## Capacity

- Any person who has the capacity to make a contract has the capacity to make a sale contract, unless expressly prohibited by law p 210 LA CC art 1918
- Fully emancipated minors have full contractual capacity p 211 art 1922
- Unemancipated minors, interdicted persons, and persons deprived of reason may not enter into sales contracts p 210 art 1918
- Unemancipated minors, interdicts, and persons deprived of reason *can* own property. Their curator or tutor can purchase property on their behalf, but the curator or tutor can only dispose of their property with court approval p 210 art 230, CCP art 4271

## Possession, presumption of ownership; good faith

- Buyer is presumed to be in good faith unless he knows or should have known that the seller did not own the thing p 211 art 1759, 523
- A good faith buyer of a corporeal movable who paid fair value gets to keep the thing purchased even if there was another vice of consent p 211 art 522 For example, if my 9-year-old niece wants to sell her baseball glove to a neighbor but I handle the cash transfer portion, and the neighbor has no idea that the glove came from a 9-year-old, the neighbor can keep the glove even though the 9-year-old has no capacity to enter into a sale. The vice of consent is a lack of capacity, but the neighbor is a good faith purchaser who paid fair market value.
- Possessor of a movable is presumed to be the owner. This is Louisiana's version of "possession is 9/10 of the law" p 211 art 530 The previous possessor is presumed to be the previous owner.
- If someone sells something that he does not have, he is obligated to get that thing at his expense and deliver it to the buyer p 212 art 2482

## General rules

- The thing sold must be fit for its ordinary use p 212 art 2524
- If a buyer makes known to a seller a particular reason for the purchase, the thing must be fit for that intended purpose p 212 art 2524 For example, if I buy a van off of an internet listing, it should be fit for use as a van, but if I tell the buyer that I am buying a van to convert to a food truck, the seller must sell it subject to my specific needs; the seller tacitly agrees that this van will fit my needs.
- If there is not a specific provision to cover an issue on a contract of sale, the Civil Code articles on obligations will apply p 212 art 2438
- If there is a conflict between the rules governing contracts of sale and other rules, like Revised Statutes Title 9 or Civil Code articles on lease, the Code articles on contracts of sale will prevail p 212 LA RS 9:3192

### *Titled movables*

- Transfer of titled movables registered in the public records (such as cars and trucks) are governed by specific statutes p 213 LA RS 32:701
- The seller must deliver to the buyer a properly endorsed title (see Chapter 23 on Titled Movable Transactions) p 213

## Form of contract of sale: movables

- Does not have to be written, unless it is a titled movable. Oral sales of movables are valid and legally recognized p 213
- Can have a "Bill of Sale" for a movable, which includes the parties, the expression of their consent, the description of the thing, and the price p 213

## Form of contract of sale: immovables

- A sale or promise of sale for an immovable must be in an authentic act or act under private signature ( a signed writing) p 213 art 2440
- The details and different versions of transfer of immovable property (cash sale, credit sale, quitclaim, etc.) are discussed in Chapter 21; for now, keep in mind the required form for the transfer:
  - Authentic act; or
  - Act under private signature; or
  - Oral transfer if the property has been delivered and the transferor recognizes the transfer under oath p 213 art 1839 (not involving the notary)
- Sale of property makes it effective between the parties immediately, but it is only effective against third parties once it is recorded p 213 art 2442

## What can be bought or sold?

- All things may be sold except those things prohibited by law p 214 art 2448
- Future things can be sold. The coming into existence is a suspensive condition p 214 art 2450
- A succession of a living person cannot be sold or be the object of a contract p 214 art 1976
- A hope may be the object of a sale contract. This is an aleatory contract p 214 art 2451
- A person cannot sell a thing, movable or immovable, that does not belong to him. Trying to do that does

not transfer ownership of that thing, and the person pretending to sell something he does not own can be liable for damages (although this may satisfy the buyer's "just title" for acquisitive prescription, see Chapter 8) p 214 art 2452
- A person cannot sell a thing (movable or immovable) *to himself* or buy a thing he already owns. But he can buy the rights of a person who has an adverse claim on a thing he owns p 213 art 2443

## Perfection of the contract of sale: when does ownership transfer?

- Ownership is transferred *between the parties* as soon as there is agreement as to the thing and a fixed price, even without delivery or payment p 215 art 2456
- Ownership of an *immovable* is effective against third persons as soon as there is agreement as to the thing, a fixed price, and filing in the registry in the conveyance records of the parish in which the immovable is located p 215 art 517
- Ownership of a *movable* is effective against third persons as soon as there is agreement as to the thing, a fixed price, and delivery to the buyer p 215 art 518
- An expression of acceptance is all that is required for a movable if there is an agreement on the thing and the price, even though the terms of the offer were different than when the thing was first offered p 215 art 2601

### *Perfection: when does ownership transfer between merchants?*

- The above rules apply, but the below rules are specific to contracts between merchants.
- Between merchants, additional terms become part of the contract unless they materially change the contract, then it is presumed the offeror would not have contracted on those terms p 215 art 2601
- If the things sold are unspecified or not individualized, ownership does not transfer until the things are individualized p 216 art 2457 For example, if you buy a gross of beads, the ownership does not transfer until they are broken down into individual dozens, if the contract is worded such that you are buying them as dozens.
- In a sale of goods sold by weight, tale, or measure, once the weighing, counting, or measuring is completed, the sale is perfected. In a lump sale, the sale is perfect even though the items are not weighed, counted, or measured p 216 art 2458
- A buyer can reserve the right to view or try the goods; then the sale is not perfected until the buyer has approved the goods p 216 art 2460
- A sale of a thing includes all of its accessories, for example, a lock would include the key to open it p 216 art 2461

## Price

- Price is an essential element of the sale p 217 art 2464
- Price must be fixed by parties, or determinable by the parties p 217 art 2464
- Price must not be out of proportion to the value of the thing sold p 217 art 2464
- Price can be determined by a third party if the buyer and seller agree p 217 art 2465
- If the buyer and seller are in a business where they habitually buy and sell movables without setting a price until later, the price will be a reasonable price at the time and place of delivery p 217 art 2466

### *Expenses incidental to sale*

- Buyer is responsible for expenses incidental to the sale p 217 art 2463

## Delivery

- Delivery of an immovable takes place upon the execution of the act that transfers ownership p 217 art 2477
- Delivery of a movable takes place by manually handing the movable over, or in another manner as the parties decide p 217 art 2477
- Delivery of an incorporeal movable, like a stock or bond, takes place upon negotiating or endorsing instruments to the buyer p 218 art 2481
- Seller pays the cost of delivery. Buyer must pay the cost of taking delivery, if there is no agreement otherwise p 218 art 2483
- A buyer who does not take delivery is liable to the seller who has to preserve the thing p 218 art 2555
- Delivery is to the place agreed upon or intended by the buyer and seller, or at the place where the thing is at the time of the sale p 218 art 2484
- If the seller doesn't deliver the thing, buyer can demand specific performance, or seek dissolution of the sale and damages p 218 art 2485
- The seller can refuse to deliver until he gets paid p 218 art 2487
- The seller must deliver the thing in the condition it was sold in p 218 art 2489

### *Transfer of risk*

- Risk of loss is transferred from the seller to the buyer at the time of delivery p 218 art 2467

## Obligations of the seller

- Clarity in the contract. Ambiguities are interpreted in favor of the buyer p 219 art 2474

### *Seller's warranties: delivery of the thing sold (immovables)*

- Immovable delivery takes place upon the execution of the writing that transfers ownership p 219 art 2477
- Seller delivers the full extent of the immovable sold; he can't retain possession of a portion of it, unless otherwise agreed upon p 219 art 2491
- If the seller sells by measure, and delivers less than promised, the sale will be reduced accordingly. If the seller delivers more than promised, the buyer will pay the overage, but can back out if there is an overage of more than 5% extra in the contract p 219 art 2492
- If the seller sells by a lump price, and the sale is within 5% of the lump amount promised, there is no change in price. If there is more than 5% lump difference less, the buyer can pay less. If there is more than 5% more, the buyer can pay the overage, or exit the contract p 220 art 2495
- If the buyer wants to rescind the sale but has already paid, the seller must return the money plus expenses p 220 art 2497
- There is a 1-year prescriptive period for an action on action for supplement or diminution of price or for dissolution p 220 art 2498

### *Seller's warranties: delivery of the thing sold (movables)*

- Seller warrants that the thing conforms to the contract p 220 art 2603
- Buyer has a right to inspect p 220 art 2604

# 13 • SALE

- Buyer has a right to reject nonconforming things after giving reasonable notice to the seller p 220 art 2605
- Buyer can accept nonconforming things, and cannot reject them as nonconforming once he does accept, unless his acceptance was in the belief that the nonconformity would be cured p 220 art 2606
- If the buyer rejects nonconforming things, the seller can cure the nonconformity if the time for performance has not expired; or the seller reasonably believed that the nonconformity would be acceptable to the buyer p 221 art 2610 For example, if the buyer ordered grey sweatshirts but they delivered charcoal instead, the seller may reasonably believe that the buyer would accept charcoal as a reasonable alternative; or if the seller still is within the delivery period, the seller may replace them with grey.
- Buyer can accept a partial delivery if that is all that conforms to the contract p 221 art 2607

## *Seller's warranties: warranty of ownership and peaceful possession*

- Eviction is not just a physical removal or loss of control over property; eviction is also when a third party has perfect title and seller has no title p 221 art 2500
- Seller warrants against the buyer's loss of, or danger of losing, the whole or part of the thing sold because a third person had a right in that thing at the time of the sale, including undeclared nonapparent servitudes p 221 art 2500
- This warranty exists in every sale even though it is not expressly stated p 221 art 2503
- A person can do a transfer of whatever rights they may have without warranty of eviction, but the warranty must be expressly waived. Even in that situation, the seller may still be liable to the buyer in the event that an eviction occurs, unless the buyer is expressly aware that he is buying at his own risk and that an eviction may occur p 221 art 2502
    - o The quitclaim deed arises from article 2502 (see Chapter 21)

## *Seller's warranties: warranty against hidden or redhibitory defects*

- A redhibitory defect is a vice in a thing that renders the thing useless or so inconvenient that the buyer would not have bought it in the first place had he known about the defect; or diminishes its usefulness or its value so much that the buyer would still have bought it but for a much lower price p 222 art 2520
- Buyers and sellers can opt out of a warranty against redhibition p 222 art 2548
- Seller must deliver the thing in the condition it was in at the time the sale was made p 222 art 2489
- The essentials of redhibition are that the defect in the thing must not have been apparent to the buyer, not have been known to the buyer at the time of the sale, must have existed at the time of delivery, and must have rendered it so useless or inconvenient that the buyer would not have bought it, or would have only bought it at a lower price art 2520

## *Seller's warranties: warranty of fitness for its intended use*

- Seller is obligated to deliver the thing as it is reasonably fit for its intended use p 222 art 2524
- If the buyer has a particular use in mind for the thing, and the seller knows or should know the buyer's particular purpose, and the seller knows or should know that the buyer is relying on the seller's skill and judgment in selecting the thing for the particular purpose, the thing must be fit for that particular purpose p 222 art 2524

# Obligations of the buyer

- Pay the price and take delivery of the thing p 223 art 2549

- Payment is due when and where it is stated in the contract; if none is stated, then at the time and place of delivery p 223 art 2550
- If the buyer doesn't take delivery, he owes damages to the seller p 223 art 2555

## Dissolution of sale

- If the buyer doesn't pay the price, the seller can sue to dissolve the sale p 223 art 2561
- If the seller seeks to dissolve the sale of an immovable in court, the court may grant the buyer an extension of up to 60 days if circumstances warrant p 223 art 2562
- If the sale of an immovable has a dissolution clause in the contract, the buyer can still pay, as long as the seller has not given the buyer official notice that he is seeking to dissolve the contract or is dissolving the contract in court p 224 art 2564

## Rescission for lesion beyond moiety

- Lesion beyond moiety allows the seller of an immovable property or real estate to undo the sale when the price is less than one half of the fair market value p 224 art 2589
- Only the seller can sue for this when selling corporeal immovables p 224 art 2589
- Value is determined at the time of the sale p 224 art 2590
- If the sale is lesionary, the buyer can either:
  - Return the thing to the seller
  - Keep the thing and pay the seller the difference in price so the sale is no longer lesionary p 224 art 2591
- If the buyer opts to return the thing in a lesionary sale, he must also return all the fruits from the time the demand for rescission was made. If he keeps the thing, he must pay interest on the price difference paid p 224 art 2592
- An action for lesion must be brought within 1 year of the sale p 225 art 2595
- If the buyer has sold the thing to a third party, the action for lesion is available against the original buyer only, and recovery is limited to the *profit* made by the buyer on the resale p 224 art 2594
- If the immovable has been encumbered, the rescission can't hurt that third party with the new right on the property, so the original seller receiving the property back has to take it subject to the rights of the third person. This original seller would have a right to recover diminution in value from the original buyer p 225 art 2596
- If rescission is granted, the original seller takes the property back in the condition it is; buyer is not responsible for deterioration, unless the buyer profits from it. Seller reimburses for expenses of sale p 225 art 2597
- Buyer keeps possession until seller reimburses buyer the price and recoverable expenses p 225 art 2599
- Each seller in a co-ownership situation may sue for lesion, whether they concurred in the sale or if they sold individually p 225 art 2600

# 14

# Lease

A lease is a bilateral (between two parties) contract by which one gives the use of a thing in return for a price p 226 LA CC art 2668

Must have three basic things, just like a sale contract: the thing, the price (rent), and consent of the parties p 226 art 2668

## Definitions

- *Lessor* is the person who leases out the property. The lessor does not have to own the property, he can be an agent of the owner. Commonly the lessor is called the *landlord*.
  - Sublessor is a person who has a lease on a property but leases to another person.
- *Lessee* is the person who leases a property. They may also be known as the *tenant*.
  - Sublessee is a person who leases a property from a person who is the lessee or tenant of the property.

## Form and recordation

- A valid lease can be in writing or oral p 226 art 2681
- Leases are subject to the public records doctrine, so an unrecorded lease cannot be enforced against a third party who purchases the property from the lessor p 226 art 2681
- Can file a "Notice of Lease" with some bare bones information instead of the entire lease, which is still binding on third persons p 226 LA RS 9:2742
- If the lease or "Notice of Lease" isn't recorded, only the lessee and lessor are bound by its terms p 228
- If the lease or "Notice of Lease" *is* properly recorded, and the lessor sells the property, the new landlord is bound by the terms of the lease, unless lessor and lessee agree otherwise p 228 art 2711
- A third person is not bound by an unrecorded lease, but lessee may have an action against lessor for losses sustained as a result of the sale of the immovable. For example, if I lease an office, but don't record my lease, and the building is sold, the new owner does not have to honor my lease. The old owner, the one I rented my office from, may owe me some damages from the contract of lease I signed with him because of the losses I sustain from having to relocate p 228 art 2712

## Essential elements: thing

- Anything that can be owned (without being destroyed by use or prohibited by law) can be leased p 228 art 2673
- Lessor does not need to own the thing he leases, as in the case of subleases p 229 art 2674

- Consumable things generally can't be leased. Examples in the code are: money, harvested agricultural products, food, beverages p 228 art 536
- Specifically prohibited items that cannot be leased are:
  - Right of habitation p 229 art 637
  - Predial servitude separate from its dominant estate p 229 art 650
  - Spouse's undivided interest in a community p 229 art 2337

## Essential elements: rent

- Rent must be serious and proportional to the value of the thing p 229
- Rent does not have to be in money. It can be in fruits, commodities, services, or other performances p 229 art 2675
- Rent must be certain or determinable; it can be tied to an index (like the Dow Jones), or left to a third party to determine; but if the third party does not determine the rent, the lease will fail p 229 art 2676

## Essential elements: term

- Term is the duration of the lease; it does not need to be specified in the contract p 230 art 2678
- Lease can terminate on a certain date or on an occurrence of an event p 230 art 2678
- Lease cannot be longer than 99 years. If it states longer than 99 years, it is automatically reduced to 99 years p 230 art 2678, 2679
- Leases without a stated term have terms as follows:
  - Agricultural leases are year to year p 230 art 2680
  - Residential immovables are month to month p 230 art 2680
  - Movables are day to day, unless fixed by longer (not to exceed 1 month) or shorter periods p 230 art 2680

## Laws governing lease

- Any laws regarding lease not covered in the specific lease title are covered by the Civil Code articles governing "Obligations in General" or "Conventional Obligations or Contracts" p 231 art 2669
- Specific statutes on lease are found in LA RS 9:3201 *et seq*

## Contract to lease at a future time?

- Yep. It is allowable to make a contract to enter into a lease at a future time p 231 art 2670

## Types of leases

Characterization depends on the agreed use of the thing; primary purpose determines the character of the lease p 231 art 2671

- Residential: when the thing is to be occupied as a dwelling
- Agricultural: when the thing is a predial estate to be used for agricultural purposes
- Mineral: when the thing is to be used for the production of minerals
- Commercial: when the thing is to be used for business or commercial purposes

## 14 ▪ LEASE

- Consumer: when the thing is a movable intended for the lessee's personal or familial use outside his trade or profession

## Obligations of the lessor and lessee

## Lessor's principal obligations

Lessor is bound to:

- Deliver the thing to the lessee p 232 art 2682
- Maintain the thing in a condition so it can be used for its intended purpose p 232 art 2682
- Protect the lessee's peaceful possession for the duration of the lease p 232 art 2682
- Pay taxes and other charges p 234 art 2689

### *Lessor's obligations: delivery*

- Lessor must deliver the thing at the agreed time and in good condition p 233 art 2684
- The thing must be free from the need for repairs to render it fit for its intended use p 233 art 2684
- If an immovable is not physically as the lessee was expecting it, then the Code articles on "Sale" govern how the discrepancy is handled p 233 art 2685

### *Lessor's obligations: alterations, repairs, and additions*

- Lessor may not make any alterations in the thing during the term of the lease p 234 art 2690
- Lessor must make all necessary repairs to maintain the thing in a suitable condition for its intended purpose p 234 art 2691
- If a necessary repair cannot wait until the end of the lease, the lessor may make it during the term of the lease, even if it inconveniences the lessee. The lessee may get a reduction in the rent or dissolution of the lease if the situation warrants p 234 art 2693
- If the repairs are necessary and the lessor fails to make them, the lessee may make them and demand reimbursement, but only to the extent that the repair was necessary and the amount expended was reasonable p 235 art 2694

### *Lessor's obligations: warranty for peaceful possession and suitability*

- Warranty against disturbance by a person asserting a right to ownership, possession, or any other right interfering with the thing. Basically, this can be an eviction or other prevention of enjoyment of use of the leased thing p 237 art 2700
- In a residential lease, this includes disturbances by neighbors p 237 art 2700
- Lessee must notify lessor of a breach of this warranty if he intends to hold the lessor to this warranty. If the lessor doesn't fix the problem, then the lessee can sue the person causing the breach of the warranty of peaceful possession *and* still hold the lessor responsible p 237 art 2701
- If a third party claims they have a right to the leased thing, the lessee may force the lessor to join a lawsuit to defend his right to peaceful possession p 237 art 2701
- The lessor only has to protect the lessee for peaceful possession when the third party claims a right in the thing leased. If the third party does not claim a right in the thing leased and still causes a disturbance, the lessor is out of it and the lessee only has a right of action against the person causing the disturbance p 237 art 2702

- The lessor is liable if the leased thing is not suitable for its intended purpose
- The lessor is liable if the premises cease to be fit for its intended purpose p 235
- These principles mimic the ones on Sales

### *Lessor's obligations: warranty against vices or defects*

- The lessor warrants that the thing is free from defects that prevent its use. It does not matter whether the lessor knew of the existence of the vice or defect at the time of the lease p 236 art 2696, 2697
- Lessor must repair defects he did not even know about p 236 art 2697
- The lessor is not responsible for if the vice or defect is the fault of the lessee p 236 art 2696
- If the lessee knows of defects and doesn't notify the lessor, lessee's recovery for redhibitory defects is reduced p 236 art 2697
- Warranty against vices or defects extends to all residents p 236 art 2698
- Warranty against redhibition can be waived but must be done so in clear and unambiguous language p 236 art 2699

## Lessee's principal obligations

Lessee is bound to:

- Pay the rent as agreed to
- Use the thing as a prudent administrator
- Use the thing in accordance for the purpose for which it was leased
- Return the thing at the end of its lease in the same condition, except for usual wear and tear p 232 art 2683

### *Lessee's obligations: alterations, repairs, and additions*

- Lessee is obligated to repair damage to the thing if he damages it or his guests damage it p 234 art 2692
- Lessee is obligated to make repairs to the thing for deterioration beyond normal deterioration p 234 art 2692

### *Lessee's obligations: use of the thing by the lessee*

- The lessee must use the thing leased for the purpose he leased it and in a way so as not to damage it, or he can be stopped from doing the thing that violates the lease, lose the lease, or be liable for damages p 233 art 2686
- The lessee is responsible for his guests if they cause damage p 234 art 2687
- The lessee must notify the lessor right away if the thing needs repairs or has sustained damage, or if his possession has been disturbed by a third person p 234 art 2688

### *Lessee's obligations: payment of rent*

- Rent is due and payable in advance at the address specified by the lessor p 237 art 2703
- If there is no address specified by the lessor, rent is due by usage or custom p 237 art 2703
- If the rent is not paid, the lessee is in default of the lease contract, and lessor may dissolve the lease and take possession of the leased thing p 238 art 2704

- *Agricultural leases only*: Without an agreement to the contrary, the agricultural lessee may claim a reduction in rent for the loss of unharvested crops, unless the loss was due to an unforeseeable and extraordinary event that destroys at least ½ the value of the crops. If the lessee receives insurance or governmental assistance, this factors into the rental abatement p 238 art 2705 If the rental agreement in this situation calls for the rent to be paid in crops and the crop loss is not the fault of lessor or lessee, then the cost is borne by both parties in proportion to their shares p 238 art 2706

## Termination of the lease: removal of attachments, additions, and improvements

- Lessee may remove all improvements he made to the leased thing as long as he fixes the leased thing to its former state p 235 art 2695
- If the lessee does not remove the improvements, the lessor may:
  - Take ownership of the improvements by reimbursing the lessor for their cost or enhanced value of the leased thing, whichever is less; or
  - Demand removal and restoration of the leased thing to its former state within a reasonable time. If the lessee fails to do so, the lessor may do it and sue for the cost of removal, or claim ownership of the improvements without owing the former lessee anything after notification by certified mail, etc.
  - Until the lessor decides which route he is going to go, the lessee owns the improvements and lessee is responsible for harm caused by improvements p 235 art 2695

## Lessor's security rights

- The *lessor's privilege* in Louisiana is a security device that secures the payment of rent. It applies to rent only, and cannot be used to secure other damages (like to recover physical damage to a property). The privilege applies to the lessee's movables (and crops in an agricultural lease) found in and upon the leased premises p 238 art 2707
- Enforcement of the lessor's privilege requires a judicial procedure, with a seizure and sale, unless the lessee has waived this in the lease p 238
- If the thing has been sublet, the privilege extends to the sublessee's movables to the extent the sublessee owes the original lessee p 239 art 2708
- The landlord lessor may also seize the property of a third person found on the premises, but only if the landlord does not have knowledge that it belongs to a third person p 239 art 2709
- To enforce the lessor's privilege, the lessor may, after going through the judicial procedure:
  - assert the privilege against the movables while they are in the seized property; and he may have them seized for up to 15 days after they have been removed, provided the lessee still owns them, and the movables can be identified; *or*
  - if they have been seized by the sheriff, he may enforce his privilege as long as the possessions remain in the possession of the officer who removed them from the premises p 239 art 2710

## Transfer of ownership of the thing leased by lessor

- If the lessor sells the thing being leased, the lessor and lessee are still bound by the terms of the lease, unless they have a prior agreement to terminate the lease upon a sale p 240 art 2711 But remember, it is only binding on a new owner if the lease is recorded. If it is not recorded, the new owner can accept the lease terms, or make a new deal with the lessee, or the lessor may be liable to the lessee for damages p 240 art 2712

## Sublease or assignment of rights by lessee

- Unless the lease expressly prohibits sublease, the lessee may do so p 240 art 2713

## Termination and dissolution

### Termination and dissolution: loss, destruction, expropriation

- If the thing leased is lost, destroyed, or expropriated in whole or in part, the lease terminates p 241 art 2714
- If one of the parties caused the loss, destruction, or expropriation, he may owe damages to the other p 241 art 2714
- If the lease terminates through no one's fault, no one owes damages; the lease just terminates p 241 art 1876
- If the thing is not completely destroyed, the lessee may continue to lease it, but with a reduction in rent p 241 art 2715

### Termination and dissolution: lease granted by usufructuary

- Lease granted by the usufructuary terminates with the usufruct p 242 art 2716

### Termination and dissolution: contracts with reservation of right to terminate lease

- Some leases are written with one or both parties reserving the right to terminate the lease with special notice before the technical end of the lease date p 242 art 2718

### Termination and dissolution: breach of contract

- The lease is terminated if either party breaches the terms of the lease agreement p 243 art 2719

### Termination and dissolution: death of party to lease

- If a lessor or lessee dies, or juridical person to a lease ceases to exist, the lease *does not terminate*.

## Lease with a fixed term: reconduction

- *Reconduction* means that the terms of the lease are automatically renewed if the lessee remains in possession and continues to make payments p 243 art 2720, 2721
- All of the original provisions of the lease remain in place, except the terms. In a reconducted lease, the new terms are month-to-month for residential leases, year-to-year for agricultural leases p 243 art 2721, 2722
- Termination of the reconducted lease is the same as a lease with an indeterminate term, so a residential reconducted month-to-month lease requires a 10-day notice for termination p 243 art 2727

## Leases with an indeterminate term

- Leases terminate as follows:
    - Leases longer than a month need a 30-day notice
    - Leases that are month-to-month need a 10-day notice
    - Leases between a week and a month need a 5-day notice

## 14 ▪ LEASE

- o Leases shorter than a week just need a notice before the week is up
- Notice given to terminate these indeterminate time leases will terminate the lease at the end of the period specified in the notice, and if none is mentioned, then the first period after the notice is given p 244 art 2728
- Notice must be in writing for a termination of lease for an immovable or a movable used as a residence; for all other leases, the termination notice can be oral p 245 art 2729

## Lease of movables

- Lease of movable property may be governed under the Louisiana Lease of Movables Act, LA RS 9:3301 et seq. if they are financed leases, or lease-purchase p 245 (True Leases vs. financed leases)

### *Lease of movables: True Lease*

- If the lease is not a lease-purchase or rent-to-own movable lease, it is a True Lease and is governed by the Civil Code articles on Lease p 245
- This is the leasing of a thing for rent or compensation, not intended for security (no UCC security interest in it). So, think of things like a rental car, or oilfield equipment, or anything movable that can be rented, where the lessee does not have an interest in it and the lessor does not have a financing agreement with the lessee, and ownership is not transferred at the expiration of a term.

### *Louisiana Lease of Movables Act: not applicable to immovables*

- The LMA (Lease of Movables Act) does not apply to immovables, but does apply to movables that:
  - o Become part of an immovable
  - o Are immobilized by declaration
  - o Are equipment that is subsequently incorporated into other movable property p 246 LA RS 9:3304
- The LMA does not apply to incorporeal movables, like leases of computer software p 246 LA RS 9:3304
- Financed leases are governed under the laws of Lease p 246 LA RS 9:3310
- Financed leases are considered secured transactions (transactions with a security interest) in favor of the lessor and subject to additional rules in LA RS 10:9-101 et seq.
- Lessor retains title to the movable until the lessee complies with the obligation to purchase the leased equipment p 246 LA RS 9:3310

# 15

# Mandate and Representation: "Power of Attorney"

If a person cannot represent themselves, they can appear before a notary public and execute an act to allow someone else to represent them in a "power of attorney" p 247

The terms "power of attorney," "agent," and "attorney-in-fact" are not used in the Civil Code, but are the commonly understood terms used for *mandate* (a bilateral contract) and *procuration* (a unilateral juridical act) p 247

## Representation defined

- Representation is the authority of one person to act on behalf of another in that person's legal relations p 247 LA CC art 2985
    - Unilateral juridical act is a procuration p 248 art 2987
    - Bilateral juridical act is a mandate p 250 art 2989
- Representation can occur by such a juridical act, or by operation of law p 247 art 2985
- Authority of the representative may be: conferred by law; created by a contract called mandate; or created by the unilateral juridical act of procuration p 248 art 2986

## Procuration

- Procuration is a unilateral juridical act by which a person, the *principal*, confers authority on another person, the *representative*, to represent the principal in legal relations, which may be addressed to the representative or to a person with whom the representative is authorized to represent the principal in legal relations p 248 art 2987
- A juridical act is unilateral when it is the product of the will of one party and its completion or effectiveness does not depend on the will of another party. So, the procuration is effective when the principal signs the authority. The procuration's existence, validity, and interpretation will be judged by focusing exclusively on the principal's expression of will, and not that of the representative.
- The procuration does not need to be in a specific form, unless the law requires a certain form for the authorized act p 248 art 2987 rev comment c
- The recipient of the procuration does not bind himself to do anything, but if he accepts the procuration, a contract may be formed and this may become a mandate p 249 art 2987 rev comment d
- The term legal relations includes creating, modifying, or terminating legal relations p 249 art 2987 rev comment e

### *Procuration may be conditional on disability*

- Conditional procuration is a procuration conditioned on the disability of the principal p 249 LA RS 9:3890

- The conditional procuration must be in writing p 249 LA RS 9:3890
- The conditional procuration becomes effective upon the disability of the principal p 249 LA RS 9:3890
- The disability must be established by an authentic act signed by 2 physicians licensed by the state medical board who have personally examined the principal, or by the attending physician and the agent p 249 LA RS 9:3890 *(The act establishing disability is tested, apart from the procuration.)*
- The conditional procuration has the same effectiveness as any other procuration p 249 LA RS 9:3890
- A conditional procuration is subject to all provisions of the Civil Code and all laws which govern procuration p 249 LA RS 9:3890

# Mandate

- Mandate is a bilateral contract between the principal (the person granting the authority) and the representative or agent (the person accepting the authority) where the principal confers authority on the agent to transact one or more affairs for him p 250 art 2989
- The agent is also called the *mandatary*.
- A procuration does not bind the agent (because it is a unilateral contract), but once a mandate has been signed, the agent has accepted that he will act primarily for the benefit of the principal in a particular endeavor. A procuration can become a mandate, if it is accepted by the agent and follows the rules of mandate p 250
- If there are no special rules for mandate, the rules for "Obligations in General" or "Conventional Obligations or Contracts" should be followed p 250 art 2990 (see Chapter 11)
- The mandate (or "power of attorney") can be exclusively for the benefit of the principal or mandatary, or for the benefit of both the principal and mandatary, or for a third person, or for all of them p 250 art 2991
- A mandatary is not entitled to compensation, unless the principal agrees to compensate him p 250 art 2992
- Mandate is not subject to any particular form, but when the law prescribes a form for a certain act, the mandate must be in that form. For example, if the mandate is to allow a donation, which requires an authentic act, then the mandate must be in an authentic act p 250 art 2993

## *General authority by mandate*

- Mandates can grant a general authority to an agent to act, phrased in a way such as "my agent is authorized to handle any and all matters on my behalf." This will allow the agent to perform most, but not all, actions and incidental actions, to take care of business for the principal p 251 art 2994, 2995
- There are other acts which must be *expressly* granted, so make sure the mandate is crafted in the form necessary for the acts intended. For example:
    o Authorization to make a donation must be in an authentic act and must be express under article 2997 p 252
    o Authorization to accept a donation must be in writing, but can be included in a general grant of authority p 252
    o Authorization to make a manual gift must be expressly authorized, but need not be in writing or in authentic act p 252
    o Mandate to alienate, acquire, encumber, or lease a thing must be express and in writing p 252

- o Mandate that gives the power to transfer or convey principal's interest in immovables, but *NOT* stating the power to donate, does not give him the right to donate. This is tested often. The authority to donate must be specifically granted p 251 art 2997 (and in an authentic act)

*A testament may never be executed by a mandatary* p 251 art 1571 (Other actions that cannot be done by agents: marriage, affidavits, and consent to adult adoption.)

## *Express authority required to be stated in the mandate*

- Alienate, acquire, lease, or encumber immovable property p 251 art 2996
- Make an inter vivos donation or revoke a donation p 251 art 2997
- Accept or renounce a succession p 251 art 2997
- Contract a loan, acknowledge or remit a debt, or become a surety p 252 art 2997
- Draw or endorse promissory notes or negotiable instruments p 252 art 2997
- Enter into a compromise or enter a matter into arbitration p 252 art 2997
- Make health care decisions involving surgery, medical expenses, nursing homes, and medications (this is why health care mandates are often separate documents) p 252 art 2997
- Prevent or limit reasonable communications, visitations, or interactions between the principal and relatives with whom they have affectionate relations p 252 art 2997
- Mandatary must be the one who carries out the duties. But if circumstances are beyond his control, or if the authority is expressly granted, he may appoint an alternate mandatary p 254 art 3006

## *Special situations*

- Except when fulfilling a duty to the principal, the mandatary may not bind the principal to a contract with the mandatary (no self-dealing) p 252 art 2998
- A person of limited capacity can still act as a mandatary for matters of which he is capable p 253 art 2999
- A person can be a mandatary of two parties, such as dual agent for buyer and seller, but he must disclose this agency to both parties p 253 art 3000

# Relations between principal and mandatary

## *Duties of the mandatary*

- A mandatary is bound to fulfill his duty with prudence and diligence, and is responsible for loss caused from his failure to properly perform that duty p 253 art 3001
- If the mandatary is not getting paid, the court may reduce any losses caused by him p 253 art 3002
- A mandatary is accountable to the principal and is bound to provide information about what he has done, notify the principal when the mandate if fulfilled, and provide an accounting upon request or when the circumstances require p 253 art 3003
- The mandatary must give the principal everything he received over and above his expenses for carrying out his duties p 254 art 3004
- The mandatary has to return any interest earned from sums of money from the principal p 254 art 3005
- Mandatary must be the one who carries out the duties. But if circumstances are beyond his control, or if the authority is expressly granted, he may appoint an alternate mandatary p 254 art 3006

- If the mandatary appoints an alternative and this was authorized by the principal, the original mandatary is liable for damages if he did not exercise diligence in choosing the substitute or instructing him.
- If the substitution was not authorized, the mandatary is automatically responsible for the substitute's acts.
- In all cases, the principal always has recourse against the substitute p 254 art 3007
- The mandatary must not exceed his authority; if he does, he is responsible to the principal p 254 art 3008
- If there are multiple mandataries acting on behalf of the principal, they are not solidarily (jointly) liable if they exceed their authority p 254 art 3009
  - An obligation is *solidary* when each obligor is responsible for the whole obligation. For example, if a group of people are responsible for a debt, each one may be responsible for the payment of the entire debt if it is not paid p 255 art 1794

## *Obligations of the principal*

- Principal must perform obligations that the mandatary/agent lawfully contracted within the limits of his authority p 255 art 3010
- Principal is bound by acts performed by the mandatary after the termination of the mandate but before the mandatary knows of the termination p 255 art 3010
- The principal is liable to the mandatary for unauthorized obligations *only* if he ratifies them p 255 art 3010
  - It is not unauthorized for the mandatary/agent to act in a manner more advantageous to the principal than was authorized p 255 art 3011
- Principal owes the mandatary reimbursement for expenses and charges incurred in carrying out his duties p 255 art 3012
- The principal must reimburse the mandatary for any loss sustained by the mandatary without fault (but not for the mandatary who is at fault for the loss) p 255 art 3013
- The principal must pay interest on any personal money the mandatary spent on performing his duties p 256 art 3014
- If there are several principals, they are solidarily liable to the mandatary p 256 art 3015 (solidary liability is the liability of any one debtor among two or more joint debtors to pay the entire debt if the creditor so chooses, until the debt is paid p 256 art 1790)

# Relations between principal, mandatary, and third persons

There can be 3 situations:
- a disclosed mandate and disclosed principal, where all the parties involved know that each party is represented by someone else;
- undisclosed mandate, where the agent does not notify third parties that he is acting on behalf of a principal; or
- disclosed mandate but undisclosed principal, where the parties know that the agent is working on behalf of a principal, but the identity of the principal is unknown

## *Relations between the mandatary and third persons: disclosed mandate and principal*

- If the mandatary discloses the mandate and discloses the principal, and if the mandatary's acts are authorized, the mandatary is *not personally bound* to the third person. Only the principal is bound p 256 art 3016

### *Relations between the mandatary and third persons: undisclosed mandate*

- If the mandatary contracts in his own name without disclosing the mandate, he is *personally* bound to the third party p 256 art 3017

### *Relations between the mandatary and third persons: disclosed mandate but undisclosed principal*

- If the mandatary informs the third party that he is acting as a mandatary for a principal whose identity he does not disclose, the mandatary is *personally bound* to the third party *until* the identity of the principal is disclosed to the third party p 257 art 3018

### *Acts exceeding the mandatary's authority*

- The mandatary who exceeds his authority is personally bound to the third party, except where:
  - The third party knew that the mandatary was exceeding his authority; or
  - The principal ratifies the contract p 257 art 3019

### *Relations between the principal and third persons*

- The principal is bound to third parties to perform the contract that the mandatary makes within the limits of his authority p 257 art 3020
- If, in the absence of a mandate, someone (the "putative principal") causes a good faith party to believe that another person is his mandatary ("putative mandatary"), then the putative principal is bound to the third party p 257 art 3021 Putative means assumed to be or supposed to be. This is the same as "apparent authority" in other states.
- A third party who contracts with a mandatary is bound to the principal if
  - the mandatary contracted in the principal's name (disclosed mandate and disclosed principal); or
  - if the mandatary disclosed the mandate but not the identity of the principal p 258 art 3022
- The third party is bound to the principal even in the case of the undisclosed mandate *unless* the obligation is "strictly personal" (see Chapter 11) or the right is assignable p 258 art 3023

## Termination and revocation of the mandate and of the authority of the mandate

- The mandate and its authority terminates upon:
  - Death of the principal
  - Death of the mandatary
  - Interdiction of the mandatary
  - Qualification of the curator after the interdiction of the principal
  - Any cause for termination of contracts p 258 art 3024
- Principal may terminate the mandate at any time p 258 art 3025
- A contract for the interest of the principal may be irrevocable, if the parties agree p 258 art 3025
- In Louisiana, powers of attorney (whether procurations or mandates) are *durable*, meaning that neither the contract nor its authority terminates on the principal's disability or incapacity unless the mandate provides otherwise (this is different from many other states, and tested) p 258 art 3026

## 15 ▪ MANDATE AND REPRESENTATION

- If a mandate has to be filed to be effective against third persons, then a notice of that revocation must also be filed p 259 art 3027

- If the principal revokes or terminates the mandate, he must notify everyone that relied on the mandatary's authority to act on behalf of the principal. If he doesn't, the principal is still bound to perform acts committed to by the mandatary p 259 art 3028

- If the mandatary terminates or resigns the mandate, his mandate is not terminated until he notifies the principal. If the mandatary believes the principal lacks capacity, the mandate is not terminated until there is a successor mandatary or a person who can help with the welfare of the principal p 259 art 3029

Normally, the agent's power ends when the principal *dies*, but if the principal dies after the mandatary begins an act authorized by the mandate, the mandatary must complete the act if the delay would cause injury p 260 art 3030 For example, if the agent is defending a lawsuit or selling a house on behalf of the principal, and the principal dies, the mandatary is bound to complete the representation. Failing to do so may bring irreparable harm and loss of rights, so the authority continues.

## Miscellaneous

- If the mandatary does not know that his mandate has been terminated, his contracts with third parties are usually enforceable p 260 art 3031

- Upon termination of the mandate, the mandatary must make an accounting for his performance to the principal, but this can be expressly dispensed with in the contract of mandate p 260 art 3032

# 16

# Suretyship

Suretyship is an accessory contract, which means it is not a contract by itself, but part of another contract p 261 art 3035, 1913

The purpose of the suretyship is to guarantee performance of an obligation, the promise to pay the debt of another if the principal fails to do so p 261 art 3035

There are 3 parties involved in a suretyship contract:

- The *principal*. This is the party who is doing the work and is required to get the surety to ensure performance of the obligation. Examples of this are when a contractor is constructing a building, the contractor may be required to get a bond to ensure completion. The contractor in this case is the principal. Also known as the *debtor*.
- The *obligee*. This is the party who is requiring the principal to get the surety to ensure performance of the obligation. In the above example, the party for whom the contractor is building is the obligee. It could be the state, or a homeowner. Also known as the *creditor*.
- The *surety*. The surety is the insurance company, or other company or person, who provides the surety bond for the protection of the obligee. The surety offers a financial guarantee to the obligee that the principal will fulfill their written obligation and uphold their duty. Also known as the *guarantor*.

## General nature of suretyship

- Surety is not obligated to the creditor unless the principal fails to discharge or fulfill his primary obligation p 261
- The surety contract is between the surety (guarantor) and the creditor (obligee) p 261
- Examples of suretyship contracts are: bonds (like the notary bond, which generally protects the public from any errors or fraud resulting from the actions of a notary public) and contracts of guaranty (like personal guarantees that one may give) p 261
- Suretyship can be established for any lawful purpose p 261 art 3036
- The principal obligation may be in existence, or may arise in the future p 261 art 3036
- Surety=guarantor, suretyship=guaranty p 261

### *Contract of guaranty*

- A contract of guaranty (which is a suretyship) may be continuing and remain in full force and effect until it is cancelled by one of the methods used to cancel a contract (kind of like a home line of credit) p 261

# 16 ▪ SURETYSHIP

## *Guarantor (surety) is not a joint debtor*

- A promisor becomes primarily responsible for a debt if he unconditionally obligates himself to pay the debt of another p 262 art 3037 (like a father co-signing a car loan for a daughter, the cause for the contract and the guarantors are obvious)
- The creditor can assume that the signors of a contract are sureties until the true nature of the contract is discovered, if it is not apparent in the four corners of the contract p 262 art 3037

## Formal requirements

- Suretyship must be express and in writing p 262 art 3038
- Acceptance of suretyship is not necessary, nor is notice of acceptance p 262 art 3039

## *Provisions of contract*

- Suretyship can be qualified, conditioned, or limited in any lawful manner that does not limit the imperative requirements such as the express and writing requirements, or the surety's right to recover what he paid to the creditor p 263 art 3040

## Three kinds of suretyship

- Commercial
- Legal
- Ordinary p 263 art 3041

## *Commercial suretyship*

- The surety is engaged in a surety business;
- The principal obligor is a corporation, partnership, or business entity;
- The principal obligation arises out of a commercial transaction; or
- The suretyship arises out of a commercial transaction of the surety p 263 art 3042

## *Legal suretyship*

- Legal suretyship is one pursuant to legislation (statutory) or a court order (judicial) p 263 art 3043
- If there is not a special rule regarding legal suretyship, then the rules on commercial suretyship will apply p 264 art 3063, 3064
- Legal surety can only be given by:
    o a surety engaged in a surety business in Louisiana; or
    o a personal surety by way of a natural person, evidenced by an affidavit by the principal obligor and the natural person surety, who owns property in this state of sufficient value to cover the amount of the obligation p 264 art 3065
- Surety is not liable for more than the suretyship is for p 264 art 3067
- A legal suretyship may be more favorable to the creditor or obligee than required by the law, but may not extend the time for bringing an action against the surety p 264 art 3067
- A cash bond in the same amount may be substituted for a surety bond p 264 art 3068

- The creditor first must obtain a judgment against the principal to be able to obtain a judgment against the surety, but the creditor can do that in one suit by joining them p 264 art 3069

**Special procedural rules for legal suretyship**

- If a party to a judicial proceeding must post a bond, the surety bond (or cash bond in lieu) is payable to the clerk of court. Any party in interest can sue for the surety p 264 LA CCP art 5121
- Any party to a judicial proceeding requiring a property bond must present to the judge in the parish where the immovable is located the following, which will be recorded in the conveyance of that parish, before the bond can be presented to the court having jurisdiction over the judicial proceeding p 265 LA CCP art 5121.1
    - An assessment certificate
    - A homestead waiver if applicable
    - Mortgage certificate
- Personal bonds in judicial proceedings must be accompanied by affidavits attesting to the personal worth of the party furnishing the surety p 265 LA CCP art 5122

## *Ordinary suretyship*

- An ordinary suretyship is one that is neither commercial nor legal. Despite its name, it is not the usual form of suretyship p 265 art 3044
- An ordinary suretyship must be strictly construed in favor of the surety p 265 art 3044
- An example of an ordinary suretyship is a parent who guarantees the personal, nonbusiness debt of a child or friend.

# Effects of suretyship: liability of surety

- Unless the contract or Civil Code article 3055 provides otherwise, the surety is liable for the full performance of the principal obligation. The creditor may recover from the surety for the debtor/ principal's failure to perform p 266 art 3045
- The surety can assert any defense that the principal could, except lack of capacity or bankruptcy p 266 art 3046 So, for example, if the principal was unable to complete construction on a building because of a natural disaster, or because of an interruption in the supply chain, the surety can assert that as a defense, just as the principal can.

## *Effects between surety and principal debtor*

- When a surety pays the principal's obligation, he gains 3 distinct rights: the right of subrogation, the right of reimbursement, and the right to require security from the principal obligor p 266 art 3047

**Surety's right to subrogation**

- A surety who pays the principal's obligation is subrogated. Subrogation is the legal right for a third party to collect a debt or damages (or in this case, performance) on behalf of another party p 266 art 3048
    - Subrogation arises by operation of law (it is not something that is contracted into) p 266 art 3048

**Surety's right to reimbursement**

- A surety who pays the principal's obligation is entitled to reimbursement, provided that he pays the obligation after it is due and not before p 266 art 3049

- A surety for multiple solidary obligors (joint debtors) may recover from any of them reimbursement of the whole amount he has paid the creditor p 266
- If a good faith surety pays a creditor when the debt has been extinguished (for example, if the debtor has been released from the obligation or the debt has been paid), or if the principal obligor had a means to defeat the obligation (a valid defense against it), the surety is still entitled to reimbursement if the surety made a reasonable effort to notify the principal obligor that the creditor was still hounding them for payment p 267 art 3050
- A surety does not have a right for reimbursement or subrogation if the principal obligor also pays the creditor and the surety warned the principal obligor that they were paying the creditor. In that case, the surety can only recover from the creditor p 267 art 3051
- The surety can't recover more than what he paid from the principal obligor, but by subrogation, he can recover attorney's fees and interest p 267 art 3052

**Surety's right to require security**

- The 4 instances in which a surety may obtain security even prior to payment include:
  - when a suit is brought by the creditor against the surety
  - when the principal obligor is insolvent (such as filing bankruptcy proceedings)
  - when the principal obligor fails to perform an act promised in return for the suretyship
  - when the principal obligation is due according to its terms and the surety has not consented to an extension of time p 267 art 3053
- If the principal obligor does not provide security as required by the surety within 10 days after written demand, the surety can cause the principal obligor to deposit funds into the registry of the court p 267 art 3054

## *Effects among several sureties*

- Unless otherwise stated, multiple co-sureties are presumed to share the obligation equally p 267 art 3055
- If one surety pays the debts of the obligor, he can recover by means of subrogation from his co-sureties p 268 art 3056
- If a co-surety pays more than his proportional share, he can recover the excess that he paid from each of the co-sureties in a proportional amount p 268 art 3057

# Termination of suretyship

- Obligations of a surety are extinguished in the same way as contracts are extinguished, with some modifications p 268 art 3058
- The *extinction of the principal obligation* extinguishes the suretyship p 268 art 3059 For example, if you co-sign a loan for a car, and the car is paid off, the surety for that loan is extinguished because the principal obligation no longer exists.
- The *prescription of the principal obligation* extinguishes the suretyship p 268 art 3060 A suit for contribution by co-sureties and a suit for reimbursement from the principal obligor both expire in 10 years.
- Surety may terminate the suretyship *by giving notice to the creditor* p 268 art 3061 Termination is prospective only: it can't relieve the surety of debts already incurred
- Knowledge of the *death of the surety* is the same as a notice of termination p 268 art 3061

## *Effect of modification of principal obligation*

- Modification or amendment of principal obligation by the creditor (like a change order) has the following effects:
    - An ordinary suretyship is extinguished
    - A commercial suretyship is extinguished only to the extent of prejudice to the surety, but the creditor has the burden to prove the extent of prejudice p 268 art 3062

# 17

# Security (UCC 9) and Pledge

*Security* is an accessory right (not a primary contract in itself) created by legislation or by contract over property, or an obligation undertaken by a person who is not the principal obligor, to secure the performance of an obligation p 270 LA CC art 3136

All of a person's property is generally available to a creditor to fulfill an obligation they are personally bound for: movable, immovable, present, future p 270 art 3133

If there is no preference established by law or otherwise, the creditors get to share the debtor's property *ratably* (they each get an apportioned or proportional share, a pro rata share) p 270 art 3134

## Pledgor and pledgee

- *Pledgor* is the person who grants the rights in the property, the one who owes the debt (the debtor, in essence)
- *Pledgee* is the person who owns the security interest, who is owed the obligation, often money (the creditor)

## Types of security p 271 art 3138

- Suretyship (Chapter 16)
- Privilege (several chapters including, importantly, Chapter 21 on vendor's privilege)
    - Privilege is a right to be preferred over other creditors, even mortgagors p 271 art 3186
    - Privilege must be expressly granted for it to be claimed p 271 art 3185
- Mortgage (Chapter 18)
- Pledge and UCC 9 (this chapter) because today, UCC 9 has replaced pledge.

## Pledge

- Pledge is a real right, established by contract, over certain types of property, creating preferences in favor of securing performance of obligations (usually collection of a debt) p 271 art 3141
- Historical principles:
    - Usually, the object of a pledge was a movable, and the owner of the movable (the pledgor) would grant a security interest in the property to the pledgee by giving him the property, so that the creditor (the pledgee) would have an automatic first-in-line ranking if the pledgor failed to make good on his obligation (as in a pawn shop) p 272
    - Now, most corporeal movables are secured by a security interest instead of a physical handover p 272

- o Pawn shop transactions are outside the scope of notary and pledge.
- o Antichresis (pledge of the civil and natural fruits of an immovable) is no longer a term we use, but the concept still exists, although it does not create real rights in immovable property p 272 This is now codified as the pledge of the lessor's rights in the lease of an immovable and its rents, discussed later in this chapter.

## *What property can be pledged?*

- According to the Civil Code: movable property that cannot be encumbered by a UCC 9 interest, rights in a lease of immovable property and the civil fruits (rents) thereof, and those things specifically allowed to be the object of a contract of pledge p 272 art 3142
- Because most things in the world can be encumbered by a UCC 9 lease, some of the only things left that can be pledged are:
  - o Rights in insurance policies other than life insurance (because life insurance is excluded from coverage under UCC 9); and
  - o The lessor's interest in the lease of an immovable and its rents

## *The nature of the contract of pledge*

- Pledge is an accessory contract, so a valid, underlying debt must exist p 273 art 3144
- If the underlying debt is extinguished, the pledge is also extinguished p 273 art 3144

## *Capacity of pledgor*

- Pledgor (debtor) must have capacity to enter into a contract (see capacity in Chapter 11 on Contracts), and have the power to alienate the object of that contract (i.e. ownership, or agency with the power to alienate) p 273 art 3151

## *The higher preference granted by the contract of pledge*

- Creditor or obligee gets the right to have his debt satisfied from the property pledged before any unsecured creditors, and anyone who has rights in the pledged property, but those rights were acquired *after* the property was pledged p 273 art 3145
- This preference extends to natural and civil fruits of the property, and these fruits can be retained as additional security p 273 art 3145, 3159

## *Pledge may be given to secure a third party's obligation*

- You can pledge property to secure the payment of an obligation of a third person p 274 art 3148

## *Pledgee's right of retention*

- The pledgee (creditor) can retain the property until the debt has been satisfied p 274 art 3156
- Partial payment does not require the pledgee to release part of the property p 274 art 3156
- The pledgor cannot demand return of the pledged items until the debt has been paid in full because the contract of pledge is indivisible, even if the pledged items are divisible p 274 art 3157

## *Care of pledged property*

- Probably "reasonable care," though the code no longer addresses this p 274

## 17 ▪ SECURITY AND PLEDGE

### *Default of underlying obligation and pledge*

- The pledgee (creditor) does not automatically become the owner of the pledged items. The pledgee has the right to dispose of the items pledged at an auction or private sale, but he must act reasonably in disposing of the items and account to the pledgor for proceeds in excess of the debt owed p 275 art 3158
- Any prior agreement that ownership of the pledged goods will transfer upon default is unlawful and null p 275 art 3140

### *Formalities of the contract of pledge*

- Does not have to be in writing – unless it is an incorporeal, then it must be in writing p 275 art 3149
- Does require delivery of possession of the thing by the pledgor (debtor) to the pledgee (creditor) or a third party that holds it for the pledgee. If the thing pledged is an incorporeal, no delivery is required p 275 art 3149
- No signature is required for acceptance by the pledgee (creditor), whose consent is presumed p 275 art 3150

### *Effectiveness against third parties*

- To be effective against third parties, the contract must be in writing, but need not be recorded unless required by law p 276 art 3153
- If the thing pledged is another person's obligation that is not arising under a lease of an immovable, the pledge is effective from the time the obligor has actual knowledge of it p 276 art 3155

### *Pledge as a security agreement under the UCC*

- The default rule is that a security interest is a UCC 9 security interest. You can call a contract a pledge, but it is probably just creating a valid UCC 9 agreement in the property, unless it truly meets the very limited transactions that pledges actually are p 276 art 3143

### *Pledge of the lessor's rights in the lease of an immovable*

- When the property pledged is the lessor's interest in the lease of an immovable and its rents, the terms of the contract must be very specific and precise as to what exactly is the object of the pledge and the obligation it secures p 276 art 3168
- The contract of pledge may include the lease itself, the civil fruits (rents), only one of them, or both of them p 276 art 3168

#### **Variations in the lease of an immovable and its rents**

- The contract of pledge may be included in an act of mortgage, but is only effective against third persons when effectively recorded, and is extinguished when the mortgage is satisfied p 277 art 3170
- A pledge may be established over all or part of the leases of an immovable, even those that don't exist yet – and the pledge will encumber them once they do come into existence p 277 art 3171
- The pledge will have effect to third persons, even for leases not yet in existence, from the time that the contract establishing the pledge of future leases is properly recorded p 277 art 3171
- Contract of pledge under a mineral lease (mineral leases are immovable) may have bonuses, delay rentals, royalties, and shut-in payments as its objects, but these must be recited with specificity p 277 art 3172

### Effects between the parties, and between third parties for pledges affecting immovables

- When the object of the pledge is the lessor's rights in the lease of an immovable and its rents, the pledge is effective against third persons other than the lessee upon recordation in the mortgage records p 278 art 3346, 3169

## UCC 9 Security Agreements

- Pledge is *almost entirely replaced* by Louisiana's adoption of the Uniform Commercial Code and its Article 9. Now, we are more consistent with other states.
- UCC 9 was adopted in 1990, to give uniformity to security devices.
- UCC 9 covers everything that is not specifically excluded from it. It covers: all goods, transactions, fixtures, agricultural liens, sales of accounts, chattels, consignments, etc. p 279 LA RS 10:9-109
- It does not cover:
  - Security interests created by a law of the United States government
  - Nonconsensual liens (legal mortgages or privileges like the lessor's privilege)
  - Interests in real estate, except for fixtures and movables by anticipation (see Chapter 18 on security interests in immovables)
  - Other specific financing transactions provided for in other laws or not intended to be governed by UCC 9

### *Security interest*

- Under UCC 9, a security interest is an interest in personal property created by contract which secures payment of an obligation p 280 LA RS 10:1-201
- *Attachment* is the term given when a security interest becomes enforceable against a debtor. A security interest "attaches" when 3 things occur:
  - The debtor has rights in the collateral, which means he has the legal right to create a security interest in the property
  - There is a security agreement
  - Value is given p 281 LA RS 10:9-203

### *Formal requirements of a security agreement*

- Must be in writing, unless the secured party is in possession of the property p 281 LA RS 9-203
- It must grant or create a security agreement p 281 LA RS 9-203
- It must be signed or authenticated by the debtor p 281 LA RS 9-203
- It must contain a description of the collateral p 281 LA RS 9-203
- If there are fixtures or timber secured, the description of the immovable must be included p 281 LA RS 9-203
- The secured party must give value to the debtor p 281 LA RS 9-203

### *Perfection of a security interest*

- A perfected security interest is any secure interest in an asset that cannot be claimed by any other party, that way it has priority over other creditors. There are several ways a security interest can become perfected:

- A security interest becomes "perfected" when it attaches to the property under LA RS 10:9-309;
- A financing statement has been recorded p 281 LA RS 10:9-310;
- The creditor has possession of the property (no filing is necessary) p 281 LA RS 10:9-313; or
- The UCC states that, "a security interest in investment property, deposit accounts, letter-of-credit rights, or electronic chattel paper may be perfected by control of the collateral," for example, giving a creditor control over a bank account LA RS 10:9-314

## *What is a financing statement?*

- A financing statement is a legal document that is used by lenders or financing agencies to announce their rights to collateral or liens on secured loans.
- The secured party may file the security agreement itself as the financing statement p 281
- The secured party may file an abbreviated form of the security agreement p 282
- The financing statement must include:
  - Name of the debtor, name of the secured party, collateral covered by the financing statement, and if the collateral is timber or fixtures in immovables, the description (legal description or address) of the immovable must be included p 282 LA RS 10:9-502

## *Where is the financing statement filed?*

- Department of Safety and Corrections, Office of Motor Vehicles, if the collateral is a motor vehicle not kept in inventory;
- Department of Wildlife and Fisheries, if the collateral is a titled, numbered vessel valued at more than $2500, or a titled outboard motor; or
- The clerk of court of any parish

# 18

# Mortgage

Mortgage is a nonpossessory right created over property to secure the payment of a debt or performance of an obligation p 285 LA CC art 3278

Mortgage gives the mortgagee the right to seize and sell the property if the debt or failure of performance is defaulted on p 285 art 3279

Mortgage is a real right that burdens the entirety of the property, and it follows the property until the obligation is satisfied p 285 art 3280

## Mortgagor and Mortgagee

- *Mortgagor* is the borrower of a mortgage loan and agrees to a lien. Also sometimes called a debtor or an obligor. Often it is the home buyer.
- *Mortgagee* is the lender and is the lienholder. Also called the secured party or creditor or obligee. Often it is the bank.

## Kinds of mortgages

- Mortgages can be *special* or *general*.
  - A special mortgage burdens a specific piece of property p 286 art 3285
  - A general mortgage burdens all present and future property of the mortgagor p 286 art 3285 A judicial mortgage is a general mortgage, because it will burden all of the property of a judgment debtor.

## Types of mortgages

- Conventional mortgage: created by contract p 285 art 3284
  - There are 3 types of conventional mortgages:
    - An ordinary conventional mortgage is one that is secured by a single one-time extension of credit with a promissory note (like your typical home loan). This is discussed in depth below.
    - A collateral mortgage is one that is used to secure multiple extensions of credit on a cross-collaterizated basis, multiple loan advances extended on a revolving line of credit basis, as well as single, one-time extensions of credit. This is discussed below as well.
    - Multiple indebtedness mortgages are similar to collateral mortgages, but there is no need for a collateral note or for a collateral pledge agreement.
- Legal mortgage: created by operation of law p 285 art 3284
  - Secures an obligation specified by the law that provides for the mortgage p 285 art 3299

## 18 • MORTGAGE

- Judicial mortgage: arising from the recordation of a judgment p 286 art 3284
  - Secures a judgment for the payment of money p 287 art 3299

## *Conventional mortgages*

- Created by written contract to secure the performance of an obligation, usually the payment of money p 286 art 3287
- Mortgage is an accessory contract to the obligation that it secures, enforceable up to the amount of the obligation it secures p 286 art 3282
- Must be in writing, but with no special wording p 286 art 3287
- The conventional mortgage can secure future property p 286 art 3298
- The conventional mortgage can secure obligations, the breach of which will result in damage that the mortgagee sustains p 286 art 3294 For example, the mortgage can be used to secure the timely closing of an act of sale, and if the sale does not take place in the time stated in the act of sale, the mortgagee can sue for damages up to the amount stated in the mortgage.
- Termination: when the underlying obligation is terminated, the mortgage is terminated p 286

## *Legal mortgage*

- Arises by operation of law p 287 art 3299 For example, by law, a minor has a mortgage over the property of his tutor; in case the tutor defaults, the minor has the right to be paid, or a mortgage on property that is the subject of inventory of a succession until a partition has been completed.
- Legal mortgage:
  - is a general mortgage p 287 art 3302
  - generally, is securing an obligation to be performed instead of money due p 287 art 3299
  - is limited to the amount represented to the value of the of the property administered, if that is the obligation p 287
- Examples of legal mortgages from the book: notary's bond when sued upon, special mortgage for a tutor in favor of a minor whose property is being administered, special mortgage for an interdict whose property is being administered, and special mortgage for a succession representative p 287
- Legal mortgages are rarely used (most curators and tutors substitute a surety bond in lieu of the legal mortgage).

## *Judicial mortgages*

- Created unilaterally when a judgment is filed with the recorder of mortgages against a debtor p 288 art 3300
- Notary public does not have anything to do with judicial mortgages, but may see Affidavits of Distinction from time to time, which are when a person has a name similar to a judgment debtor p 288
- The judicial mortgage secures only payment of money, not performance of any other obligation p 288 art 3299
- Judicial mortgage is a general mortgage, attaching to immovable property then owned or subsequently acquired by the judgment debtor, *once it is properly filed for recordation* p 288 art 3303
- The judgment should be recorded in all parishes where the judgment debtor owns immovable property p 288 art 3346
- Movable property cannot be the subject of a judicial mortgage p 289 art 3286, 3302

### Difference between tax lien and judicial mortgage

- The tax lien mortgage is created when the taxing authority files a notice of tax lien (instead of a judgment) in the mortgage records p 289
- The tax lien mortgage extends to all movable property as well as immovable property p 289 LA RS 9:47:1577, LA RS 9:5504

### Validity of judicial mortgages

- A judicial mortgage is valid from the time it is recorded p 289 art 3300
- The judicial mortgage remains valid even though the judgment may be appealed, and enforcement can't proceed until after the time has elapsed for the suspensive appeal p 289 art 3304, LA CCP art 2252
- An out-of-state judgment (called a "foreign judgment") must be recognized by a Louisiana court before it can be recorded and recognized as a judicial mortgage p. 289 art 3305
- Judgments of federal courts can be recorded in Louisiana without the need to be recognized as foreign judgments p 290 LA RS 13:4204
- Judicial mortgages are good for 10 years, and must be revived every 10 years to remain valid or they prescribe (die) p 290 art 3359, 3362
- If a judicial mortgage is revived and reinscribed, it is valid for another 10 years p 290

### Cancellation of a judicial mortgage

- Judicial mortgage is extinguished by satisfaction of the judgment (paying off the debt) or the lapse of 10 years if the judgment is not revived p 290 art 3319, 3368
- Because it is created by a judgment, it is not subject to the normal formalities of mortgage p 290

## Property susceptible to conventional mortgage

- Usually, immovables and other associated incorporeal **im**movables (such as usufructs, predial servitudes, and rights in a lease) are able to be mortgaged p 290 art 3286 *(note the typo in the study guide: it says "incorporeal movables" but in fact those are financed under UCC 9)*
- Predial servitudes: Only the right of use servitude may be separately mortgaged without mortgaging the corporeal immovable it is related to p 290 art 3286
- Buildings can be owned by someone different from the person who owns the land. The building is an immovable, as is the land, and each can be subject to mortgage p 290 art 464
- Standing timber and mineral rights: If they are owned by the same person who owns the land, they can be mortgaged as component parts of the land p 290 LA RS 31:203 If the standing timber or mineral rights are owned by someone other than the landowner, they are not capable of being mortgaged. Instead, they can be the object of a UCC 9 secured loan p 290 LA RS 31:204
- Any movable which is a component part of an immovable (including an immovable by declaration) can be the subject of a mortgage of the immovable p 291 art 3286 *(but most movables are secured under UCC 9, not a mortgage – this is tested)*
- A usufruct of a corporeal immovable may be subject of a mortgage p 291 art 3286
- A lessee's rights in a lease of an immovable, with his rights in the buildings and other constructions on the immovable, may be mortgaged p 291 art 3286
- Present and future component parts of an immovable may be mortgaged p 291 LA RS 9:5391

## 18 ▪ MORTGAGE

### Effect and rank of mortgage

- Mortgage, or default on a mortgage, does not transfer ownership or possession of the mortgaged property from the mortgagor to the mortgagee p 291

- The mortgagee has a right over the mortgaged property to secure performance of the obligation (usually, payment of the debt owed) p 291 art 3279

- When the mortgage is granted, the mortgagor grants a security interest in the property for performance of an obligation, which could be his obligation or the obligation of someone else p 291 art 3293, 3295

- If the obligor (mortgagor or another party obligated to perform) defaults, the mortgagee has a right to cause that property to be seized and sold according to the judicial process (usually, a sheriff's sale), and to have the proceeds put towards paying off the mortgage p 291 art 3279, 3307

- Once a mortgage is recorded, it is effective against third parties and creates a privilege for payment of obligations. This means the lender gets in his place in line for payment in the event of default and anyone else with claims against the property will get paid after him. Unsecured creditors are always last in line p 291 art 3307

- Mortgaged property cannot be sold to the prejudice of the mortgage. This means the mortgage either must be paid off, or the mortgagee must agree to the sale and assumption of the mortgage p 292 art 3307

- If a new obligor assumes the first mortgage, the ranking of the mortgage is not extinguished or subordinated even though the original obligor may have been released (a new obligor just stands in his place, in effect) p 292 LA RS 9:5384

### Third possessors

- A person who acquires a mortgaged property but is not liable for the mortgage debt is a *third possessor*, or a *third party possessor* p 292 art 3315 For example, someone who gets a property by any means, by sale or donation or almost any method, and takes it either without knowing of the mortgage, or takes it subject to the mortgage but without assuming or becoming personally bound by the mortgage, is a third possessor.

- The third possessor is said to buy the property *cum onere*, or "as burdened." The mortgagee can foreclose on the property but cannot enforce the debt on the third party. If the third party pays off the debt (fulfills the obligation), he can recover from the mortgagor who owes the obligation p 292 art 3317

- The third possessor has an obligation to maintain the property to keep it from deteriorating and is liable to the creditors if it does p 293 art 3316

- If the third possessor makes improvements that enhance the value of the property, he can recover the cost of those if the proceeds of the enforcement of the mortgage (forced sale) exceed the unenhanced value of the property p 293 art 3318 So, if the house before the sale was worth a little bit of money, and the third possessor makes it worth a lot more, and the house goes into foreclosure, the third possessor is entitled to the proceeds above what the house was worth before any improvements were made.

### Recordation

- A mortgage has no effect against third persons (i.e. other people, not the parties or "third possessors" mentioned above) until it is recorded with the recorder of mortgages in the parish where the property is located p 294 art 3338, 3347

- The effect of recordation is limited to property located in the parish in which the recordation occurs; if it is not filed in the correct parish, it has no effect p 294 art 3341, 3346

- Recordation of a mortgage is not evidence of the validity of the obligation the mortgage secures, and gives the creditor no greater rights against third persons than he has against the owner of the property secured by the mortgage p 294 art 3320 Just because a debt is recorded does not mean it is valid. Sometimes debts don't get cancelled, or may be recorded incorrectly.

### *Mortgages affecting property in more than one parish*

- To affect third persons, the mortgage must be recorded in each parish.
- Mortgage instruments can be executed in multiple originals so they can be recorded in several parishes; or a certified copy from the clerk of court can be filed in another parish p 294 art 3355, LA RS 13:103

## Mortgage Certificates

- A Mortgage Certificate is a listing of all uncancelled mortgages affecting a particular immovable property p 294 LA RS 9:2743
- The clerk of court (acting as the ex-officio recorder of mortgages) is required to furnish this to anyone who asks.
- When a notary executes an act that is to be recorded with the clerk of court, it must contain the printed names of the witnesses or the clerk of court may refuse it (please don't forget this), and you must record your encumbrances promptly as required by law p 295 LA RS 35:12, LA RS 9:5212

## Extinction of mortgages

There are 7 methods by which a mortgage may be extinguished. The mortgage still must be cancelled in the public records, because extinction does not automatically cancel a mortgage p 295 art 3319

1. Extinction or destruction of the thing mortgaged;
2. Confusion, which is the obligee acquiring ownership of the thing mortgaged;
3. Prescription of all the obligations that the mortgage secures;
4. Discharge through execution or other judicial proceeding in accordance with the law;
5. Consent of the mortgagee;
6. Termination of the mortgage of future things by reasonable notice that an obligation does not exist and neither the mortgagor nor the mortgagee is bound to the other; or
7. When all the obligations, present and future, for which the mortgage is established have been extinguished

## Establishing a conventional mortgage

### *Form and content of contract of mortgage*

- There is no special wording p 296 art 3287 Generally, the mortgage may be under private signature, without witnesses, recorded or not, to be valid between the parties.
- In Louisiana, the mortgage is usually in an authentic act. If there is a default, the parties can avail themselves of the executory process instead of an ordinary process which requires a trial and judgment p 296 art 3287, LA CCP 2631 (So, if a mortgage contains a "confession of judgment" clause, it must be in an authentic act to be able to use the executory process; see Chapter 21.)
- The contract of mortgage must include:
    - The parties' intent to mortgage;
    - The nature and situation of each of the immovables (legal description);
    - The amount secured or the maximum amount secured at any one time; and

## 18 ▪ MORTGAGE

　　　　o   The signature of the mortgagor

### *Acceptance of the mortgage by the mortgagee*

- Acceptance by the mortgagee is not necessary, it is presumed p 296 art 3289
- Even though acceptance is presumed, get all the parties to sign the mortgage document.

### *Who can create a conventional mortgage?*

- The person who can alienate the property can mortgage it p 297 art 3290
- A person can give a mortgage over property they don't own, but the mortgage doesn't have any effect until the person takes ownership of the property p 297 art 3292 An example of this is when you mortgage future property, or property you are acquiring by adverse possession. The mortgage takes effect once ownership kicks in.

### *Specific things are presumed to be mortgaged*

- Specific things are presumed to be the subject of a conventional mortgage unless otherwise stated in the mortgage p 297 art 3291

## Mortgage Cancellation

### *Production of a note or release for cancellation*

- Once a mortgage has been satisfied, a mortgagee has 30 days upon written request to provide the original promissory note, or a cancellation document sufficient to bring about the cancellation of the mortgage in the mortgage and conveyance records. If the note is held by a federal agency, they get an additional 60 days p 298 LA RS 9:5385

### *Methods of mortgage cancellation*

Request for cancellation varies by parish, but generally must be accompanied by a uniform mortgage cancellation form created by LA R.S. 9:5166. Please note that most parishes have information available on the internet to assist in filing these forms. Jefferson Parish has a detailed package that describes each of these methods and forms as examples.

- *Method of cancelling a non-paraphed obligation* (a paraph is a signature by a notary on the evidence of an obligation, typically a mortgage, to identify the note with the mortgage securing the note; see Chapter 21) p 298 LA RS 9:5169
    - o   The person requesting the release must submit a request for cancellation, along with an act signed by the mortgagee or obligee stating that he acknowledges the satisfaction or extinction of the secured obligation, releasing or acknowledging the extinction of the mortgage or privilege, and directs the recorder to cancel its recordation
- *Method of cancelling a paraphed obligation* p 298 LA RS 9:5170
    - o   The person requesting the cancellation must file a request for a cancellation, along with either
        - The original obligation marked "paid," or "cancelled," or
        - An *authentic act* describing the paraphed obligation with sufficient particularity to reasonably identify it as the one paraphed for identification with the act of mortgage or privilege and containing: (a) The appearer's declaration that he is the holder and owner of the paraphed obligation and that he releases or acknowledges extinction of the mortgage or privilege or directs the recorder to cancel its recordation; and (b) A declaration by the notary that the appearer presented him with the paraphed obligation and that he paraphed it for identification with his act; or

- The affidavit of the obligee of record, declaring that the obligation has been paid, forgiven, or satisfied and that the obligation has been lost or destroyed and cannot be presented
- *Method of cancelling an obligation pursuant to a certificate by a public officer* p 299 LA RS 9:5171
    - If the cancellation is because of a judicial sale, like a sheriff's sale or public auction, the request for cancellation shall have attached to it a certified copy of the order of cancellation
- *Method of cancellation by a licensed financial institution* p 299 LA RS 9:5172
    - Instead of complying with the provisions of RS 9:5169, 5170, and 5171, a request for cancellation or partial cancellation may have attached to it the signed, written act of a licensed financial institution represented by one of its officers and executed or duly acknowledged before a notary public with or without witnesses (or an act under private signature by two authorized officers of the licensed financial institution), declaring that the obligee is a licensed financial institution, with some particular criteria being met
- *Method of cancelling a prescribed mortgage not reinscribed* p 300 art 3367
    - If a mortgage has prescribed and not been reinscribed (a mortgage must be reinscribed, or re-recorded, so to speak, to keep it active in the records, arts 3357 and 3358), a written application to cancel must be signed and submitted by the person requesting cancellation
- *Method of cancelling a prescribed mortgage not revived, or revival demand rejected* p 300 art 3368
    - The person requesting the cancellation must submit a request for cancellation accompanied by a certificate from the clerk of court that no revival suit has been filed, or shall submit a final judgment of the court rejecting the demand for revival
- *Method of cancelling on affidavit of notary or title insurer where paraphed note or other evidence is lost or destroyed* p 300 LA RS 9:5167
    - When the notary public has received the funds and satisfied the obligation for a note paraphed for identification with a mortgage or vendor's lien, the recorder of mortgages can cancel the mortgage with an affidavit from the notary stating those facts, and describe the note that was lost or destroyed
- *Method of cancelling on affidavit of title-insurance-company officer, closing notary, or attorney for mortgagor that obligation was satisfied* LA RS 9:5167.1
    - When a *mortgagee* receives the full payoff but no documentation, the closing notary may request that the mortgage be cancelled by submitting the request for cancellation on an affidavit along with a payoff statement

# Obligations that can be secured by conventional mortgage

## *Securing payment of money or act*

- Generally, the mortgage is granted to secure the payment of money.
- A mortgage can also be granted to secure the performance of an act p 304 art 3294
- A mortgage can be given to secure the performance of a person other than that of the mortgagor p 304 art 3295

## *Secure future obligations*

- A mortgage can be used to secure future obligations p 304 art 3298
- The mortgage for future obligations is effective
    - between the parties from the time the mortgage is established p 304 art 3298
    - as to third persons from the time the mortgage is recorded p 304 art 3298

- The mortgage for future obligations continues until the mortgagor terminates the mortgage by giving the mortgagee reasonable notice of termination, and is conditioned on 2 things: p 304 art 3298
    - no obligation exists; and
    - no agreement exists to permit an obligation secured by the mortgage to be incurred
- A mortgage for future obligations can be extinguished in any other lawful manner, however p 304 art 3298

## "In Rem" mortgage

- The mortgage can be tied not to a person, but only to the property, so the mortgagee only has recourse to seize the property and not sue anyone personally. This is an "in rem" mortgage p 305 art 3297, LA RS 9:5391
- This is not typical, though, because lenders want borrowers to be personally liable in addition to being able to seize the property.

## Collateral mortgage

- Like all other mortgages, it is an accessorial contract p 307
- A collateral mortgage combines elements of pledge and mortgage; it is a conventional mortgage with a security interest in the note that the mortgage secures, to secure present *and future* indebtedness p 306 LA RS 9:5550
- The collateral mortgage may be used over and over with new funds lent at any time, so there is no effective reduction of the mortgage limit.

### *Two essential elements of a collateral mortgage*

- The collateral mortgage note can be issued and reissued without extinguishing the collateral mortgage; and
- It incorporates a UCC 9 security agreement controlling the collateral mortgage note p 306

### *Mechanics of creation*

- The collateral mortgage involves 4 elements:
    - Borrower grants a mortgage in favor of a specific person, or any holder of the mortgage, which is where the mortgagor acknowledges the debt. The mortgage secures the mortgage note.
    - A collateral mortgage note, sometimes called the "ne varietur" note, which is where he intends to use the "ne varietur" to raise funds. The collateral mortgage note is the collateral (not the property itself). The collateral mortgage note is usually payable to bearer on demand.
    - A hand note or promissory note, which is paraphed (signed by the notary) for identification with the act of mortgage. This is the evidence of the debt. This identifies the indebtedness intended to be secured by the pledge of the collateral mortgage note. This is generally where the language regarding current and future loans, lines of credit, extensions of credit, liabilities, and any other obligations, etc., may be found.
    - A UCC 9 security agreement (formerly a pledge).
- The mortgagor then grants a security interest in (pledges) the "ne varietur" note to the creditor and customarily executes a promissory note for the loan: the note that actually represents the debt is commonly called a "hand note."

- This is where a collateral mortgage is different from a mortgage to secure future advances and from an ordinary conventional mortgage. In those two cases, the money is directly advanced on the note that is paraphed or identified with the mortgage. In the collateral mortgage, the money is advanced on the collateral mortgage note, which is pledged to secure a debt. The hand note or promissory note is what is paraphed p 308

## *Purpose and durability of the collateral mortgage*

- Purpose is to make a mortgage note that can be given as security for pre-existing debt, contemporaneous debt, future debt, or a combination of any of those three (like an older form of a line-of-credit home loan) p 308
- Origins of the collateral mortgage: There was no code article for the collateral mortgage, but it was a made-up creation from several laws to provide flexibility in financing and security instruments. Today, it is recognized by statute p 307 LA RS 9:5550
- The collateral mortgage "package" is a combination of mortgage and UCC 9 security agreements.

## *Combining a UCC 9 security agreement and mortgage*

- The grant of a security interest in a negotiable collateral mortgage note secured by a mortgage is a movable, hence the UCC 9 interest p 309
- Sometimes the UCC 9 agreement and other parts of the package are combined into 1 document, so there are not always 4 separate instruments p 312
- The underlying security in the case of the collateral mortgage is the right to cause the mortgaged property to be seized and sold to fund the collateral mortgage note to pay the indebtedness p 309

## *The collateral mortgage note and the mortgage*

- An acceptable method to connect the hand note to the security of the collateral mortgage is to write across the face of the hand note that it is secured by the collateral mortgage note p 309

## *Effect and recordation of collateral mortgage*

- Because the nature of collateral mortgage is kind of a hybrid of mortgages (containing real rights of security in movable *and* immovable security), there are different rules for effectiveness p 309
- Two things must occur for a collateral mortgage to be effective against third persons:
  - The mortgage must be recorded in the parish where the mortgaged property is located p 309
  - An actual debt must be incurred in favor of the creditor and a security interest granted in the collateral mortgage note to secure that debt p 309
- When these two things happen, the mortgage will affect third persons, and it will be ranked along with other liens, privileges, or mortgages burdening the property p 309
- No requirement that the grant of the security interest (the collateral mortgage note) be filed when the creditor is placed into physical possession of the hand note p 309 LA RS 10:9-322

## *Effective date*

- Effective date occurs when a security interest is perfected in the obligation secured by the collateral mortgage and collateral mortgage note p 310

## Miscellaneous provisions regarding all types of mortgages

- An original vendor's privilege *or* first mortgage, or both, is not extinguished nor ranked lowered when it is assumed by a new obligor p 311 LA RS 9:5384
- A mortgage shall secure additional funds to advance to the mortgagee if the mortgaged property needs to be protected, preserved, or repaired, etc. p 311 LA RS 9:5389
- A mortgage note under Chapter 9 of the Louisiana Commercial Laws may be combined into one form p 312 LA RS 9:5393
- The essential components of drafting a mortgage are discussed in Chapter 21.

# 19

# Juridical Acts: Authentic Acts, Acknowledgments, Affidavits

## Juridical Act

A juridical act is a voluntary act that is undertaken and intended to have legal consequences p 315 These include, but are not limited to:

- all acts that can be done before a notary under LA R.S. 35, including authentic acts and acknowledged acts
- any acts that do not require the services of a notary
- acts under private signature
- acts that do not need a writing at all, like donation of a movable

## Notarial Act

A notarial act is any juridical act that is passed before a notary p 315 The book notes that if a statute or code requires a "notarial act," without any further clarification, the authentic should be used out of an abundance of caution p 316

In any notarial act that is prepared by a notary, LA R.S. 35:12 must be followed p 329 This statute requires the printed names and identification numbers of notaries, along with the full printed or typed name of the parties and the witnesses (if any) under their respective signatures. A notary's stamp with their name and notary ID number works, too.

### *Acts in derogation of laws for the protection of the public interest*

The book states that parties cannot undertake juridical acts that are in derogation (opposition) from laws enacted for the public interest. A person cannot, for example, make a contract to force a person to work for less than minimum wage, as that is against the public interest.

- Suppletive laws – are laws that exist when parties are silent on certain matters, but these laws are capable of being modified as *supplements* to the expression of the intentions of the contracting parties' will p 316
- Imperative laws – this is not mentioned in this chapter, but helps explain suppletive laws. These are laws that cannot be modified and are not disclaimable and are indispensable to a valid contract. For example, a sale contract must have a warranty of title, that is an imperative, but warranty of redhibition (freedom from defects) is suppletive.

## Capacity

- Natural and juridical persons must have legal capacity to enter into a juridical act p 317
- Capacity is presumed, but it's a rebuttable presumption (it can be challenged at a later time) p 317

# 19 • JURIDICAL ACTS AND CLAUSES

## Consent

- To consent to a bilateral contract or execute a unilateral juridical act, a party must be able to consent p 317 LA CC art 1927  If one of the parties does not understand the consequences of their actions or is under duress or undue influence, their consent may be vitiated (destroyed) p 317 art 1948
- Consent requires that the party making the juridical act be of sound mind, lucid, capable of making decisions, free from undue influence, and free from duress.

### *Rebuttable presumption of capacity and consent*

- There is a presumption that a party appearing before a notary to sign a juridical act has capacity and consents to the act. But that presumption is rebuttable at a later time, if someone has evidence to show that the party lacked capacity or consent at the time the act was signed.
- Capacity and consent are discussed in detail in Chapter 11 on Obligations and Contracts.

## Proof of obligations

The person demanding performance of the obligation must prove that the obligation exists (for example, a creditor demanding payment of a debt has to prove that the debt exists) p 317

An instrument which has been lost or destroyed may be proved by secondary or parol evidence (oral testimony), except as provided by law p 318

- If the lost juridical act is not a contract, like an Act of Adult Adoption, special rules apply, not Civil Code article 1832 p 318
- See the chapter on Obligations and Contracts, discussing "proof of obligations" in detail.

There are 2 types of written contracts or other juridical acts: p 318

- Authentic act – which is self-proving, i.e. evidence will generally not be admitted against the authentic act except in cases of fraud, duress, forgery, or undue influence, the facts contained in the act itself are taken as true
- Act under private signature – which is proof of the obligation only when a party testifies under oath that his signature is his own, unless his signature is authenticated by being acknowledged in a form provided by law (see below, Acknowledged Acts)

## Do not create pleadings

This is the unauthorized practice of law. You can notarize pleadings brought to you by a customer, and you can represent yourself in court, but you cannot create pleadings for customers. You cannot create a 103 divorce, or any other pleadings. This can result in you facing criminal prosecution, civil liability, and loss of your notary commission.

## The Authentic Act

Notaries in other states don't typically pass authentic acts, they usually just certify that they witnessed a party sign after having been placed under oath, or they receive acknowledgments. But in Louisiana, notaries may even create and execute such acts.

The authentic act occurs when the notary and two witnesses observe, simultaneously, a party declare their intent to enter into a particular juridical act, and make a formal declaration of their intention. The authentic act occurs in a particular series of steps and in a particular format. *Next to testaments, an authentic act is the most formal of all written documents a notary can execute.*

It is generally written in the voice of the notary, since it's an account of what the notary has witnessed p 319

The authentic act does not have to be written by the notary; it can be prepared by another party, like a power of attorney prepared by a title company to effect the donation of an immovable by a party unable to attend the closing. But it *can* be drafted by a notary in this state without illegally practicing law.

The code states that an authentic act is:

- a writing
- executed before a notary public ("executing" and "signing" have different meanings. Execute means "something more" than just signing, though the code does not express what that means) p 321
- signed by each party who executed it
- simultaneously in the presence of two witnesses
- signed by each notary public before whom it was executed

The typed, printed, or handwritten name of each person signing *shall* be placed in a legible form beneath the signature of each person signing p 319 art 1833 a although failure to do so doesn't invalidate the act (but, in practice, a clerk of court may refuse to record the act if it's missing this statutory directive)

The authentic act:

- can be executed in more than one part
- each part must be executed as an independent authentic act. For example, if 2 parties are signing the act at different times, there should be 2 separate sets of signature, notary and witness areas, 1 for each of the parties, and each should be filled out when that party signs. The witnesses and notary can be different for each party. It can be 2 sets of signature lines on 1 document, or 2 documents intended to be incorporated together as 1. The documents can be separate, as a real estate transaction that is completed in different states and mailed to 1 title agency for completion. But if real estate is sold in La., the formalities for a sale of immovable property must be followed, no matter where the transaction is notarized p 319 art 1833 b

## *Executing the Authentic Act and its effect*

- If a party cannot sign his name or does not know how to sign, the notary must cause him to affix his mark to the writing. For example, if the party is a quadriplegic (but is able to read), the attorney may help him make a mark on the authentic act on the signature line. This does happen often with clients with physical disabilities, or who are elderly, or have had surgeries p 319 art 1833 c
- The authentic act is considered self-proving (mentioned above) p 319 art 1835 Evidence will generally not be admitted against the authentic act except in cases of fraud, duress, forgery, or undue influence; the facts contained in the act itself are taken as true. It is valid against the heirs and successors by universal or particular title. While validity of the authentic act is presumed, the presumption is rebuttable through credible and competent evidence p 320
- If there is a defect in the authentic act for any of the following reasons, the act may still be valid as an act under private signature: lack of competency or capacity of the notary public, lack of competency or capacity of one or more witnesses, or a defect as to the form of the authentic act p 320 act 1834
- An act under private signature or an act under private signature duly acknowledged can never substitute for an authentic act where one is required by law p 320 art 1836

## *Executing the Authentic Act: the importance of ritual*

- Reading of the act. The notary ensures that the act is properly executed by reading through the act in the presence of the witnesses) or at least assuring herself that the parties have read it) p 320
- Concluding the act. The words at the end of the act serve to reinforce the sentiments contained in the act. The statement that the act was "executed before him and in the presence of the witnesses who

signed their names with the parties after due reading of the whole" or a similar statement ensures that the act is intentional and authentic p 322

## *Using a stamp that says "attesting to signatures only"*

There is ongoing litigation on the propriety of using this stamp on documents. It's not necessary for a non-attorney notary to use them on documents that they themselves have not prepared, as it'll usually be evident to a court (in the event of litigation) that they were form documents or ones prepared by someone else. The non-attorney notary should be memorializing the intentions and sentiments of the parties, not advising them on legal matters; and the courts will recognize the limited role of the notary in that instance.

If this type of stamp is used on a testament and is stamped in the wrong place, for example, above the attestation clause, or the stamp incorrectly states that the notary did not read the document, in contravention of the rule that testaments must be read aloud before signing, it may invalidate the testament and subject the notary to litigation. This rule could be extended to authentic acts at some point p 323

*Side note to such disclaimer stamps – please be careful when signing wills prepared by others; make sure they conform with Louisiana laws and form. See Chapter 24 on Testaments.*

## *Acts required to be in authentic form*

| Act of surrender (adoption) | LA Children's Code art 1122 |
|---|---|
| Consent to adoption by alleged father/release of claims | LA Children's Code art 1196 |
| Intrafamily adoption: consent of parent to adoption of his child | LA Children's Code art 1244 |
| Acknowledgment of paternity | LA CC arts 190.1, 196, RS 40:34.5.2 |
| Adult adoption | LA CC art 213 |
| Designation of a tutor (other than in a will) | LA CC art 257 |
| Limited emancipation | LA CC art 368 |
| Modification or termination of limited emancipation | LA CC art 371 |
| Declaration of dispensation of collation* when made by separate later act (not in a testament) | LA CC art 1232 |
| Proof of conditions of partnership to exempt from collation* | LA CC art 1247 |
| Gratuitous transfer of separate property to the community | LA CC art 2343.1 |
| Donations of immovables, incorporeals, and corporeals other than manual gifts | LA CC art 1541 |
| Confirmations of donations that were supposed to be in authentic act but weren't | LA CC art 1842, 1845 |
| Acts of mortgage on immovable property that contain a confession of judgment | LA CC art 2631, 2635 |
| Declaration of immobilization of a mobile home outside of a sale, mortgage, or sale with mortgage | LA RS 9:1149.4 |
| Beneficiary's refusal of interest in an inter vivos trust | LA RS 9:1985 |
| Grant of a real right in immovable property for educational, charitable, or historic purposes | LA RS 9:1252 |
| Act to establish disability of principal in conditional procuration | LA RS 9:3890 |
| Act of sale of titled movable sold by a holder of privilege | LA RS 9:4502 |

| Act to cancel mortgage or privilege secured by a paraphed obligation | LA RS 9:5170 |
|---|---|
| Unincorporated association of authority | LA RS 12:505 |
| Act of correction by notary | LA RS 35:2.1 |
| Power of attorney which authorizes any act needing to be in an authentic act | LA CC art 2993 |

\* *Collation* is, in one context, an action that happens when a forced heir can have some gift to a sibling fictitiously brought back into the succession or considered an advance on their inheritance. It is complicated and the author of the study guide does mention it (e.g. in the context of partnerships) among the acts that must be in authentic form, but are unlikely to ever be encountered by non-attorney notaries p 325

## Act Under Private Signature (also called Private Act)

- A writing
- The writing can be by them or by someone else
- Signed between the two parties p 325 art 1837
- There are no other formalities to make it binding on the parties, except the standard contractual requirements of capacity and consent
- If there is a situation where the signature on a private act is questioned, the person who signed the act must acknowledge or deny their signature p 325 art 1838
- If they deny their signature, any means of proof may be used to prove their signature p 325
- The act under private signature need not be witnessed, but if it is not witnessed at the time it is signed, it cannot later become an *acknowledged act of a witness* p 326 but could be acknowledged by a party
- If the act is not authentic (an authentic act) or acknowledged, it is only admissible and useful in court upon proving of the signatures p 326

## Act Under Private Signature Duly Acknowledged (also called Acknowledged Act)

- Halfway between the authentic act and private act p 326
- An act under private signature is acknowledged when the party recognizes the signature as his own before a notary public, or other officer authorized to perform that function, in the presence of two witnesses p 326 art 1836
- The book makes a distinction between acts that are valid when private and continue to be valid even though they are later acknowledged, and acts that are required by law to be "under private signature duly acknowledge" *from their inception* to be valid at all (such as a matrimonial agreement) p 326

### *Acts requiring either an Authentic Act or Act Under Private Signature Duly Acknowledged*

| Act of privilege or security interest in a *movable* containing a confession of judgment | LA CCP art 2635, LA RS 9:5536 |
|---|---|
| Certain articles of incorporation for non-profit corporations | LA RS 12:205 |
| Articles of incorporation of a fraternal benefit society | LA RS 22:290 |
| Foreign (non-Louisiana) corporation's statement acknowledging a state contract | LA RS 12:304 |

## 19 • JURIDICAL ACTS AND CLAUSES

| Matrimonial agreements (premarital/post-marital agreements) | LA CC art 2331 |
| Reservation of fruits and revenues of separate property | LA CC art 2339 |
| Modification of spousal support obligation | LA CC art 116 |
| Creation of inter vivos trust | LA RS 9:1752 |
| Transfer or encumbrance by a beneficiary on his interest in a trust | LA RS 9:2003 |
| Modification, division, termination, or revocation of a trust (not in a testament) | LA RS 9:2051 |

## Acknowledgment

Acknowledgment authenticates a private act p 327 The authentic act is self-proving and admitted into evidence during litigation, *but* a private act is not without being authenticated. *But*, if an act is acknowledged, it shares the self-proving quality of the authentic act.

An acknowledgment is an affidavit with language describing the original act, original signatories to that act, and other information (see next section).

There are 2 methods of acknowledgment by a party or parties in Louisiana:

1. *Act under private signature duly acknowledged* p 327 art 1836

    - Does not substitute for an authentic act, but is regarded as the true and genuine act of the parties
    - A party (signer) to the act may acknowledge his signature to a notary public and 2 witnesses, so the original party to the act must sign it (the buyer or seller, then that person's signature is duly acknowledged)
    - This act must be acknowledged by the original signing parties, since a witness was not necessary at the original signing and need not have witnesses when originally signed

2. *Acknowledgment by affidavit of witnesses, vendor, or grantor under LA R.S. 13:3720* p 328

    - The original private act *must* have been properly witnessed (at the time of signing)
    - Either an affidavit of the vendor or grantor that the instrument was signed or executed by him; *or* an affidavit of 1 or more of the original witnesses, made at or after the signing and execution of the private act, and stating substantially that the instrument was signed or executed by the party or parties in the presence of the affiant or affiants. Note that for this form of acknowledgment, 2 witnesses must actually have observed the signing of the act by the person whose signature is being acknowledged by the witness. One witness to the execution is not sufficient;
    - If the original act was done outside of Louisiana, and the notary public was a witness to the act itself or the acknowledgement of the act, the acknowledgment is still valid

### *Statutory language for acknowledgment*

An acknowledgment is an affidavit that is signed by certain people to the act and would include information identifying the original parties entering the act, the act itself, like the date of the act, and as many particularities as possible to acknowledge the act.

General forms for acknowledgments can be found in LA R.S. 35:511 p 328

The final paragraph of LA R.S.35:511 states that the acknowledgment should be signed in conformity with LA RS 35:12 and either LA CC art 1836 or LA R.S. 13:3720; so the book states that: p 329

- a signature protocol of parties signing in the presence of 2 witnesses for the signatures of the parties is

required, to be deemed authenticated under LA CC Art 1836 (party acknowledgment) p 329 art 1836
- a private act must have already been signed by 2 witnesses for it to be properly acknowledged by a witness under LA RS 13:3720 (when accompanied by an affidavit) p 329 LA RS 13:3720
- a private act with no witnesses may only be acknowledged by a party p 330 art 1836

## Affidavits

This is a unilateral juridical act – or a statement made under oath or affirmation given by the notary – affirming that the statement is truthful p 330

- ["An oath or affirmation signed by the affiant before a notary public" is how the Louisiana election code defines an affidavit LA RS 18:200]
- Because the *affiant* (the person swearing to the oath or affirmation) is technically under oath when they sign the affidavit, they can be subject to penalties for perjury if the information contained in the affidavit is not truthful p 330 LA RS 14:123, or subject to penalties for false swearing p 330 LA RS 14:125 (see below)
- The affidavit must be signed in front of the notary, or else it is not made under oath and is not an affidavit p 331
  - If an affiant has already signed the affidavit, the notary may "receive and sign" the affidavit by the affiant's confirming that the testimony in the affidavit is that of the affiant and that the signature is his p 331
  - An affidavit may not be made valid by use of an acknowledgment p 331
  - An affidavit may not be signed for by an agent on behalf of a principal (see Chapter 15)
  - Oath is administered by having affiant raise right hand, etc., but this is just a formality; the execution of the act in front of a notary public is formality enough without a valid oral oath p 331 (see Chapter 20 on Oaths)
- The notary is not responsible for the truth of the information *within* the affidavit.

### *What is the difference between perjury and false swearing?*

*Perjury* occurs when the oath or affirmation takes place with regards to something over which there is a judicial proceeding, or a board (like a school board, etc.); and *false swearing* takes place when the sworn statement is not subject to the jurisdiction of a court or other official matter. For example, if a customer needs to have an affidavit of income and assets notarized, which is part of their child support arrangements, and that customer is not being truthful, they may subject themselves to perjury penalties. If, on the other hand, the customer is signing an affidavit that is being offered to an employer which states that they have never been arrested, but that is not true, that is the offense of false swearing.

## Components of Juridical Acts

All juridical acts will have some commonalities, with the exception of the act under private signature, which may not need the services of a notary.

Every notary-prepared juridical act should contain:

- Heading or caption
- Preamble or introduction
- Appearance clause
- Evidence of oath when necessary (especially affidavits)
- Body of act

## 19 ▪ JURIDICAL ACTS AND CLAUSES

- Conclusion
- Signatures

The language below is just an example (really, 2), but notice the differences:

|  | **Affidavit** | **Authentic Act** |
|---|---|---|
| Heading (or caption or title) | State of Louisiana<br><br>Parish of Jefferson<br><br>Affidavit of One and the Same | State of Louisiana<br><br>Parish of Jefferson<br><br>Act of Donation of Immovable |
| Preamble (or introduction) | Before me, the undersigned Notary Public, duly commissioned and qualified in and for the parish and state aforesaid, personally came and appeared… | Before me, the undersigned Notary Public, duly commissioned in and for the State and Parish aforesaid and before the undersigned competent witnesses, personally came and appeared… |
| Appearance clause | John A. Smith, a person of majority [or ABC Corporation, by and through its CEO, Jill A. Brown]… | John A. Smith, [his capacity, his domicile, marital status, plus any other necessary information, like last 4 of SS# if a mortgage is included]… |
| Evidence of oath | who after being duly sworn did depose and state the following: | who declared that he does by these presents, make, name, desire, etc. |
| Body of act | That xxx facts are true. [Here, that John A. Smith=John Smith.] | [You would state the reason, content, and required action … Here, donate xxx property.] |
| Conclusion | Sworn and subscribed before me this ___ day of _____, 2022 [this is the distinctive jurat*] | Thus, done, read and signed, this ___ day of _____, 2022 in the presence of the undersigned competent witnesses and notary after due reading of the whole. |
| Signatures | Signature lines for all parties and notary | Signature lines for all parties, witnesses, and notary [+ printed or typed names under each] |

\* The *jurat* in the affidavit is just above the signature of the attesting officer (the notary). Often a form or letter will be brought in to be notarized without a line for the notary to sign (and missing the jurat). So it is helpful to own a "jurat stamp" with the distinctive language and signature line.

## Parts to an act – definitions and rules

### *Heading or title*

- contains the *venue* clause: State of Louisiana, Parish of xxx (where it's *signed*)
- if the title of the act and the contents of the act are inconsistent, it is the *content* of the act that controls p 333 So please read what the act *says* to make sure that it is in the correct form. If its title states that it is an Affidavit, but it actually tries to make a donation of movable property, it may need to be in the form of an authentic act for it to have effect.

### *Preamble*

- the introduction to the act in which the notary establishes their qualifications, stating that they are qualified to act in the parish where the act is being signed and, if applicable, statewide p 334

## *Identification of parties*

- eliminates any doubt that the notary has identified who has appeared before them and taken whatever action the juridical act does p 335
- notary must exercise reasonable care in ascertaining identity (discussed in Chapter 7), like checking identification and signatures p 335

## *Appearance clause*

- identifies the parties by their full names
- contains declarations of marital status if necessary for that type of document
- contains declarations of domicile, capacity, and permanent mailing address, if necessary for that act
- may contain information necessary for a specific act such as social security number for a mortgage document p 335 art 3352
- a marital-status-change declaration when an act transfers ownership or rights in an immovable p 335 art 3352
- different local areas have different local customs for appearance clauses, like the order of placement of names p 335

### Full name of parties

- notary is required to put the full name (not nickname or initials) of all of the parties (notary, party to the document, witnesses, if any), along with their own full name p 336 LA RS 35:12

### Appearer's Role or Capacity

- If they are not appearing for themselves, they must list their capacity as part of the appearance clause. For example, a CEO appearing on behalf of a corporation, a tutor for a child, or someone appearing with power of attorney for another.
- The power which gives the appearer the capacity should be described with specificity (Jane Doe, as Chief Financial Officer with a resolution from the Board of Directors of XYZ Corporation).

### Domicile

- Domicile is necessary on acts which are being recorded p 336 art 3352a
- Domicile is the habitual place of residence for a natural person and state of principal place of business for a juridical person 336 art 38, and can be different from mailing address.
- It is a complex legal topic, but generally it is where you intend to reside. You can have more than one residence, like summer and winter homes; but if you are registered to vote and drive in one place, that place is usually considered your domicile.

### Marital Status

- Marital status is required on acts which are being recorded p 338 art 3352a2
- If the property that is the subject of the act is owned separately by one person who is married, that fact should be stated p 338

### Marital History

- Not legally required on most documents, but as a matter of custom, marital history is included in recorded documents, to facilitate ease of title work, which also helps narrow identity p 339

- But a transfer of ownership or rights in an immovable requires a declaration of change (or no change) in marital status p 335 art 3352, which is not the same as marital status or history. This lets those searching title records determine if there are lingering community interests.

**Social Security or Taxpayer Information Number**

- A mortgage document (or similar encumbrance like a credit sale) must contain the last 4 digits of a social security number (or entire taxpayer identification number of a business entity) p 340 art 3352(5)
- TIN must be included in articles of incorporation and some documents filed with the Secretary of State p 340
- Full SSN must be included in an acknowledgment of paternity 42 USC 652a7

## *Evidence of Oath or Affirmation (rules specifically for affidavits)*

- The act must contain a recitation that the appearer is making a sworn oath or affirmation; that he was placed under oath p 340
- If the affiant has religious objections to being placed under oath, he may "declare" or "affirm" that his testimony is true p 341 LA CCP 1633
- If the affiant has religious objections on an affidavit, the jurat can similarly be reworded to say something like "attested to before me" p 341
- You should declare in the act that the affiant has religious objections that the declarant has declined to swear, just to be safe, to show interpreters of the document that the language is intentional p 342

## *Body of Act (the content)*

- This contains the declaration or the details of the act or agreement that the parties are entering into p 342
- Must be very carefully worded, because if it needs to be judicially interpreted, it will be looked at through the "four corners" doctrine, which considers only what is contained within the four corners of the document, i.e. what is actually written on the page. The court cannot interpret what is not written, so if the parties intend something, it should be written with specificity p 342 LA CC arts 1848, 2046

## *Conclusion*

- Recites the location and date of the execution of the act and circumstances of the signing p 342
- Private act should recite that the act was signed by the parties and if it was signed by witnesses p 342

**Private act** – Witness our hand this _____ (date) at Minden, Louisiana.

**Affidavit** – Sworn and subscribed before me, this _____ (date) at Minden, Louisiana.

**Authentic Act** – Thus done and passed before me, in Minden, Louisiana in the presence of the undersigned competent witnesses, who together with the appearer, and notary, this ____ day of _____, 20___.

## *Affixing signatures*

Order of signatures is very important:

1. Parties/Affiant signs first, with typed or printed name beneath
2. Witnesses sign next, with typed or printed name beneath

3. Notary signs after all parties and witnesses have signed, with typed or printed name *and* notary ID number beneath (or stamped) p 343 LA RS 35:12 The document can be rejected for filing if the printed names/notary ID are not included p 343

## What is a signature?

"A signature is not just an ornament." p 344 These are famous words.

A signature is a person's name written in a distinctive and usual way as a form of identification p 344

- It does not have to be in cursive, although customarily it is p 344
- There is no requirement that the full name be used as a signature p 345
- If a statute *requires* a signature, it may be written, printed, or typed as long as it was authorized p 345
- If there is no statutorily required method of signing, the signature may be written by hand, printed, stamped, typed, engraved, or affixed by another method, as long as it was authorized p 345

### *Party unable to sign*

- This is covered in Obligations and Contracts, but it if a party cannot sign his name because he does not know how to or because of a physical disability, the notary must cause him to make a mark on the signature line, p 345 art 1833 except a mark is not enough in the case of an *olographic testament* p 345
- In the Louisiana tax code, a signature for person who cannot sign is a mark by the person with two subscribing witnesses p 346
- If the person who needs to sign is just having difficulty, a notary or third party may physically assist the signor, as long as the person signing is coherent, not under duress, or otherwise lacks capacity p 346
- If it is a *witness* that is unable to sign – no limitation on the use of a mark by a witness except it's not allowed in the case of a *notarial testament* p 346 art 1581

### *Acts must be signed by the parties and in the proper place*

- Acts requiring a signature (even just private acts) are not effective without one p 346 art 1833, 1837
- If not signed in the right place (which happens too often), it could appear that capacity was lacking or consent not freely given p 346

### *Electronic signatures are problematic and unsettled*

- Cannot be used with a testament, a codicil, or the creation of a testamentary trust p 347
- Can be used with an affidavit to obtain a warrant p 347 RS 9:2611
- But courts have not explained what is necessary for an act to be acknowledged or notarized under the Revised Statute to be accepted; Louisiana law states that a person does not have to accept electronic signatures except to not deny the legal effect of a writing where the party agreed to use an electronic signature p 348

## Witnesses

### *Who can be a witness?*

- A witness is a third person with respect to an act, who is not a party to or not personally bound by the act p 349 art 3343 So a party to an act cannot witness it p 349 art 3343, p 350
- Any person of proper understanding unless otherwise prohibited by law p 348 La C.E. 601, RS 13:3665

- Person of any age of proper understanding – except as a witness to testaments, where the witness has to be at least 16 p 348 art 1581
- Relatives of a party can be a witness unless
    - prohibited by law, such as in a Declaration Concerning Life Sustaining Procedures p 348
    - legatees or spouses to a testament (it would invalidate *that legacy* beyond what they would inherit from intestacy, though the will is valid; *see the Successions Chapter 24*). Naming an executor, trustee, curator, tutor or person disposing of remains is *not* considered a legacy, so the rule on witnesses does not apply to these situations – but if they are legacies in other respects, the witness rules apply in those other respects p 349 art 1582.1
    - The law is silent as to fiancés or domestic partners, but a prudent notary will not use such people as witnesses to avoid the appearance of impropriety.
- Notary cannot be a witness p 349 art 1582, p 350
- Person must intend to witness the act, p 350 and actually witness the act p 350
- Two competent witnesses are required for the validity of juridical acts requiring witnesses, unless legislation requires fewer p 350 Most acts by statute require either 2 witnesses or zero witnesses.

## *Unintended consequences for witnesses*

- A witness may be prevented from contesting the recitals in the act. For example, a witness to an act of donation of an immovable may not later claim they did not realize or know that the property was being donated; it is presumed from their signature on the document that they knew of the donation p 349
- A spouse witnessing the other spouse purchasing a property with separate funds that contains a declaration of that fact: the spouse witnessing the property purchase is deemed to have concurred in the separate nature of the property p 349 art 2342

## *Witnesses to a testament (see also Chapter 24 on Successions)* p 350 art 1581

- must be able to sign their name
- must not be insane
- must not be blind
- must be over the age of 16
- if the will is done for someone who does not know how to or cannot read under article 1579 (such as a blind testator), the witness cannot be deaf or unable to read

# Recordation

Acts are generally binding between the parties immediately, and binding on third persons upon recording in the proper registry p 350 Recordation is discussed generally in Chapters 6 and 7, and for many types of transfers in Chapter 21.

## *Notary has a statutory duty to record*

- Notary must record all acts affecting immovable property with the appropriate parish recorder so the act can be effective against third parties. The notary may be subject to penalties if they fail to do so p 351
- The notary can include language in the instrument or another writing if the parties agree to deliver the notarized documents regarding immovables to one of the parties or a third party for recordation. Not all notarial duty to record is waivable p 351
- Recording in Orleans Parish must be in 48 hours; outside Orleans is 15 days art 35:199 (this gets tested)

- Exemptions from registering p 351
  - evidence of pledge of written obligation secured by collateral mortgage or vendor's lien
  - transfer or assignment of written obligation secured by collateral mortgage or vendor's lien
  - transfer or assignment of the collateral mortgage or vendor's lien
  - security interest in a collateral mortgage of vendor's lien, or written obligation secured by either

## *Costs of recording*

- Usually are paid by the buyer, but are *suppletive*, so can be altered if circumstances warrant p 351 art 2463
- Orleans Parish Documentary Transaction Tax is imposed on the seller/mortgagor/lessor when they are recording an instrument that transfers/alienates/leases, or creates rights in and to. immovable property p 351 NO Code of Ordinances 150-366
  - There are exemptions to this, such as single residence leases, dation en paiments, judgments of possession, and transfers between spouses

## *Parish customs* p 352

- Local rules and customs should be followed when recording.
- Page lengths and margin requirements may vary, clerks may reject if not followed, and making sure it is timely filed and not rejected is the duty of the notary p 352
- Some south Louisiana parishes have "notarial act of deposit," which is a request to add a document or attachment to a recorded document and index it to the official file (not to be confused with a different meaning of "act of deposit," in which a person "deposits" a thing for safekeeping with another person) p 352

## *Information required in all recorded documents under article 3352* p 353

- Full name, domicile, and permanent mailing address of the parties
- Marital status of all the parties who are individuals, including full name of the present spouse, or a declaration that they are presently unmarried
- Declaration of change in marital status of a party who is transferring an immovable since they acquired it, and if there has been a change in marital status, when and in what manner the change occurred (widowed in 1989, divorced in Caddo Parish in 2001, etc.)
- Legal description of the property, and municipal address or postal address if there is one
- Last 4 digits of the social security number or taxpayer identification number of the mortgagor, if there is one, whichever number is applicable
- Notary's ID number and his typed, printed, or stamped name; and typed or printed names of each of the parties and witnesses (if any) underneath their signed names
  - The statute states that technically the recorder shall not refuse to record if the information is missing p 353
- The name and address of the person responsible for property taxes and assessments LA RS 9:2721 (additional information required under Revised Statute Title 9)
- If any servitudes or rights-of-way agreements cross private property for certain utilities, aerial photos, plats, or sketches must be included in the recordation or the agreement is ineffective except between grantor and grantee, their heirs, successors, and assigns LA RS 9:2726 (additional information required under R.S. Title 9)

Note: the book mentions that if the statute says that a law requires an action but is not invalid if the action is not taken (like the recorder not refusing to record in the event of missing information under C.C. article 3352 above), the notary must still do the statutory requirements, or may be liable to the parties for curative work or, even worse, a lawsuit because something else happens to cause the notarial act to fail because formalities weren't followed.

# 20
# Oaths

- An oath is a:
  - solemn promise to faithfully perform the duties of a public office or fiduciary position; or
  - solemn promise that a declaration made or about to be made either orally or in writing is the truth p 363
- Louisiana notary is authorized to administer oaths in any parish of this state, swear in persons who give testimony at a deposition, and verify interrogatories and other pleadings to be used in state courts p 363 LA RS 35:2

## Oath of office

- The Louisiana Constitution provides the oath of office that all public officials (including notaries) must swear to, which can be administered by a notary p 363
- The person administering the oath must certify the oath p 363
- The notary's oath of office must be filed with the Secretary of State's office, and then recorded in the clerk of court's office in the parish *within 1 month* after it was administered p 363 LA RS 42:161, 162

## Declaration under oath

- Person making oath can be liable for perjury or false swearing p 364 LA RS 14:123-126
- No formalities are required for giving the oath, but the notary should warn about the penalties for making false statements p 364 LA Code Evid art 603

## Oath is personal

- An oath cannot be taken by an agent or someone holding power of attorney; it is personal p 365
- This is why affidavits cannot be executed via power of attorney.
- Affidavits also cannot be executed via witness acknowledgment, because the notary did not administer the oath *to the affiant*.

# 21

# Forms of Conveyance and Mortgage of Immovables

## Sale

Actual content of the specific act of sale will vary depending on the kind of sale at hand.

- Act of sale of immovable property may be done by private act written by the parties, but is usually done by authentic act prepared by a notary p 366
- The transfer of the property is immediate as between the parties upon the act of sale, but is effective to third persons when the act of sale is recorded in the conveyance records of the parish where the immovable is situated (see Chapter 13 on Sale) p 366

### *Vendor and vendee*

- *Vendor* is the seller or transferor
- *Vendee* is the buyer or transferee

## Cash sale

- Also called cash sale of an immovable, cash deed, or cash warranty deed. It is a conveyance act (an act translative of title) whereby the vendor or seller conveys (generally, with warranty of title) the immovable, in exchange for the price paid in money by the vendee p 366
- A cash sale can be a sale with a mortgage; the mortgage does not make it a "credit sale." If the seller is paid off at the time of the sale (using funds obtained from the mortgage), it is a "cash sale." This can be confusing.

### *Content of the cash act*

- *Appearance clause:* A complete recitation of the full name, declaration of capacity, marital status, domicile, and permanent mailing address for all parties
- *Marital-status-change declarations:* A declaration as to whether there has been a change in the marital status of any owner of the property since the acquisition of the property (if any owner has died, divorced, married, etc.) and how that change occurred
- *Recitation of conveyance:* Statement that seller sells, with or without warranty of title
- *Property description:* Full legal description of the property being transferred, including municipal address, if there is one
- *Price:* The amount of money paid for the property
- *Details of the agreement:* Specific details including rights, warranties, waivers of warranties, receipt of price, and related information necessary to describe the intent of the parties

- *Property-tax-matter designee:* Designation *by name* of the person responsible to pay property taxes together with the address to which the property tax and assessment notices are mailed
- *Conclusion and signatures:* Signatures of the parties, witnesses, notary (witnesses are typical but not necessarily required)

# Credit sale

- A credit sale is where all or a portion of the sale price is not paid at the time of title transfer to the buyer, like an *owner-financed sale* p 368
- The vendor (seller) is also the creditor (financer) and the vendee (purchaser) is also the debtor p 368
- The sale will usually be accompanied by a conventional mortgage but one that is in favor of the seller instead of a bank p 368
- Credit sale also comes with a special *vendor's privilege* (or *vendor's lien*) which outranks other mortgages that may attach to the property when the buyer acquires it p 368

## *Vendor's privilege*

- This privilege arises by operation of law when there is a credit sale for an unpaid portion of the purchase price p 368 art 3249
- The vendor's privilege is independent of any right to dissolve the sale for nonpayment of the purchase price p 368
- Even if the vendor's privilege is contained in a conventional mortgage granted at the time of sale, the vendor's privilege is separate from and independent of the mortgage p 368
- If the vendor's privilege is not acknowledged in a concurrent act of mortgage, the credit act of sale showing the purchase price has not been fully paid is the proper way to preserve the vendor's privilege p 368
- If the act of sale does not show that a portion of the price is unpaid, even though it is, a separate act acknowledging the vendor's privilege and stating that a portion of the price is unpaid must be recorded with the act of sale p 368 art 3249
- The vendor's privilege extends to livestock on the land and agricultural implements of the land p 369 art 3250
- If the first seller sells to a second, the first seller has the preferred vendor's lien, provided he has timely recorded p 369 art 3251
- You should caption the credit act of sale as being a "Credit Act of Sale with Vendor's Lien or Privilege" even though it's not legally required p 368
- Rights conveyed by a vendor's privilege are greater than those granted in a conventional mortgage p 369
- Provision for a vendor's privilege fixes his position first, ahead of any general mortgages on the property p 369

## *Registry and recordation*

- Vendor's privilege must be preserved by recording the act of sale with the vendor's privilege p 369 art 3271
- When properly and timely filed, the vendor's privilege will outrank all prior encumbrances and it follows the property into the hands of third parties.
- The vendor's privilege is effective against third persons from the date of the filing of the act of sale or

the recorded act of vendor's privilege p 369 art 3273

- The credit act of sale must be recorded in the parish where the property is situated within 7 days of the act of indebtedness (the credit act of sale) to outrank intervening encumbrances (this way, it will relate back to the date of the act of sale). If it is not recorded within the 7 days (15 days if the property and sale are in different parishes), it will still outrank other encumbrances from the date of recordation p 369 art 3274, p 370
- Failure to record the credit sale in a timely manner is fatal to the claim of vendor's privilege against third parties, including tax liens, judgments, or other security interests. You lose your place as first in line if you don't file timely p 370

## *Content of act*

- When the act of mortgage recognizing the vendor's privilege is not granted simultaneously with the act of sale, the credit sale must clearly state that there is a balance due p 370
- Where the buyer gives the seller cash and a promissory note, the seller has not received the full price p 370
- The credit act of sale should contain (in addition to the traditional components of a cash sale):
  - *Buyer's taxpayer identification number:* Because the vendor's lien is a security interest similar to a mortgage, the last 4 digits of a SSN or full taxpayer ID number are required
  - *Statement of indebtedness:* a declaration that the buyer is indebted to the seller for a particular sum
  - *Description of debt instrument:* a description of the promissory note or other instrument
  - *Declaration of the paraphing of the note* if the note is presented to the notary to paraph
  - *Recitation of delivery to, and receipt of, the note by the creditor*
  - *Recitation of the vendor's privilege*
- Additionally, if the vendor wants to avail himself of the executory process in the event of default, the credit sale must be in an authentic act and should include (see later in this chapter):
  - Stipulation to executory process
  - Confession of judgment
  - Waiver of the benefit of appraisement p 371

## Bond-for-Deed

- Installment contract to sell real property where title is delivered after final payment p 372
- It is a contract *to* sell, not a contract *of* sale (so not really a conveyance of immovables, yet)
- It is also not a true credit sale, because the *title does not transfer* until the final payment is made. It is kind of like a rent-to-own sale (but not legally, that is just a similar situation)

## *Requirements when property is mortgaged*

- In a bond-for-deed where the property has a mortgage on it, the mortgagee (bank, usually, or credit sale holder) must agree in writing to release the property from the mortgage when the price is paid
  - If the seller does not get the guarantee from the mortgagee, he can be subject to a fine of up to $1000 or six months in jail, or both p 372 LA RS 9:2947
- A bank must agree to act as the escrow agent, collecting the payments from the person buying under the bond-for-deed, and applying them to the person selling who owns the mortgaged property p 371 LA RS 9:2942

- o The bank must be licensed to do business in the state of Louisiana p 372 LA RS 9:2943
- The seller of a bond-for-deed cannot require the buyer to give any promissory notes as part of the payment price if there is a mortgage on the property p 372 LA RS 9:2946

### Bond-for-deed when no mortgage

- If there is no mortgage on the property, the seller of a property in a bond-for-deed can accept a note in full or partial payment for the property p 372
- If the seller in a bond-for-deed has accepted notes for payment, when the notes are paid off, the buyer is entitled to demand a deed, and the notary passing the act of sale shall require the production of the notes and effect the cancellation of the notes p 372

### *Bond-for-deed miscellaneous*

- Bond-for-deed contracts must be registered to be effective against third persons p 373 art 3338, LA RS 9:2941.1
- Bond-for-deed sales cannot have a forfeiture clause. The only remedies in the event of a default is a demand for specific performance, or a cancellation of the bond-for-deed. Money paid towards the bond-for-deed cannot be forfeited p 373
- Bond-for-deed can trigger a due-on-sale clause in a conventional mortgage. Most conventional mortgages are written so that if a mortgagor tries to sell a mortgaged piece of property, the entire amount due under the mortgage will become due and payable immediately. This can potentially put the seller at risk of foreclosure, because the entire loan will be due and will need to be either paid back or refinanced for the outstanding balance p 374
- The Louisiana constitution prohibits a homestead exemption on a property under a bond-for-deed p 374

## Quitclaim deed

- A quitclaim deed is a transfer of whatever rights, if any, that a person has in a piece of property, without any type of warranty p 374 art 2443, 2502
- Quitclaims are prophylactic, intending to eliminate any claims the grantor may have in the thing at the time the quitclaim is given p 374
- Quitclaims are used to cure defects in titles, questions as to ownership, misspellings, etc.
- Quitclaims do not have any effect on outstanding mortgages.
- Quitclaim will contain the same components as any act of sale (so should be in the same form as any other act of sale), but the statement of conveyance should clearly set forth that the sale is made without warranty of title p 375

## Sale with right of redemption

- French *vente à réméré*, a sale in which the vendor reserves the right to take back the property sold from the vendee p 375 art 2567
- The right is a resolutory condition that expires in 10 years for immovables p 375 art 2568
- The right of redemption must be expressly listed in the act of sale by the vendor
- If the vendor making the reservation does not act in a timely manner, the buyer becomes the unconditional owner of the thing sold p 377 art 2570
- The period for redemption runs against all persons, even minors, and cannot be extended, even by a court p 377 art 2571

- The sale with right of redemption will contain all of the same components as any other act of sale, with the one additional condition of the right of redemption p 377
- A transferor's right of redemption in a quitclaim deed was held to be valid p 377
- To be effective against third parties, the right of redemption must be recorded.

# Exchange

- Exchange is a contract where property transfers for something other than money p 377 art 2660
- Exchange is effective as soon as there is agreement on the things, even though none of the things have been delivered p 377 art 2660
- Unless they interfere with articles 2660-2664, rules for contracts of sale apply to exchanges.
    - 2660 is the definition of an exchange;
    - 2661 is that each party has the same rights and obligations that a seller has;
    - 2662 is that a person evicted from a thing received in exchange may demand the value of the thing from which he was evicted or the return of the thing he gave;
    - 2663 is that a party giving a corporeal immovable in exchange for property worth less than one half of the fair market value of the immovable given by him may claim rescission on grounds of lesion beyond moiety; and
    - 2664 is that the contract of exchange is governed by the rules of sale p 378
- The content of the contract of exchange is the same as the contract of sale. Each party is treated as both a buyer (with respect to the thing he receives) and as a seller (with respect to the thing he transfers), but are called "exchangers" p 378 So, such contracts often label the parties "Exchanger 1" and "Exchanger 2."

# Dation en Paiement (or Giving in Payment)

- An agreement between a creditor and someone who owes a debt, where the creditor agrees to accept a thing of value (a movable or immovable piece of property) instead of a sum of money, to satisfy that debt. It is similar to an offer in compromise. The debtor gives a *thing* instead of money as payment for the debt due p 379 art 2655
- Unlike a sale, giving in payment is perfected by delivery p 379 art 2656
- The giving in payment is otherwise subject to the rules of sale p 379 art 2659
- The most common application is the debtor giving up the property to the creditor on which the creditor has the mortgage, to satisfy the mortgage p 379 It is often used as a "deed in lieu of foreclosure"
- An obligor may give a thing in partial payment of a debt p 379 art 2657
- For a dation to be valid, an actual debt for a *certain* amount in money must be due at the time of the execution of the dation. If not, it will be considered a donation in disguise and subject to the rules of donations p 379 (see Chapter 10)

## *Content of act of dation*

- Governed by the rules of the contract of sale, so must have the same components as the act of sale, except regarding the price paid and release of the indebted party:
    - Appearance clauses
    - Marital-status-change declaration

- o Description of the obligation: an explanation of the nature of indebtedness
- o Recitation of conveyance: a statement that the debtor conveys, with full warranty of title, the subject property
- o Property description
- o Cause: a statement that the conveyance is made for the release, discharge, and acquittal of all or part of the debt
- o Details of the agreement
- o Recitation of receipt, acquittance, and discharge: the creditor's acknowledgement that he has received the property and he discharges the debtor from all or part of the debt
- o Property-tax-matters designee
- o Conclusion and signatures
- Dation is not the same as a foreclosure. Inferior liens, mortgages, and privileges are not cancelled, and the party receiving the dation takes the property subject to any liens, mortgages, and privileges that may encumber that property p 381

# Timber sale

- Sale of the real right to harvest standing timber p 381
- Controlled by the Civil Code articles governing the sale of immovables p 381
- Standing timber may be owned by someone other than the person who owns the land p 381 art 491
  - o Timber, when owned separate from the ground, is a separate immovable p 381 art 464

## *Content of act for timber sale*

- Usually contains a condition that the buyer will have a limited time to cut the timber before it reverts back to the owner of the land p 381
- Contains all the provisions of a sale of an immovable (see above) plus:
  - o Stipulation for time to harvest
  - o Description of the particular timber sold (species of timber, size of timber, etc.)
  - o Any necessary servitudes to accommodate the harvest

# Donation inter vivos

- Donation inter vivos is an act translative of title, where the donor gratuitously divests himself of property, at present and irrevocably, in favor of the donee p 382 art 1468
- Cannot donate future property p 382 art 1529

## *Form for donation inter vivos*

- Must be done in an authentic act (unless it is onerous or otherwise falls in an exception, see Chapter 10 on Donations) p 382 art 1541
- The authentic act must identify the donor, the donee, and the property donated p 382 art 1542
- The donation must be accepted in writing by the donee during the lifetime of the donor p 382 art 1544
- If it is not accepted during the donee's lifetime, it fails, because the donee's successors cannot accept for him p 383 art 1546

# 21 • CONVEYANCE OF IMMOVABLES

- To be effective against third persons, a donation must be filed in the registry of the parish where the immovable is situated p 383 art 3338

## *Content of act of donation of an immovable*

- Appearance clauses
- Marital-status-change declaration
- Recitation of conveyance
- Expression of donative intent: the wording should be express, "I donate to," not something that can be construed in any other manner but that of a donation. Don't phrase it like "I wish" or "I desire."
- Property description
- Recitation of cause
- Acceptance
- Property-tax-matters designee
- Conclusion and signatures

## *The following elements may be in an act of donation, but must be stated so if:*

- Charges or conditions imposed by the donor p 384 art 1526-1528
- Reservation of usufruct of donation from parent to child p 384 LA RS 9:2361
- Stipulation of right of return p 384 art 1532
- Reservation (or renunciation) of right of revocation (interspousal donation only) p 384 art 1744

## Additional provisions for conveyances that may or may not be included

These add-ons apply to <u>all conveyances</u>, such as cash sales, credit sales, donations, etc.

- *No title examination* If no title examination has been made, it is customary and prudent for the notary to recite that fact in the act of sale p 385
- *Property description furnished by parties* If the parties furnish the property description instead of having the notary prepare it, the notary should notate that, just in case there are errors p 385
- *Cum onere clause* If the property is subject to an encumbrance and the buyer neither has nor assumes personal liability for the debt, this clause should be included p 385
- *Reservation of mineral rights* If the seller reserves mineral rights, the reservation must be express p 385
- *Reservation of usufruct* Must be express in the act of conveyance p 385
- *Servitudes* p 385
- *Building restrictions* p 385
- *Disclosure of existing restrictive covenants* p 385
- *Declaration of immobilization* (but if made as a separate declaration and not in the act of sale, it is usually in the authentic act) p 385
- *Right of first refusal* p 385
- *Right of redemption* p 385

## Mortgage

The definition and concept of mortgage is discussed in Chapter 18. Here, the study guide discusses the form and components of the act of mortgage.

### *Content of act of mortgage*

- *Appearance clauses* Including the last 4 digits of the SSN or the tax identification number
- *Marital-status-change declaration*
- *Statement of indebtedness*
- *Declaration of debt instrument*
- *Declaration of the paraphing of the note if presented to the notary for paraphing*
- *Recitation of delivery to, and receipt of, the note by the creditor*
- *Grant of mortgage*
- *Description of property mortgaged*
- *Signatures*

### *Additional provisions for mortgages that may or may not be included*

- *Stipulation to executory process* (see next section)
- *Confession of judgment*
- *Waiver of the benefit of appraisement*
- *Pact de non alienando* Agreement to not alienate the property to the prejudice of the mortgage. It gives the mortgagee the right to foreclose by executory process directed solely against the original mortgagor, and gives him the right to seize and sell the mortgaged property, regardless of any subsequent alienations. Not a due on sale clause p 387 LA CCP art 2701
- *Due on sale clause* This is a provision in a loan or promissory note that enables lenders to demand that the remaining balance of a mortgage be repaid in full in the event that a property is sold or transferred p 387
- *Default* Provision for what constitutes a mortgagor's default, what requirements and waivers are required, and how the default will proceed
- *Attorney's fees* Binding the mortgagor to pay attorney's fees
- *Insurance* Requiring the mortgagor to maintain insurance on the property mortgaged
- *Taxes* Binding the mortgagor to pay all taxes due
- *Waiver of homestead exemption* Provision waiving the homestead exemption in favor of the mortgagee and of future holders of the obligation

### *Executory process*

- Is a fast-track foreclosure procedure that can be used when certain requirements are met, allowing the property to be sold without obtaining a personal judgment against the debtor p 389 LA CCP art 2631
    - The mortgage must have been executed in an authentic act p 389
    - The mortgage must contain a "confession of judgment" clause in favor of the mortgagee, which is kind of a pre-admission of guilt or default, obviating the need to produce evidence regarding the matter confessed p 389 LA CCP art 2632

# 21 ▪ CONVEYANCE OF IMMOVABLES

- *Procedure for executory process* (this is not in the book, but gives context to help remember why the authentic act is so important, and why it is so often tested):
  - Petition is filed for seizure and sale, including all *authentic* evidence, then the clerk of court files notices for demand for payment to the defendant who is given 3 days to pay (which can be waived in the mortgage), there is the execution of the writ of seizure and sale; where the sheriff seizes the property, giving the defendant notice of the seizure; notice is filed in the newspaper or other place of legal filing; then the property goes to an actual foreclosure auction. This is a much easier process than an *ordinary process*, which is what happens if the authentic act or confession of judgment are not properly included in the mortgage. An *ordinary process* is what is typically thought of as a regular lawsuit, which can take months or years.

## *Promissory note*

- A written promise to pay, signed by the debtor (maker), promising to pay a specified sum of money on a specified date p 390
- A promissory note should *never* be signed by a notary p 390
- Promissory notes should include:
  - Place and date of execution
  - Amount of the debt
  - To whom the debt is payable (the "bearer" of the debt)
  - The date the debt is due
  - The place where the debt is payable
  - The interest rate
  - Provisions for putting in default
  - Provisions for attorney's fees
  - The signatures of the maker
- A promissory note is a negotiable instrument (similar to a check) p 390
- If a promissory note is issued in connection with an act of mortgage, it may be paraphed, or marked on its face that it is referencing that mortgage p 391
- The promissory note is not recorded; it is handed over to the holder of the note (the person that lent out the money). They will be the ones that mark it as paid when the money is repaid. See Chapter 18 for specifics on cancellation of notes p 391
- Because a promissory note is negotiable, it can be endorsed and negotiated, either with or without recourse. With recourse means it obligates the endorsing party, without recourse means the endorsing party does not have any liability p 391

## *Paraph*

- The notary's signature on the obligation, typically a collateral mortgage note or promissory note, to connect the note with the mortgage securing the note p 391
- Paraph is also used in connection with a partial release of certain property from a mortgage or security device p 391
- To be effective, the notary must state in the security instrument (the mortgage) that he paraphed the debt instrument (the note) p 391 art 3325
- Paraph looks like: *"Ne Varietur" for identification with an Act of Mortgage passed this ___ day of _____, 20__.*

- The notary may be liable to anyone who is harmed through improper paraphing (failure to, or paraphing incorrectly) p 391

## Corporate Resolution

- An officer of a corporation cannot act without authorization from the corporation p 392 art 2996
- To have authorization from a corporation, the corporation's board of directors must adopt a resolution allowing that officer (or other person) to act on behalf of the corporation p 392
- A *Corporate Resolution* is an actual piece of paper that shows that the corporation's board of directors have come together to address the situation at hand and formally have decided that the officer of the corporation has the power to do the job that he needs to do. This happens frequently, for example, if a company vehicle, titled in the corporate name, needs to be sold; a resolution will need to be drawn up so that the officer will have the power to alienate that vehicle p 393
- When drafting an act for a corporation, please see the appearance clauses in the study guide (Chapter 19) as to how corporations being represented by an officer through a resolution from the board of directors would appear in an act p 393
- The Corporate Resolution must be included with any acts that the notary executes (or it can be recorded and referenced) p 393
- An LLC will have something similar called a *Certificate of Authority*. Neither this certificate nor the Corporate Resolution need be done as an authentic act (unlike the following).

## Unincorporated Association Statement of Authority

- An unincorporated association is an organization, other than one created by a trust, consisting of two or more members, joined by mutual consent for a common, nonprofit purpose; a legal entity separate from the identities of its members p 394 LA RS 12:501
- They can hold an interest in immovable property in the name of the association, which can be transferred by a person authorized to do so. Authority is granted through a *Statement of Authority*, filed in the conveyance records of the parish in which the immovable is situated p 394 LA RS 12:505
- The Statement of Authority must be in an authentic act, executed by a non-authorized party, setting forth the following information: name of the unincorporated association, federal tax ID number (if any), address of the unincorporated association, name or title of the person authorized to transfer the interest in immovable property, and the fact that the transaction was duly authorized by a majority of the members.

## Counterletters

- A counterletter is a secret agreement that expresses the true intent of the parties to a simulation, especially in a donation in disguise p 394 art 2025
- *Absolute simulation* is a situation where the parties intend that their actions have no actual effect. For example, if the parties transfer a piece of property in a sale, but no price was ever paid for the properties, the sale is not actually a sale (it can be a donation in disguise, but it is not a sale) and is an absolute simulation. This happens often, because people want to protect their property in the event of lawsuits, or from judgment debts, or from tax and other liens p 395 art 2026
- A *relative simulation* is a situation where the parties intend that their actions have a different effect than what they seem. For example, if a man buys a piece of property in his name, but secretly the property is financed by someone else and the purchase is for someone else, but the "true" buyer does not want anyone to know, then that is a relative simulation. The sale is valid, but the true reason behind the sale is hidden. A relative simulation can be cured but an absolute simulation will never be valid p 395 art 2027

- Counterletters have no effect as to third persons in good faith, but recordation principles apply p 395
- Counterletters are rarely recorded, because they are usually secret.
- Try not to use counterletters, because they can be deemed to be misrepresentations or false representations of facts p 395

## Federal disclosure and reporting requirements

- TRID is the Truth-In-Lending Act, RESPA, and Integrated Disclosure statement forms all rolled into one nice neat bundle for when immovable property is sold; these are "closing documents."
- The study guide also discusses the duty to protect private information (Non-public Personal Information, or NPI), which includes the name of the client, address, SS#, and even the fact that they are your client; and discusses the process for safeguarding NPI.
- But the notary acting as a closing agent does have mandatory IRS reporting requirements.

# 22

# Property Descriptions

## Property described by Meridians, Baselines, and Townships

- This is a system that the entire country uses. Every state has its own meridians and bases. This is the Rectangular System (Public Land Survey System) established by the Bureau of Land Management.
- The state is divided into a grid pattern of townships and ranges, which is a rectangular unit for the survey of public lands generally being a square measuring 6 miles per side.
- Meridian lines runs north and south. Louisiana is divided into 2 meridians, the St. Helena Meridian (east of the Mississippi River), and the Louisiana Meridian (west of the river).
- The Principal Meridian Line is a line extending in a true north-south direction passing through the initial point along which townships were established. There are 2 Principal Meridian Lines in Louisiana.
- Baselines run east and west. The Base Line is a line extending in an east-west direction along a line of true latitude passing through the initial point along which ranges were established. The Louisiana Base Line is north of the Florida Parishes. The intersection of the Principal Meridian Line and the Base Line is called the Initial Point. This is the point of origin for the public survey of lands within a given area. There are only 2 Initial Points in Louisiana.
- Township is 6 square miles on each side. Townships run north and south. Each township (36 square miles) is subdivided into sections. There are generally 36 sections per township, square in shape, measuring 1 mile on each side, and being 640 acres in size. In Louisiana, it is not unusual to have upwards of over 100 sections in some townships, with the sections of varying shapes, sizes, and acreages.
- Section is a square area 1 mile on each side. A group of sections is called a tier.
- Range lines are parallel to each meridian, running north-south at 6 mile intervals. A range is a vertical column of townships, running north-to-south. You will often see the term Range in property descriptions.
- Township lines are parallel to each baseline, running east-west at 6-mile intervals. A township is identified by specifying how many tiers it is north or south of the baseline, and how many range lines it is east or west of the principal meridian.
- Townships are the 6-mile-by-6-mile intersection of the range lines and the township lines. Townships run north and south, while Ranges run east and west.

## Property description fundamentals

Acts affecting immovable property must describe the property with reasonable certainty p 401

### *Sections: dividing a section, quarters, halves*

- This part should be read in conjunction with the illustrations in the book.

## 22 • PROPERTY DESCRIPTIONS

- The sections are numbered in a township 6-5-4-3-2-1 left to right, but then the next row down, the numbers go the opposite way, 7-8-9-10-11-12 (this is called "as the cow plows" numbering). In the larger grid of townships, the pattern is the same.
- The number 1 in a township is always the upper right (or northeast) section of the township.
- The sections can be further divided into smaller increments, if they have been legally divided.

### *Describing a property using the rectangular system*

- Always start with the smallest piece. If the property is divided into quarters, describe first what the smallest quarter is and explain the description of that quarter. If it is further divided into eighths, describe what those eighths are, then, where those eighths are inside the quarter of the section, then where that is inside of the section, until you have described the entirety of the section. It just takes practice, but always start with the smallest piece of the property and describe *all* of the property that is situated around the portion you are describing. The property must be described so that it is not confused with any other piece of property in the country. If a step is skipped or a piece is described inaccurately, the notary can be liable.

## Property described *per aversionem*

- This is a property sale which is made from boundary to boundary; there are no specific measurements p 406
- The property is described as a certain and distinct body, and is sold for a lump price.
- This is rarely used today.
- An example would be: "All of the land between the creek and the silver mine, with the outer edges being as far as the fences for the Jonas' ranch."

## Property described by metes and bounds

- This is the oldest known method of describing land.
- A property referenced by course and distance around the tract or by natural and recorded monuments.
- *Metes* are distances.
- *Bounds* are boundaries.
- These are typically used in older, rural areas. This would be something like: "Go 300 feet to the old well, then turn south 300 feet to the edge of the mine, then west to the edge of the Miller property, then back north to the old well."
- There must still be a point of beginning, which must be the same point where the survey ends.
- A survey with metes and bounds typically starts with a primary landmark. It then describes which direction to go from that landmark and for how far. From that point, it describes the next jog in terms of its direction and angle. The process continues until the description returns the surveyor to the original starting point.
- Directions in modern metes and bounds descriptions don't just describe feet and degrees. They break distance measurements down to hundredths of feet, and directions down to degrees, minutes, and seconds.
- Metes and bounds can be used to describe land that is not either in a subdivision, or not easily described in a township and fractions of sections p 410

## *Bearings*

- Bearings are expressed as degrees, minutes, and seconds, east or west, north or south p 408
- For instance, north is a heading of 0 and west is a heading of 270, meaning that northwest would be 315 degrees or, in surveying systems, N45W. N44W is a little bit more northerly and less westerly than N45W. If you need more accuracy, you can also use fractions of degrees. 1/60 of a degree is called a minute. If describing directions in minutes isn't accurate enough, you can also break minutes down further into seconds, so there are 60 seconds in a minute.

## *Point of beginning*

- To use metes and bounds, there must be a place to start (not necessarily on the property itself, but often on the property), usually a physical feature, called the *commencing point* p 408
- The point of beginning should be a property corner that is easily accessible and identifiable by interested parties. It is the same as the commencing point if the feature is on the property, too p 408
- In recent years, artificial permanent monuments such as metal pipes, steel pins, or concrete posts have replaced natural features.

## *Closing the land*

- The description of the land must make a complete enclosure. It must start and end at the same point, the point of beginning, and the description must travel in a clockwise direction p 410
- If the description does not end at and mention the point of beginning, or if it does not travel in a clockwise direction, it is incorrect.

## Property described by subdivisions, or by lot and block

- This is the most modern way of describing property. Municipal address is insufficient for a legal description because municipal addresses often change.
- A survey, called a plat, will create the subdivision name.
- A plat map shows the detailed size and boundaries of each lot, easement, location of utilities, and streets. Each lot (parcel) of land is given a lot number, and each group of contiguous lots is given a block number.
- A lot is an individual piece of land which is intended to be conveyed in its entirety to a buyer. A *block* is generally a group of contiguous lots bounded by streets, such as a city block.
- The legal descriptions that we most commonly see in property transactions (in real life) will contain both a metes and bounds description and a lot and block description. Because cities often have subdivisions with similar names, it is prudent to include as much of the information from the survey as possible.

## Boundaries

- A boundary is the separation between contiguous lands p 421 art 784
- A boundary marker is a natural or artificial object that marks on the ground the line of separation of contiguous lands p 421 art 784
- Fixing the boundary may involve determining the line of separation between contiguous lands p 421 art 785 Often, this involves calling in a surveyor.
- The boundary may be fixed by demand of either owner p 422 art 786

## 22 ▪ PROPERTY DESCRIPTIONS

- The right to fix the boundary never expires p 422 art 788
- Boundaries can be fixed in court, or out of court (by written agreement between the parties) p 422 art 789
    - If the boundary if fixed by agreement (extrajudicially), this is what is considered a "compromise" p 422 art 795
    - If the boundary is fixed out of court, the costs are split equally between the 2 landowners p 422 art 790
    - If the boundary dispute has to go to court, the costs are determined by the rules in the Code of Civil Procedure p 422 art 790

# 23

# Titled Movable Transactions

## The Office of Motor Vehicles

- Operates under the Department of Safety and Corrections p 423
- Is run by the Commissioner of Motor Vehicles p 423
- Louisiana R.S. Title 32 is the title containing all of the motor vehicle laws in Louisiana p 423
- A certificate of title is a negotiable instrument (meaning that it can be endorsed and transferred, like a check) p 423
- Anyone falsifying or forging a certificate of title, or in a bill of sale or sworn statement of ownership, is guilty of forgery p 424 LA RS 32:730

## The law of vehicle certificate of title

### *Endorsement and delivery of certificate of title*

- No person may convey ownership in a motor vehicle without delivering to the buyer a Certificate of Title issued by the OMV in the name of the seller, properly endorsed by the seller or donor of the vehicle p 424 LA RS 32:705
- There are 2 methods of endorsement:
  - The seller signs the completed title assignment *in the presence of a notary* who attests to the seller's signature; or
  - The seller signs the completed title assignment *in the presence of two subscribing witnesses* and one of the witnesses then goes to a notary public and that witness (who saw the seller sign) then completes the acknowledgment on the title in the presence of the notary. This is commonly how car dealerships deal with titles p 425

### *Ownership vs. merchantability*

- The language of R.S. 32:705 is not a condition of sale (see Chapter 13: how we transfer a movable by delivery). But the courts view this statute as an additional requirement to validly title and register a movable as to make them merchantable (sellable on open market) p 425
- Failure to comply with R.S. 32:705 makes the titled movable unmerchantable, but does not invalidate the sale. (It can bring about some liability if the sale was made with warranties of title, though.) p 425

### *Requirements for obtaining certificate of title*

- Certificate of title is the official negotiable document of ownership for motor vehicles p 426

- Buying a **new**, previously unregistered vehicle: p 426
    1. Persons buying a new, previously unregistered vehicle must fill out a DPSMV Form 1799, Vehicle Application, which you see if you are at a dealership or a used car lot purchasing a car but you're not trading in one (asking you all of your personal information)
    2. Manufacturer's Statement of Origin bearing the completed seller's assignment in favor of the buyer
    3. Original itemized invoice from dealer to buyer
    4. Odometer disclosure statement
    5. Lien and copy of the UCC-1 form (if the sale is financed)
    6. Copy of driver's license
    7. Taxes and fees
- The requirements for a new owner to obtain a Louisiana certificate of title on a **used** vehicle are: p 429
    1. DPSMV Form 1799, completed and signed by applicant
    2. Current certificate of title, with completed seller's assignment of title to purchaser properly endorsed
    3. Odometer disclosure statement
    4. Conveyance document:
        - Original bill of sale or invoice, with actual price and full description of vehicle; or
        - Act of donation
    5. If a lien is to be recorded, a copy of the UCC-1 financing form
    6. Proof that the buyer has liability insurance, unless the purchase was from a dealer
    7. Copy of driver's license
    8. Taxes and fees
- Out-of-state vehicle titles have the same requirements, *except* when the certificate of title has no requirement for a seller to appear and sign the assignment *before a notary public* (as in many states). Their residence can be determined by: p 430
    - An affidavit of non-residency which shows their true address; or
    - Showing their out-of-state driver's license to the motor vehicle officer; or
    - Dealer's invoice lists the out-of-state residence on the trade-in invoice.
- The out-of-seller's state must be determined to determine taxes and fees. Their taxes and fees are calculated as a single out-of-state transfer p 430
- If the seller is a resident of Louisiana, for in-state taxes and fees, the use and title fees due from the seller for bringing the vehicle into Louisiana will be charged in addition to the sales tax and fees for the sale transaction p 430

## Supporting documentation

Forms for Bill of Sale and Act of Donation are available on the OMV website at *www.expresslane.org*.

### *Bill of sale*

- A bill of sale executed before a notary supports the assignment of title and its endorsement by the seller p 430
- Must contain:

- Name and capacity of the seller
- Recitation of the date of sale
- Price
- Recitation that the seller is selling the titled movable
- Whether there is a warranty of any kind (title, redhibition, etc.) . . . or not ("as is")
- Liens and encumbrances
- A full description of the titled movable (VIN, make, model, year, color)

- Buyer does not necessarily have to appear, but it is customary p 430
- Names on the title must conform to that on the bill of sale p 430
- Bill of sale is not *required* except when claiming a tax credit for an out-of-state transfer (ask your accountant), p 431 but it is a good practice

## *Act of donation*

- Act of donation for a titled vehicle must be accompanied by an authentic act of donation that is properly accepted by the donee p 431
- Must contain:
  - Name and capacity of the seller
  - Recitation of the date of donation
  - Value of the donated vehicle
  - Recitation that the donor is donating the titled movable
  - Whether or not there is a warranty of any kind (title, redhibition, etc.)
  - Relationship between the donor and donee
  - A full description of the titled movable (VIN, make, model, year, color)

## *Memorialization of manual gift*

- The OMV will recognize a manual gift without an authentic act of donation in *certain, limited* situations as part of a transaction involving a licensed new-car dealer. For example, when a father donates a vehicle to his daughter for use as a trade-in on a new-car purchase p 431
- Otherwise, a donation can be made without an authentic act in terms of transferring ownership, but the OMV will not recognize the transfer of title

## *Odometer disclosure statement*

- All title transfers on *non-exempt* vehicles must contain an odometer statement with the printed names and signatures of the transferor (seller or donor) and the transferee (buyer or donee) p 431
- An *exempt* vehicle is one that is one of the following:
  - Vehicles having a gross weight rating of more than 16,000 pounds
  - Vehicles that are not self-propelled (e.g. trailers)
  - A vehicle with a model year of 2010 or before, that is transferred at least ten (10) years after January 1st of the calendar year corresponding to its designated model year; for example: A vehicle transferred in 2020 is exempt from odometer requirements if the vehicle is a 2010 model year or older

- Effective January 1, 2021, a vehicle with a model year of 2011 or newer that is transferred at least twenty (20) years after January 1st of the calendar year corresponding to its designated model year; for example: A 2011 model year vehicle will become exempt January 1, 2031, a 2012 model year vehicle will become exempt in 2032, and so on (*this is a testable change in the law*)
- Dealer-to-dealer trades, on new vehicles only

## Affidavit of heirship

- When a vehicle owner dies, and *no judicial succession has been opened,* nor judgment of possession has been issued, the surviving spouse, heirs, or legatees may obtain title to his vehicle by filing an affidavit of heirship on the approved DPSMV Form 1696 p 434
- The following documents must be submitted for an affidavit of heirship:
    - DPSMV Form 1696
    - Copy of the death certificate or published obituary
    - Copy of the will if the deceased died testate
    - Certificate of title and registration (affidavit if these are not available)
    - Completed odometer statement, unless exempt
    - Any other documents such as vehicle application or act of donation
    - Copy of renunciation documents, if any
    - Copy of everyone's driver's licenses
    - Taxes and fees
    - Completed Form DPSMV 1799

## Power of attorney

- If someone is authorized to act on behalf of another through a power of attorney, the OMV will recognize that power of attorney. They are authorized to keep the original, or they can make a copy and keep the copy on file at the request of the person submitting the power or attorney p 435
- Thus, for example, an agent can transfer a vehicle on behalf of the principal and sign in that capacity on the back of the title, if that power of attorney grants him that power
- A certified true copy is sufficient for the OMV p 435
- The power of attorney should specifically authorize transactions with the OMV p 435

## Security agreements and financing statements

Vehicle liens may be recorded with OMV by filing any of the 4 following:

1. UCC-1 financing statement
2. Any security agreement
3. A lease agreement when the leasing company is both the owner and the lending institution
4. A combination bill or sale and lien document p 436
    - If any documents submitted, such as a Manufacturer's Statement of Origin or invoice, indicate a lien, a lien instrument must be included with the file p 436
    - An out-of-state title indicating a lien is considered a lien instrument when the vehicle is being moved into Louisiana and no ownership is taking place p 436

- Security agreements may be filed in any form, provided the information conforms to OMV requirements; forms do not need to be notarized or witnessed p 436
- UCC-1 documents are acceptable if they contain:
    - Name and address of lienholder
    - Name and address of debtor
    - Complete description of vehicle
    - Terms of the agreement

## Affidavit of correction

- Errors happen. When an error is made in a title assignment or other signed instrument, a correction is made and explained in an affidavit of correction (see the sample in the study guide) p 436
- The affidavit of correction must make specific reference to:
    - The document or documents being corrected
    - The title number or certificate-of-origin number
    - The subject vehicle by year, manufacturer, model, and VIN
    - The explanation of the specific error and the correction made
- The affidavit must be made by the party whose recitation is in error (the person who wrote their name incorrectly, the notary who signed in the wrong place, etc.) p 437
- This is not the same kind of Act of Correction made under LA R.S. 35:2.1 (clerical error in a notarial act affecting movable or immovable property), because this affidavit is being made by the person who made the error and does not need witnesses p 437

## Affidavit of one and the same person

- When the name usage on documents is inconsistent in OMV transactions, this affidavit is used. For example, if a woman gets divorced and changes her last name, her name may be inconsistent with the title on a vehicle p 437

## Affidavit of non-purchase and delivery

- When an assignment has been completed but the sale does not take place, this affidavit is filled out. For example, if the financing falls through, or the vehicle is not as promised p 438

## Affidavit justifying selling price

- If the price appears to be too low to the OMV (because they want to collect taxes on the fair market value of the vehicle), the seller may have to provide an affidavit justifying why the price is so low p 438

## Name usage on document

- The applicant's full legal name is defined as the name on his driver's license, unless they provide proof of a name change p 438 La Administrative Code Title 55 § III-1301
    - Full given first and last name. *no initials in place of the first name*, like A.J., *or nicknames*
    - Full legal name of the business
    - Names must correspond on all of the documents

## 23 • TITLED MOVABLES

- No titles or rank can be used: cannot say Dr., Mrs., etc.
- Suffixes such as Jr. or III can only be used if it is a legal part of their name
- Except for a hyphen (-) and ampersand (&), no punctuation is allowed
- In care of (c/o) is not allowed
- Last names such as O'Donnell must be entered without spaces or punctuation
- An abbreviated form of a name must be used when there are more than 28 characters
- Standard abbreviations apply for companies, such as LLC, LLP, or Corp
- Entities such as trusts and DBA shall be classified as businesses

## Sales and use tax

- The OMV is the agency responsible for collecting *sales tax* on all transfers of new and used motor vehicles based on the selling price shown on the bill of sale or invoice passed before a notary public *and* in compliance with rules, regulations, and law as construed by the Department of Revenue p 439
- Tax is calculated based on where the vehicle is domiciled, not where it is purchased p 439
- Vehicles transferred to Louisiana from other states are subject to a road use tax based on the loan value in the printed NADA used car guide, or the average trade-in value if using the online edition. If the vehicle is too new, the value for road use tax is 85% of the original invoice price p 439
- Sales or use tax can be lower if the vehicle has sustained major damage, but documentation is required p 439

### *Road use tax credit*

- Louisiana has reciprocal agreements with other states that allow a credit for out-of-state road use taxes p 439
- Sales tax is not charged on trade-in value, provided the traded vehicle is titled in Louisiana and the sale document expressly recites the trade-in and description of the vehicle taken in trade. This avoids double taxation p 440

### *Even and uneven exchanges*

- Sales tax is not charged in an even exchange of vehicles p 440
- Sales tax is charged on the net difference on an uneven exchange of vehicles p 440

### *Penalties and interest*

- Sales tax must be paid on all vehicles by the 40th day following the date of sale p 440 LA RS 47:306
- If sales tax is not paid timely, penalties are due of 5% per 30 days, up to 25%; and interest of 1.25% per day p 440

## Duplicate titles

- If an original title has been lost, destroyed, or never received, a duplicate can be applied for p 440
- DPSMV Form 1799 must be completed and signed by all registered owners and notarized p 440
- A duplicate title can be requested by any one of the following:
  - The owner

- o A mandatary or agent for the registered owner when a POA is attached with the application
- o A curator or tutor, when a copy of the Letters appointing him are attached
- o A trustee for a bankruptcy, but the copy of the referee's order must be submitted
- o A representative of the company, provided his position with the company has been proved
- o The recorded lienholder
- Witness acknowledgment before a notary for the purpose of duplicate title request will be acceptable only if the witness signs the application before a notary attesting that he witnessed the *owner* sign the duplicate title affidavit p 441
- If there is an unsatisfied lien, the lienholder must file an Affidavit of Non-Possession in addition to the owner filing for the duplicate title p 441

## Cancelled or rescinded sales

- When a manufacturer sells a new vehicle, but submits an incorrect Manufacturer's Statement of Origin or Certificate of Origin, the "sale" may be rescinded or cancelled and the dealer may correct the sale with the correct documentation p 441

# 24

# Successions and Testaments

## Succession

Succession is the *transmission* of the *estate* of the *deceased* to their *successors* p 443 LA CC art 871, 934

The person who dies is the *decedent*, not to be confused with *descendant*, who is the person left behind.

- Can be *testate*, which results which results from a will contained in a testament executed in a form prescribed by law p 443 art 874
- Can be *intestate*, which results with no valid will, and operates by provisions provided by law p 443 art 875
    - *Intestate* successors are called **heirs** p 444 art 876
    - *Testate* successors are called **legatees,** p 445 art 876 who receive by a will
    - Will = testament in the study guide p 443 (they're synonyms, but the book uses "testament" more)
- *Estate* means all property, rights, obligations that a person leaves after his death, whether that is a positive or a negative. This includes anything that accrues since death and obligations that occur after death p 444 art 872 (estate is sometimes also called "patrimony")

## *Seizin*

Seizin can be a confusing concept. Immediately upon the death of the decedent, the deceased's proper successors are legally invested with (a) ownership of the decedent's property and (b) the right to possess the property. The "seized" successors stand in the decedent's shoes. For example, an executor once appointed may possess the property but have no ownership in it. The seizined successors are custodians of the decedent's property until the transfer of ownership is complete p 444 art 935, LA CCP 3211

- Universal successors acquire ownership of entirety of complete estate upon death of decedent p 444 art 935 Universal successors are successors who take the entirety of the estate after death of the decedent
- Particular successors acquire ownership of particular legacy upon death of decedent p 444 art 935 Particular successors receive a specified item or class of items under a testament
- Before a succession representative is qualified, a universal successor may represent a decedent about their heritable rights and obligations p 444 art 935
- A succession representative has possession of all succession property and shall enforce all obligations in favor of the succession p 444 ccc p 3211
- Relevance of seizin to the notary is to know that the succession representative becomes person who can enter into juridical acts on behalf of the estate, not decedent's successor p 444

# Intestate succession

## *Basic principles*

Intestacy happens when the decedent has died with no will – or the decedent has died with a will that is invalid p 445 art 880

- Descendant – person in direct descending (down) line of birth or adoption from the descendant p 445
- Ascendant – person in direct ascending (up) line of birth or adoption from the descendant p 445
- Collateral – person who is related by blood or adoption but not a direct ancestor or descendant p 445 art 901
- Spouse – person to whom decedent was legally married to at the time of the death, p 446 and not legally separated from under a covenant marriage p 446 LA RS 9:272, LA RS 9:307b
  - If an action for divorce was pending but not final, the divorce action is null because divorce is a strictly personal action, but consult an attorney before doing an affidavit for small succession during pendency of a divorce because certain actions within the divorce may not die with the decedent p 446

## *Heirs*

- Must be in existence at the time of death of decedent (born alive and not yet dead) p 446 art 939
- Juridical persons can never be successors, therefore not heirs, of an intestate succession
- Unborn child is in existence if later born alive, p 447 art 26, 940 regardless of length of life if there is heartbeat, movement of voluntary muscles p 447 RS 40:32(9)
- Stillborn children cannot be heirs, p 447 nor can child who suffers fetal death p 447 RS 40:32(3)
- Embryo is a juridical person until implantation into womb; p 447 RS 9:123 after implantation becomes a natural person subject to rules above
- Donated embryo does not retain inheritance rights from donors unless it would inherit under intestacy p 447 RS 9:133
- Must not have been declared or presumed dead by court of law p 446 art 54 If they are and later reappear, though, they can recover their inheritance p 447 art 54, 58, 59 A 5-year absence is required for declaration of death.
- Citizenship or non-citizenship in the U.S. does not prevent a person from inheriting p 448

### Those called to the succession as heirs: degrees of relationship

Nearness of relationship to decedent is called the *degree*. Nearness is determined by the number of generations, each one generation being a degree. The closest degree, in an intestacy situation, will inherit first. First degree, sons or daughters (if any), will inherit everything before second degree p 448 art 900

- Direct line are the descendants of the deceased p449 art 901
- Collateral line is the line formed by the series of degrees of person related to – but not directly descended or ascended from – the decedent p 449 art 901 (moving sideways rather than up and down)

### Representation

Generally, the rule in intestacy is that the closest degreed relation inherits. But, if certain persons predecease the decedent, *representation* can take place.

- Representation does not take place in the ascending (upward) line, only in the descending (direct downward) line p 449 art 883, 884

## 24 ▪ SUCCESSIONS AND TESTAMENTS

- In the descending line, representation can take place as long as there are grandchildren, great grandchildren, etc. p 449 art 882

- Representation can take place in the collateral (brothers and sisters) line if there are no descendants that can inherit; p 449 art 881 but descendants always succeed to the property of ascendants p 449 art 888

- Descendants take (inherit) property in intestacy in equal shares p 449 art 888 But if one of the successors has predeceased the decedent and the predeceased's child or children is taking by representation, they take "per stirpes" or *by root* p 449 art 885 This means that the group of people who step up to represent the successor who would have originally inherit only split his or her original portion, not that the entirety of the inheritance is redivided among the successors including those who represent the predeceased successor. So, for example, if Mom dies and Jack and Jill would inherit equally, but Jill is already dead, Jill's 3 children would split her one half of Mom's estate. They would not redivide the estate into 4 parts. The estate is divided into 2 roots, one for Jack and one for Jill, and Jill's root is represented by her 3 children.

- A descendant may never represent a living person p 450 art 886

- A quasi-representation of a living person can take place if a person renounces a succession: in that case, the renouncing successor is treated as if they died before the decedent and the renouncing successor's heirs may represent in the succession p 450 art 887

## *Community Property vs. Separate Property*

Community property: acquired during a marriage subject to a community property regime p 450 art 2338

Separate property:

- Acquired before marriage (before the establishment of a community)
- Acquired with separate funds
- Inherited by one spouse alone or donated to one spouse alone p 450 art 2341
- Among other ways as noted on p. 204

How property is distributed in intestacy depends a lot on whether it is characterized as community or separate p 450

| Community Property | With spouse, no descendants | Entirety goes to surviving spouse p 451 art 889 |
|---|---|---|
| Community property | With spouse, with descendants | Descendants get naked ownership, surviving spouse gets usufruct until death or remarriage, unless testament has disposed of his share of community property p 451 art 890 |
| Separate property | Spouse, no descendants, but parents and siblings with or without nieces and nephews | Siblings get naked ownership, parents get usufruct; if there are 2 parents, the usufruct is joint and successive (lasts until they both die) but they cannot pass it on p 452 art 891 |
| Separate property | Ascendants, spouse, no descendants, who donated immovable to the decedent | A case where the ascendant can inherit from the decedent. They have the right to inherit an immovable back that was given to the decedent, in line before descendants of a more remote degree p 452 art 897 |

| Separate property | Spouse, no descendants, but siblings from different parental lines | Property is divided equally between paternal and maternal lines. Those who share both parents with deceased sibling take in both lines. Half blood siblings take in their respective lines p 452 art 893 |
|---|---|---|
| Separate property | Spouse, no parents, no descendants, but siblings | Siblings receive property in full ownership p 453 art 892 |
| Separate property | Spouse, no descendants, no siblings, no nieces or nephews, but parents | Parents receive property in full ownership p 453 art 892 |
| Separate property | Spouse, no descendants, no parents, no siblings, no nieces or nephews | Surviving spouse receives property in full ownership to the exclusion of all other collaterals p 453 art 894 |
| Separate property | No spouse, no descendants, no parents, no siblings, no nieces or nephews; but collaterals in the same degree | One half of property goes to ascendants on maternal side, one half of property goes to ascendants on paternal side p 454 art 895 |
| Separate property | No spouse, no descendants, no siblings, no nieces or nephews, no ascendant, no collaterals in the same degrees | Collateral relations in the nearest degree exclude all others and take equally by heads p 454 art 896 |
| Separate property | No spouse, no siblings, no nieces or nephews, no ascendants, no collaterals | Property *escheats* to the state of Louisiana but the state is not considered an heir p 454 art 902 |

## *The 890 usufruct*

When community property is passed through intestacy, the article 890 usufruct enters the picture.

- The surviving spouse must be survived by descendants
- The surviving spouse shall have a usufruct over the decedents share of the community property
- The property or the usufruct itself can be disposed of by testament
- The usufruct exists until the surviving spouse remarries or dies, although this can be modified in a will

This alters the rights of the descendants who would inherit that portion of the decedent's estate, because it is burdened with a usufruct. The surviving spouse is not a forced heir; if there is a testament and not an intestate situation, the testator can dispose of this usufruct.

The 890 usufruct is one that is created by law, not by contract between two parties, so there is no requirement that the surviving spouse post a bond.

## *Renunciation*

- Heir or legatee is not obligated to accept property in a succession p 455 art 947
- Heir or legatee may accept all or part of property p 455 art 947
- Acceptance is presumed by a minor but a legal guardian may renounce with court permission p 455 art 948
- May not renounce in advance of the decedent's death; p 455 art 949 this attempt would be an absolute nullity p 455 art 951

## 24 • SUCCESSIONS AND TESTAMENTS

- Renunciation must be express and in writing, p 455 art 963 but not necessarily an authentic act p 455
- Renunciation in intestacy creates a situation where the renouncer is presumed to have predeceased the decedent p 456 art 964
- Renunciation in *testate* situations (but no governing testamentary disposition) similarly creates the situation where the renouncer is deemed to have predeceased the decedent p 456
- When the renunciation is intestacy and a will is later found, the renunciation is set aside; and if there is a will and someone renounces and the will is found to be invalid, that renunciation is also set aside p 455-456 art 952 They may of course choose to renounce again
- Renouncing in favor of another person is considered an acceptance plus donation and should follow the rules applicable to donations p 456 art 960

### *Intestate accretion*

- Accretion is when a successor receives more of a portion in the succession because another successor has predeceased the decedent, or the original successor in question has been deemed unworthy, or ineligible to inherit, or the legacy to that successor has lapsed or been declared invalid p 456

| Intestate accretion – unworthy successor | The new or replacement successors rights are as if the unworthy successor had predeceased the decedent p 456 art 946 and no usufruct is available |
|---|---|
| Intestate accretion – heir dies before decedent | Property passes by laws of intestacy p 456 art 880 or by representation p 456 art 881 |
| Intestate accretion – heir renounces | Property passes to those who would have succeeded the renouncing successor as if he predeceased the decedent p 457 art 964 |

### *Unworthy Successors* (this applies to both testate and intestate situations)

Sometimes an heir can be legally prohibited from inheriting p 457 art 941 *This is different from disinherison!* The law prohibits the heir from inheriting whether or not the decedent wants him to p 457

A successor is unworthy if p 457 art 941

- He is *convicted* of a crime involving the *killing* or *attempted killing* of the decedent; or
- He is *judicially determined* to have participated in the intentional, unjustified killing or attempted killing of the decedent
- Must bring an action to declare successor unworthy in the succession proceeding of the decedent
- Official pardon will not restore worthiness p 458 art 941
- If an unworthy successor can prove reconciliation with or forgiveness by the decedent, he can be redeemed and considered worthy p 458 art 943
- Unworthy successor cannot act as executor or administrator p 458 art 945 He must also return any property, fruits, reimburse for any losses, among other restrictions p 458 art 945
- In any succession in which he otherwise would have been involved as a successor to the decedent he harmed, the succession property passes as if the unworthy successor had predeceased the decedent, p 458 art 946 and no usufruct is available

## Testate succession

Person making the testate or will is called the *testator*.

Intestacy laws can be modified by the writing of a testament (will) p 459 art 1469

- The donation *mortis causa* takes place at the death of the donor
- But the donation *mortis causa* is revocable during the life of the donor
- The person executing the act must show testamentary (contemplation of death) intent p 459 in the language of the instrument
- The donation can dispose of all or part of the donor's property
- If the entirety of the property is not disposed of in the will, what is not disposed of passed by the laws of intestacy

<u>*Formalities must be followed or the testament will be absolutely null*</u> p 459 art 1573

## *Capacity*

- It is presumed all persons have capacity, with certain exceptions p 459 art 1470
- Capacity requires that the person understand the nature and consequence of the disposition they are making p 460 art 1477
- The totality of the circumstances regarding the person will be considered when determining capacity p 460
- Mental capacity must exist at the time the testament is executed even though it may come and go or be fleeting p 460 The testament must be made during a lucid moment
- Being an interdict or being interdicted is not an impediment to making a testament p 460 The testament must be made during a lucid moment, though then capacity is not presumed but must be proved
- Illness, old age, Alzheimer's, etc. are also not impediments to testaments, but will be factors in determining capacity p 460
- Alcohol or drugs can affect capacity p 460
- Generally, the ability to read, write, and sign their name is sufficient for capacity, but be careful p 461

### Exceptions to capacity

- Persons under 16 – may make a testament only in favor of his spouse or children p 459 art 1476
- Persons age 16 to 18 (up to age of majority) – may make a testament in spite of lack of contractual capacity in other areas p 460 art 1476
- Persons fully emancipated – may make testaments p 460
- Persons with limited emancipation – may make testaments if this is provided for in the emancipation act p 460

## *Types of legacies*

- Universal legacy: the whole estate, or everything left in the estate after particular gifts have been given out p 461 art 1585
- General legacy:
  o where the testator fractions out their estate to the legatees, or after giving out particular gifts, fractions out the balance. Like, I give 1/3 to each of my 3 children (after any particular legacies are distributed) p 461 art 1586
  o a disposition of property described by the testator at all; p 461 art 1586

- o or a fraction or certain proportion of separate or community property, movable or immovable property, or corporeal or incorporeal property p 461 art 1586
- Particular legacy: a particular thing to a particular person or organization. Like $50,000 to my favorite charity (named), or my engagement ring to my granddaughter (named) p 461 art 1587

Type of legacy determines preference given to one legacy over another and whether or not court approval may be needed p 461

## Testaments: general rules for olographic and notarial wills

- Testaments may only be made in the form authorized by law p 461 art 1570
- If they fail to follow the required formality, they are absolutely null p 462 art 1573
- Oral wills are absolutely null p 462 art 1570
- Wills may not be made through an agent with a power of attorney p 462 art 1571
- Only one testator per will p 462 art 1571

### *Forms of testaments*

There are two legal forms of testaments in Louisiana, olographic and notarial p 462 art 1574

## Olographic will

- Entirely written in the handwriting of the testator
- Dated in the handwriting of the testator; the date must sufficiently indicate day, month, and year
- Date may appear anywhere on the olographic will
- Signed in the handwriting of the testator
- Testator *must* sign the olographic will *at the end*
- If anything is written after the testator's signature, the court, as the court chooses, can consider the additional writing as part of the will based on the totality of the circumstances that there was no improper purpose or undue influence p 462 art 1575, p 464
- Additions and deletions on an olographic will may be effective only if made completely in the handwriting of the testator p 462-463 art 1575

While this is one of the most foolproof methods of confecting a will, you still must show testamentary intent to dispose of the property.

Additional notes for olographic wills:

- The olographic will does not have to be done all in one sitting p 463
- Writing doesn't have to be done in pen or pencil p 463
- Additions or deletions don't require an additional signature as long as they are in the hand of the testator p 463
- A mark is not a sufficient signature, nor is an electronic, stamped, or typed signature p 463
- Signature does not need to be full name of testator, as long as actual identity can be ascertained p 463

*Preprinted forms* – Louisiana does not like preprinted forms. If an olographic testament is prepared on one, the preprinted words will generally be ignored and the testament will be upheld only if the handwritten remaining words meet the requirement of an olographic will p 464 This also applies to wills prepared with both printed and hand filled-in blanks.

## Notarial testament

One that has been passed before a notary, executed in accordance with formalities required by law p 464 art 1576 (whether or not it's *drafted* by a notary)

If the proper form is not followed, the testament will be absolutely null p 464 art 1573

Requires in this order:
1. Appearance of testator with capacity clause
2. A dispositive portion
3. Signature of the testator
4. Date
5. Attestation clause
6. Signature of the witnesses
7. Signature of the notary p 464

Some basic rules:

- The notarial testament must be in a writing. It can be typed, handwritten, written in crayon, etc., but it must be written in accordance with the formalities prescribed by law p 465

- It does not have to be written in English, nor use Roman characters, but if it is in a language *not native to the testator*, then he must be able to read and understand the language in which it is written p 465

- The notarial testament does have a requirement to be dated, but does not have to be dated on each page – or even dated by the testator themselves, p 465 unlike an olographic will

### *Attestation clause*

*In the presence of the testator and each other, the notary and the witnesses shall sign the following declaration, or one substantially similar: "In our presence the testator has declared or signified that this instrument is his testament and has signed it at the end and on each other separate page, and in the presence of the testator and each other we have hereunto subscribed our names this ____ day of _____, ____."* p 466 art 1577

- It is *technically* allowable to use a "substantially similar" clause to the one found in LA C.C Art 1577. But there is continual ongoing litigation, and to avoid any unnecessary potential conflicts, it is best practice that the attestation clause be the one contained in the code article.

### *Formalities for notarial testaments*

Depending on the ability of the testator, the formality (and attestation clause) for the testament may differ. There are 5 notarial wills listed in the study guide.

1. <u>The testator knows how to read, sign his name, and is able to do both</u> p 466 art 1577
   (This is the most common will.)

   - Prepared in writing

   - Dated

   - Testator shall declare or signify in presence of notary and two witnesses that this instrument is his testament

   - Testator shall then sign his name at the end of the testament and on each separate page

   - In the presence of the testator and each other, the notary and the witnesses shall sign the general attestation clause quoted above.

If the testator is sighted and able to read and write the language in which the testament is received, there is no requirement that the testament be read aloud in the presence of the witnesses p 467

2. <u>The testator knows how to read and sign his name, but is physically unable to sign</u> p 466 art 1578
   (The Steven Hawking will.)

   - Prepared in writing
   - Dated
   - Testator shall declare or signify in presence of notary and two witnesses that this instrument is his will
   - Testator shall declare that he is unable to sign because of a physical infirmity
   - Testator shall then affix his mark or direct another person to assist him in affixing a mark at the end of the testament and on each separate page; that person may be a witness or the notary
   - In the presence of the testator and each other, the notary and the witnesses shall sign the attestation clause which reads, slightly differently:
     - *In our presence the testator has declared or signified that this is his testament, and that he is able to see and read and knows how to sign his name but is unable to do so because of a physical infirmity; and in our presence he has affixed, or caused to be affixed, his mark or name at the end of the testament and on each other separate page, and in the presence of the testator and each other, we have subscribed our names this ___ day of _____, ____.*

If the testator is sighted and able to read and write the language in which the testament is received, there is no requirement that the testament be read aloud in the presence of the witnesses p 467

3. <u>The testator does not know how to read, or is unable to read because of a physical condition, whether or not he can sign his name</u> p 466 art 1579
   (The Forrest Gump – or my husband graduated from the University of Alabama – will.)

   - Prepared in writing
   - Dated
   - Testament must be read aloud in the presence of the testator and the notary and the competent witnesses AT THE SAME TIME who follow along reading copies of the testament if they are not the ones reading aloud
   - After the reading, the testator must declare that he heard the reading and that this is his testament
   - In the presence of the testator and each other, the notary and the witnesses shall sign the attestation clause which reads
     - *This testament has been read aloud in our presence and in the presence of the testator, such reading having been followed on copies of the testament by the witnesses [, and the notary if he isn't the person who reads it aloud,] and in our presence the testator declared or signified that he heard the reading, and that the instrument is his testament, and that he signed his name at the end of the testament and on each other separate page; and in the presence of the testator and each other, we have subscribed our names this ___ day of _____, ____.*
   - If he is able to sign, he shall sign at the end of the testament and at the bottom of each and every page. If he is unable to sign, he shall declare so and affix his mark, or cause it to be affixed and the required attestation shall be modified to read
     - *This testament has been read aloud in our presence and in the presence of the testator, such reading having been followed on copies of the testament by the witnesses [, and the notary if he isn't the person who reads it aloud,] and in our presence the testator declared or signified that he heard the reading, and that the instrument is his testament, and that he is unable to sign his name because of a physical infirmity; and in our presence he has affixed, or caused to be affixed, his mark or name at the end of the testament signed his name at the end of the testament and on each other separate page; and in the presence of the testator and each other, we have subscribed our names this ___ day of _____, ____ .*

A person who can execute a testament under Article 1577 (standard notarial testament) or Article 1578 (physically unable to sign) can also execute a valid testament under this article p 469

4. <u>The testator knows how to and is physically able to read braille regardless of whether he is physically able to sign his name</u> p 466 art 1580  (The Stevie Wonder will.)

    - Testator must know how to and be physically able to read braille
    - Testament must be written in braille
    - In the presence of the notary and two competent witnesses, the testator must declare or signify that the braille testament is his will
    - In the presence of the notary and two competent witnesses, the testator must sign his name at the end of the testament and on each separate page
    - In the presence of the testator, the witnesses and the notary must execute the following attestation clause (but ***this shall be in writing, not in braille***):
        - *In our presence the testator has signed this testament at the end and on each other separate page and has declared or signified that it is his testament; and in the presence of the testator and each other we have hereunto subscribed our names this ___ day of _____, ____.*
    - If he is unable to sign, he shall declare so and affix his mark, or cause it to be affixed and the required attestation shall be modified to read
        - *This testament has been read aloud in our presence and in the presence of the testator, such reading having been followed on copies of the testament by the witnesses [, and the notary if he is not the person who reads it aloud,] and in our presence the testator declared or signified that he heard the reading, and that the instrument is his testament, and that he is unable to sign his name because of a physical infirmity; and in our presence he has affixed, or caused to be affixed, his mark or name at the end of the testament signed his name at the end of the testament and on each other separate page; and in the presence of the testator and each other, we have subscribed our names this ___ day of _____, ____.*

5. <u>The testator is deaf, or deaf and blind</u> p 466 art 1580.1  (The Helen Keller will.)

    - One of the witnesses MUST be a CERTIFIED interpreter for the deaf as provided for in LA R.S. 46:2361 p 469 art 1580.1 e 1
    - This testament may be executed ONLY for someone who has been declared physically deaf or deaf and blind AND who is able to read sign language, braille, or visual English
    - Notarial testament must be written
    - Notarial testament must be dated
    - There must be a notary and two competent witnesses present (one of whom is a certified interpreter for the deaf, as noted above) and in their presence the testator shall declare that the instrument is his will and shall sign his name at the end and on each separate page
    - The following attestation clause shall be used:
        - *The testator has signed this testament at the end and on each other separate page, and has declared or signified in our presence that this instrument is his testament, and in the presence of the testator and each other we have hereunto subscribed our names this ___ day of _____, ____.*
    - If the testator is unable to sign because of a physical infirmity, then they shall make a mark, and use the following attestation clause:
        - *The testator has declared or signified by sign or visual English that he knows how to sign his name but is unable to sign his name because of a physical infirmity and he has affixed his mark at the end and on each other separate page of this testament, and declared or signified in our presence that this instrument is his testament and in the presence of the testator and each other we have hereunto subscribed our names this ___ day of _____, ____.*

- Attestation clause must be in writing not braille.
- Testator shall be given choice of either use of large print, braille, or tactile interpreter p 470 art 1580.1 Tactile interpreter is sign language interpreter who does sign language in the blind person's hand.

# Legacies

A legacy is a donation of personal property, rights, or obligations, through a will, from the estate of the deceased p 471 art 872 A person's body after death is not property of the estate, p 471 but a testator can make certain arrangements for disposition of his remains under certain circumstances.

This was covered earlier, but it is touched on again here. The 3 types of legacies are:

- Particular legacy: Easiest to understand – it is when a certain thing is donated in a testament. Any legacy that is not universal or general p 471 art 1584
- General legacy: A legacy is general when it is, for example, a division of the whole of the estate, like 1/3 to each of my 3 children (after particular legacies are parceled out) p 471 art 1586
- Universal legacy: A legacy is universal when the whole thing or the remainder of the estate after particulars are divided out goes to 1 person or entity p 471 art 1585

### *Giving to 2 or more people to share a legacy: conjoint legacy*

In Louisiana, we don't use the term "share and share alike." It means something specific in common law, and not necessarily what we would think it means, but courts here have come to recognize it as a division of assets among the legatees of the same degree. Please use the term *conjoint* in Louisiana p 472 when you want 2 or more people of the same degree to share something equally

Lapse in legacy, accretion, preferential payments, and reduction of legacy to satisfy debts all depend on the classification of the legacy as particular, general, or universal p 472

### *Debts*

- If a debt is not attributable to an identifiable or encumbered piece of property (example, a mortgaged immovable, or movable like a car), then debts are paid from the balance of the estate in this order:
    o Debts are first satisfied from property that is the subject of general or universal legacies (valued at the date of death) p 472 art 1423
    o If that property is insufficient, then the debt will be satisfied from the fruits or products of the property that is the subject of the general or universal legacy (picture a person inheriting a factory: if the factory is indebted, first the estate will satisfy the debts from the factory itself, like perhaps cash from its operating capital, but if that is not sufficient, then debts may be satisfied from the fruits of the factory, i.e. its output)

### *Testamentary accretion (as opposed to intestate accretion discussed earlier)*

Takes place when a legacy lapses p 473 art 1590

- Two or more people may have a joint legacy, but one cannot receive his share
- A successor is deemed unworthy
- A successor predeceases the testator
- A successor renounces the legacy
- A successor is added to or incorporated in other legacies in accordance with rules particular to various types of legacies

| Particular or general legacy lapses | Accretion takes place in favor of the successor who, under the will, would have received the thing had the legacy not been made p 473 art 1591 |
|---|---|
| Accretion among joint legatees | Accretion takes place ratably (proportionally) in favor of the other joint legatees with some exceptions p 473 art 1592 |
| Exception to testamentary accretion | If a legatee (joint or otherwise) is a child or sibling of the testator, accretion takes place *per stirpes* (by roots) unless the legacy is invalid because of fraud, duress, or undue influence p 473 art 1593 |
| Accretion to universal legatee | Any legacies that lapse and not disposed of to legatees under other articles go proportionally to the universal legatee p 473 art 1595 |
| Accretion to intestate successors | Any legacies not disposed of according to the above rules devolve according to intestacy p 474 art 1596 |

## *Satisfaction of legacies*

Governed by the testament, but if not, then there are rules p 474 art 1599

- Contradictory provisions in the testament? The one written last prevails p 474 art 1615
- Particular legacies trump general legacies p 474 art 1600
- Order of legacies: 1. Particular, 2. General, 3. Universal p 474
- The particular legacies must be paid first. If there is not enough to satisfy them, here is the order of payment:
  - Legacies of specific things
  - Legacies of groups and collections of things
  - Legacy of money for recompensation of services that has been expressly declared
  - Legacies of money in proportion to amounts of their legacies

# Legatees

Please see Chapter 10 on donations (because a legatee is just a donee given property after a donor's death, and the donations chapter covers this extensively).

- Any natural person who is alive at the time of the death of the testator p 475
- Any juridical person in existence at the time of the death of the testator p 475
- A fertilized ovum cannot be a legatee or an heir p 475 unless it is in utero at the time the donation is made ultimately becoming a born child p 475 art 1474

All persons have the capacity to make donations mortis causa with certain exceptions, p 475 art 1470 and to receive. Capacity to receive a donation mortis causa must exist at the time of the death of the testator p 475 art 1471

## *Capacity to receive*

- An unborn child must be in utero and later born alive p 475 art 1474
- Non-citizen of Louisiana or the U.S. does not prevent capacity to receive a donation mortis causa p 475

- A notary may not be a legatee of a testament in which he is the notarizing agent; the will is not null, only the portion to which the notary would have received is invalidated p 476 art 1582

- A witness or a spouse of a witness may not be a legatee p 476 art 1582 But if they do by accident witness the will, they will take the lesser of: the legacy given to them in the will, or what they would have taken under intestacy rules

## Witnesses to testaments

- Cannot be a legatee (inherit) in the will p 476 art 1582

- Notary cannot be a witness p 476 art 1582

- Cannot be a witness if you are insane p 476 art 1581

- Cannot be a witness if you are blind p 476 art 1581

- Cannot be a witness if you are under the **age of 16** p 476 art 1581

- Cannot be a witness if you are unable to sign your name p 476 art 1581

- Cannot be a witness if you are the legatee or spouse of a legatee p 476 art 1581

- In the special case of a will prepared under Article 1579 (where the testator does not know how to read or cannot read because of a physical condition), a person who is deaf or unable to read cannot be a witness to this type of will p 476 art 1581, 1579

The code does not address long-term partners, cohabitants, or marriages not recognized in Louisiana, but to avoid potential protracted litigation and potential failure of the testament, it is best to have neutral witnesses.

Designation of a succession representative or trustee is not a legacy p 477 art 1583 Therefore the notary or a relative can be the executor or trustee.

## Revocation of testaments, legacies, and appointments

These revocations are subject to special rules.

1. Revocation of *entire* testament by testator p 477 art 1607

    - The testator physically destroys the testament or has it destroyed at his direction p 477

    - The testator declares the testament revoked in one of the forms prescribed for testaments (like by writing a new testament and stating that all previous wills are revoked), or in an authentic act p 477

    - The testator identifies and clearly revokes the testament by a writing that is entirely written and signed by the testator in his own handwriting p 477

2. Revocation of a legacy (*part* of testament) or other testamentary provision p 478 art 1608

    - So declares in one of the forms prescribed for testaments (like a codicil that is in a form prescribed for testaments) p 478

    - Makes a subsequent incompatible testamentary disposition or provision p 478

    - Makes a subsequent inter vivos donation and does not reacquire it p 478

    - Clearly revokes the provision or legacy by a *signed writing on the testament itself* p 478 This should be in the testator's own handwriting, p 478 and should be dated although not required by statute p 478

    - Is divorced from the legatee after the testament is executed unless the testator provided to the contrary. Divorce does invalidate spousal legacies. The divorced parties are free to name each other as legatees or executors. But this may be done after the divorce, or with language such as "my former spouse," since the law presumes that former spouses would not be included as legatees

While the entire testament can be revoked in an authentic act, particular provisions cannot; they can only be revoked in one of the ways provided in Article 1608 (above).

3. Revocation of *a revocation*

- A revocation of a testament or any legacy that is made in any way other than pure and complete physical destruction, inter vivos donation of the thing, or divorce, can be un-revoked prior to the testator's death

## Prohibitions and limits of testamentary provisions, or *what you can't do in a testament*

### *The testator cannot alienate the forced portion*

- If there are forced heirs, the testator cannot dispose of the forced portion p 479 art 1495
- The forced portion is also sometimes called the *legitime*
- The portion that is not the forced portion is called the disposable portion, or the remainder
- Forced portion is fixed at moment of death

### *How much is the forced portion?*

- If there is 1 forced heir, the forced portion is ¼ of the estate
- If there are 2 or more forced heirs, the forced portion is ½ of the estate p 479 art 1495
- *However*, if the forced portion (the ¼ or the ½, depending on the number of forced heirs), is greater than the fraction the forced heirs would get by intestacy, then the forced portion shall be determined by intestacy rules p 479 art 1495
  - For example, Joe dies leaving 5 children, one of which is a forced heir. The normal rule calculates the forced portion as one-fourth (25%) of the estate However, because Joe died leaving 5 children, the forced portion is one-fifth (20%) of the estate assets, which is the portion the forced heir would have received under intestacy rules

### *Who is a forced heir?*

- A descendant of the first degree (child, natural or adopted, filiated or not) who has not yet reached their 24th birthday (23 years, 364 days of age or younger) p 479 art 1493
- A descendant of the first degree who is disabled p 479 art 1493
  - Physically or mentally; and the impairment must be so severe that the disabled child is either permanently incapable of taking care of his affairs *or* permanently incapable of taking care of his person *at the time of the death of the decedent*
  - Grandchildren are never forced heirs in their own right, but only by representation p 479 But a grandchild may be a forced heir and represent the parent if the parent predeceased the decedent and the deceased parent would have been younger than 24 years of age at the time of the decedent's death p 479 art 1493 b; or
  - The grandchild of the deceased parent (the deceased parent could have been any age when they died) if the grandchild is disabled and the impairment is so severe that the disabled child is either permanently incapable of taking care of his affairs *or* permanently incapable of taking care of his person *at the time of the death of the decedent* p 480 art 1493 c

Permanently taking care of their person or administering their estate means there is medical documentation of an inherited, incurable disease or condition that may render them incapable of caring for their person or estate p 480 art 1493 e Controlled bipolar disorder may fall under this disability p 480

If there is no testament, forced heirship is *irrelevant* because descendants inherit to the exclusion of others p 480

The forced portion must go to the forced heir unless the forced heir has been disinherited in accordance with law, p p 480 art 1494 and it must be in a testament and not an authentic act unless it meets the requirements of a will p 480 art 1618

The forced portion can be placed in trust p 481

## *Prohibited substitutions*

- A disposition not in a trust by which the donee, heir, or legatee is charged to preserve for and *then* pass along a thing *to a third person* p 481 art 1520
    - It is a double disposition of the same thing in full ownership
    - The legatee is charged to preserve it and transmit it to another person designated by the testator
    - The testator establishes a successive order that causes the property to leave the inheritance of the first person and enter that of another person (for example, I give my Zulu coconut collection to my daughter, and when she dies, then to my grandson)
- A *vulgar substitution* is allowable. This is where I would give the collection to my daughter, but if she were unable to take it because she doesn't have room, then my grandson would take it p 481 art 1521 (Or, say, a backup legatee conditioned on one donee's death.) Technically, this is a disposition whereby a third person is called to take a gift or legacy in the event the original donee does not take it

## *Illegal, impossible, or immoral conditions*

- Testator cannot dispose of property that has an impossible, illegal, or immoral condition. If they are included in the testament, they are stricken as if not written p 482 art 1519
- You *can* include penalty clauses if heirs object to a disposition in a testament p 482 For example, you can include a clause that states something like an *in terrorem* clause such as
    - *If any legatee or beneficiary hereunder should directly or indirectly object to or contest this Will or the disposition or distribution of my Estate hereunder, or in any way hinder the carrying out of the letter and spirit of this Will, then such person or persons shall take nothing under this Will and all provisions hereof shall be interpreted as if such contesting or objecting party had predeceased me and left no descendants.*

## *Designating to a third party the power to dispose of property generally not allowed*

- Allowing a third party to make testamentary dispositions is null, except for an executor allocating assets to satisfy legacies p 482 art 1572
- The testator may delegate to his executor the ability to allocate a legacy to a trust, or impose conditions on those legacies

## *A Living Will is not a will but an advance directive and is not subject to form*

Clients often confuse a "will" with a "living will," but they have fundamentally different purposes. A living will is an advanced medical directive that goes into effect while the party is living, designating for example that they should not be kept on life-preserving machines p 483 No notary is needed, though often one is used to draft and witness it.

# Permissible testamentary provisions, or *what you can do in a testament*

1. Change the order of intestate succession (unless there are forced heirs). You can change which descendants receive property, skip generations, provide for a natural heir who is deemed unworthy, and change the rules of representation and accretion otherwise fixed through intestacy p 483
2. Modify, terminate, or change legal usufructs. You can extend an 890 usufruct beyond the time the law allows, keep it in place if the spouse remarries, eliminate it completely, impose additional restrictions (as long as they

are not immoral, illegal, or impossible), extend a usufruct over separate property, and waive security for the modified usufruct p 484

3. Make bequests to non-family members

4. Revoke a previous testament, or revoke or modify an existing legacy or testamentary provision (such as affirmatively providing that the automatic revocation in an amicable divorce does not occur)

5. Designate an executor. Choose your executor and a second one in case the first cannot serve. They cannot be a minor, an interdict, mentally incompetent, a convicted felon, or a person of bad moral character p 485 LA CCP 3097 They can be a non-resident if they have a resident agent for service of process and can be a corporation if the Louisiana articles of incorporation allow them to do so p 485

6. Authorize an independent administration without the necessity of court approval for most transactions, p 486 LA CCP art 3396.1 et seq. or prohibit independent administration

7. Make conditional legacies, like donating a car only if a child has a driver's license at the time of death, p 486 although the legacy may lapse if the suspensive condition fails

8. Make a bequest (legacy) subject to a term that is not a suspensive condition. This is a legacy that has effect but is not executed until the term or condition.

    - Very, very hard to distinguish between this and suspensive condition, but this usually has a time specification, like: I bequeath my car to Susie when she gets her driver's license or turns 21 p 487

9. Provide for alternative dispositions in the event of a lapsed legacy, instead of the way the code provisions make the disposition p 487

10. Impose survivorship terms. Testator may impose a requirement that the legatee survive the testator for a period of up to 6 months p 487 art 1521 This is often done for tax purposes in case of simultaneous or near simultaneous death to avoid taxation on more than one estate at a time; preventing the estate from passing and thus creating a passage by intestacy to the heirs of the originally intended legatee can avoid that tax. This survivorship clause can also provide for property to pass to certain legatees instead of going to a spouse or passing through intestacy.

11. Impose no-contest clauses (called *in terrorem*) clauses. This is done to provide a penalty in case someone wants to contest the will. There is an example quoted above (previous page).

12. Disinherit a forced heir under limited circumstances – see below.

13. Forgive an unworthy successor. A successor is declared unworthy as a result of the law (see above in Intestate section) and makes the successor ineligible to inherit by intestacy p 492 art 941 The testator and successor can reconcile and the testator can make this known in the testament to allow him to inherit.

14. Relieve legatees of specific debt. The testator can change the order of payment of debts from his succession if sufficient assets exist in the estate. For example, the testator may dictate that a mortgaged piece of immovable property be paid off from the assets of the estate.

15. Appoint tutor to minor children ("Tutorship by Will"). If the parent of the child dies before the child reaches the age of majority, the parent can designate (in a testament) a tutor p 493 art 257 The appointment may be made in any of the forms authorized for testaments, or an authentic act that the surviving parent(s) executed prior to their death p 493 (see sections on tutorship and designation of tutorship in Chapters 12 and 29)

16. Partition property. A testamentary bequest may partition property p 493 art 1725, 1727

    - To partition property in a testament, the partition must include all of the children; if any are excluded, the partition is null p 493 art 1729

    - Testator can partition in kind (like shares) but if he has to partition in quantum or value, the testator can delegate to the executor the authority to parse out assets to satisfy that p 493 art 1725

    - Partitions made by testament are still subject to rules of partition formalities p 493 art 1727

17. Prohibit (within limits) or place limits on condition on the partition of property. By testament, can prohibit a partition on a property not to exceed 5 years or the happening of a condition, p 494 art 1300 or an ascendant may

dictate that a descendant's (child or grandchild) property not be partitioned for 5 years or until at least 1 of the descendants reaches the age of majority, whichever is longer p 494 art 1301

18. Modify an inter vivos trust. If the testator is the settlor of a trust and has retained the power to modify or revoke a trust, he may do so in a testament p 494 LA RS 9:2051 b

19. Provide for disposition of remains. *Human remains are not succession property*, but the control for the right for disposition of human remains is provided for in R.S. 8:655 and may be modified in a notarial testament or a written "notarized" declaration (not needing witnesses) p 495 An olographic testament is not permissible for disposition of remains since it is not notarized. Without changing it in a will, the normal decision-flow is:

- The surviving spouse, if no petition for divorce has been filed by either spouse prior to the death of the decedent spouse
- A majority of the surviving adult children of the decedent, not including grandchildren or other more remote descendants
- The surviving parents of the decedent
- A majority of the surviving adult brothers and sisters of the decedent
- A majority of the adult persons respectively in the next degrees of kindred as established in Civil Code art 880 *et seq.*

Note that you can't specifically control *how* your body gets disposed of, only *who* can make that call (often tested).

## Disinheriting a forced heir

The disinherison must be done in one of the forms prescribed for testaments (olographic or notarial) p 488 art 1618

- Name the child expressly or in a manner that clearly identifies him p 488 art 1619
- Testator must make it clear and unambiguous that they are legally invoking the power to deprive the heir of the forced portion p 489
- Declare the reason p 488 LA CC art 1619
- The reason for disinherison had to have happened before the testament containing the disinherison is executed, it cannot predict a future situation p 489 art 1621b
- The reason for disinherison must be recognized under C.C. art. 1621. You can't just say you disapprove of the forced heir or don't want to leave them property; it has to be one of the 8 legally valid reasons.
- Must express the reasons, dates, facts, or circumstances that constitute the disinherison or else the disinherison is null (the facts expressed are presumed to be true, though the disinherited legatee can rebut them in a legal proceeding) p 489 art 1624

### The 8 reasons for disinherison

1. The child has raised his hand to strike a parent, or has actually struck a parent; but a mere threat is not sufficient
2. The child has been guilty, towards a parent, of *cruel treatment*, crime, or grievous injury
3. The child has attempted to take the life of a parent
4. The child, without any reasonable basis, has accused a parent of committing a crime for which the law provides that the punishment could be life imprisonment or death
5. The child has used any act of violence or coercion to hinder a parent from making a testament
6. The child, being a minor, has married without the consent of the parent
7. The child has been convicted of a crime for which the law provides that the punishment could be life imprisonment or death

8. The child, after attaining the age of majority and knowing how to contact the parent, has failed to communicate with the parent without just cause for a period of two years (unless the child was on active duty in any of the military forces of the United States at the time)

Any *one* of these are reasons to disinherit a forced heir from their forced portion, but only these reasons.

"Cruel treatment," mentioned above, can be:

- Physical mistreatment
- Abuse
- Injury
- Mental harassment
- Emotional harassment

Cruel treatment has not been found to include prolonged indifference, but that may qualify under #8.

Communication under #8 includes any communication that is respectful and made known or conveyed to the parent. A child does not have to try and communicate if the attempt would be futile. The code article does not require that the parent contact the child p 492 art 1621 a  Electronic communication is problematic (Facebook, Twitter, etc.).

# Preparing and Receiving a Notarial Testament

Notaries have the responsibility to faithfully perform all the duties of their office p 497

Use phrases that convey the intention expressed by the testator. Use clear and unambiguous language p 497

### *Just because you can do it, doesn't mean you should do it*

Please don't make a testament unless you are confident in drafting one. If you are not completely sure that you can draft one effectively, ask an attorney.

### *Determining capacity*

Try to make sure the testator has the mental and legal capacity to make a testament.

- Is the testator over the age of 16? If not, is he bequeathing to his spouse or children?
- Is the testator suffering a medical or mental condition like Alzheimer's, dementia, or a disease that limits oxygen flow to the brain?
- Is the testator sober?
- Is the testator suffering a mental illness and not lucid at the time of the testament?

### *Determining conflicts of interest*

Does the testator desire to will something to the notary or the notary's close family or friends? Does the testator want to will something to the notary in exchange for the notary to do something perhaps a bit illegal?

### *Determining undue influence*

A testament is null if it is the product of undue influence. If other people come to the initial interview, and appear to be influencing the testator, watch for this. Keep an eye out for threats, whether physical or nonphysical, and bribes.

### *Signature of testator*

In any and all testaments, the testator's signature must appear at the end of the will. If not, the testament will be null, or any dispositions after the signature will be null p 500  Signature on outside of sealed envelope is not the same as a signature at the end. Must sign at end of *dispositive portion* of will p 500

- No requirement to sign attestation clause, but if he has signed this it is considered at the end of the will, because this comes after the dispositive portion of the will p 500
- Testator must *sign* on each page, too, even if the printed on both sides (don't just initial, this could lead to litigation) p 500
- The notary may assist the testator in signing as long as the testator does intend the signing p 500

The signature rules are very different for olographic testaments, so please don't mix them up.

## *Comprehension of the language in which a testament is received*

Testator must be able to comprehend the language in which the will is prepared p 501 art 1579

## *Donative intent*

In addition to form, testator must show testamentary donative *intent* – to dispose of his property at his death by the testament. Acceptable phrases include

- I bequeath to
- I leave all to
- Upon my death I pay to

Terms like only "all to" are considered insufficient, considered precatory (wishes and desires) p 501 Don't phrase it in terms of "would like" or what "should" happen at death.

## *Sufficient date*

Must be a certain date containing the day, month, and year. For example, if it says "on my mother's birthday" or something like that, but if no extrinsic evidence can be found for any date at all, the testament will be invalid. Preferably don't use a date like 3/7/22, where it may be ambiguous; *write* out the month to be clear. If there are two dates in the testament, and one can be ascertained through extrinsic evidence, that date will be used.

## *Contradictory and unclear provisions*

Contradictory provisions – the last one written rules p 502 art 1615

- Try to avoid them, make sure that dispositions make sense. Remember the priorities of dispositions p 502 art 1600
- Use particular legacies rather than a general legacy if possible p 503

## *Incorporation of other acts*

If the will refers to another writing for a bequest and that bequest cannot be ascertained without reference to that writing, that legacy will fail p 503

- The will can refer to another writing to identify a particular property to which the testament refers p 503

## *Videotape execution of testament*

Not valid as a testament itself, but as evidence of

- The proper execution of the testament
- The intentions of the testator
- The mental state or capacity of the testator
- The authenticity of the testament

- Matters that are determined by a court to be relevant to the probate of the testament p 504 CCP art 2904

## Codicils

An addition, deletion, or qualification to a testament and is a part of the testament it amends. It must be made in one of the 2 forms prescribed for a testament with the same formalities p 504 art 1608

- May not contain the phrase "last will and testament revoking all others"
- Can be used to make corrections, such as misspellings or omissions p 504 art 1610

Codicils and wills can be in either form, and do not have to be like kind. A notarial will can have an olographic codicil attached (as long as each is properly executed), and vice versa. The codicil below can be adapted to be an olographic codicil, following the rules applicable to olographic testaments.

An example of the body of a notarial codicil will look like this, with the heading and attestation being in the same form as a testament:

*I, JANE JONES, do hereby make this a codicil to my Last Will and Testament which is dated June 22nd, 1994, and confirm that no other codicils to my Last Will and Testament have been made previously.*

*I hereby amend Article III (3.1) by replacing the existing paragraph with a new paragraph as follows:*

> *I name and appoint my daughter JENNY JONES as executrix of my estate with full seizin and without the necessity of posting bond. Should JENNY JONES be unable or unwilling to serve, then I appoint my son JACK JONES to be my executor with full seizin and without the necessity of posting bond.*

*All the other provisions of my Last Will and Testament are to remain in full force and effect.*

*This Codicil consisting of one (1) page has been prepared and typewritten under my direction by Maxwell Smart, Notary Public, on this 19th day of March 2022.*

_____

JANE JONES

*The testator has signed this codicil, consisting of one (1) page at the end of each separate page and has declared or signified in our presence that it is her intention to make this amendment to her last will and testament and that the codicil does make those changes, additions or deletions which she desires to make, and in the presence of the testator and each other we have hereunto subscribed our names this 19th day of March 2022. [+ Witness signatures/names, then Notary...]*

## Will Registry

The Louisiana Secretary of State keeps a will registry, where the testator (or his attorney if the testator allows her to) can record in strict confidence:

- testator's name
- social security number
- address
- date
- place of birth
- where testament is located, or name of someone who knows where testament is located p 505 LA RS 9:2446

This is kept in confidence until after the death of the testator and then it can be made available to anyone who presents a death certificate or judicial declaration of death. *The will itself is not recorded.*

## Sample testament

The study guide presents a useful template for writing a will, with explanatory footnotes that should be read closely.

# 25

# Trusts

The Louisiana Trust Code is established under Title 9 of the Revised Statutes, 9:1721-2252 p 510

- A trust is a fictional creation of the law that allows the transfer of title from one person to another, the relationship resulting from the transfer of title to property to a person to be administered by him as a fiduciary for the benefit of another p 510 LA RS 9:1731
- The trust is *not* a juridical person, it is only a legal relationship p 510 (different from common law; tested)
- The trust operates to separate the responsibility of owning property from the benefits one receives from owning that property p 510
- The property transferred into the trust is often called the principal (or *res* or *corpus*) p 510

## Definitions

- *Settlor* is the person who settles or creates the trust p 511 LA RS 9:1781
- *Trustee* is the person to whom the title is transferred and who manages the trust p 511 LA RS 9:1783
    - If it is an individual, it must be a U.S. citizen LA RS 9:1783
    - If it is a bank, it must be organized under the laws of the U.S. and be federally insured (FDIC) LA RS 9:1783
    - Charities may be trustees of charitable trusts
- *Beneficiary* is the person for whose benefit the trust is established p 511 LA RS 9:1801
- Principal is also known as the *corpus* or *res*: this is the body of what is in the trust.
- Income is sometimes also called interest: this is the interest earned on the principal that is in the trust.

## *3 types of trusts*

- *Private trusts* p 511
    - Ordinary trusts
    - Class trusts are in favor of a class of people
- *Charitable trusts* benefit educational, charitable, or literary institutions p 511
- *Mixed trusts* have both a private and a charitable purpose p 511

# Forms of trusts

## *Inter vivos trust*

- Created by the settlor with the intent that it come into existence when the trust documents are created p 511
- Must be created by authentic act; or by an act under private signature executed in the presence of 2 witnesses and duly acknowledged by the settlor or by the affidavit of one of the attesting witnesses p 511 LA RS 9:1752

## *Testamentary trust*

- Created by the settlor with the intent that the trust come into existence when the settlor dies p 511
- Must be created only in one of the forms prescribed by the laws regulating donations mortis causa, meaning in a testament p 511 LA RS 9:1751

## *Trustee must accept the trust*

- The trustee may accept the trust in the same document or in a separate document p 512
- The trustee's acceptance must be express and in writing. It is not presumed p 512 LA RS 9:1755
- If the trustee was not a party to the trust documents, and does not accept in a reasonable time, the court may appoint a trustee p 512 LA RS 9:1824
- Trustee can resign in writing by giving notice to the beneficiaries p 512 LA RS 9:1788

# Creation of trusts

- A trust is effective from the time it is created p 512
    - Inter vivos at the execution of the trust document p 512 LA RS 9:1822
    - Mortis causa at the moment of the testator's death p 512 LA RS 9:1821
- Acceptance of the trustee is necessary for the creation of the trust, but if she doesn't accept, the trust is still effective. A substitute trustee will be appointed p 512 LA RS 9:1731
- Once accepted, the trustee's acceptance is retroactive to the date of the creation of the trust p 513 LA RS 9:1823

## *For whom may trusts be created?*

- For any person, natural or juridical, that is in existence at the time the trust is created p 513 LA RS 9:1803
- Trusts can be created for the benefit and care of an animal

## *Technical language*

- No technical language is needed, except the clear intention to create a trust p 513 LA RS 9:1753

## *Reference to other trusts*

- A trust may incorporate by reference the terms of another, existing trust (unlike a testament) p 514
- On the day the new trust incorporates the older trust by reference, the trust is deemed incorporated and all terms are incorporated. But after that date, any amendments to the older trust document or termina-

tion of the old trust no longer affect the new trust p 514 LA RS 9:1754

## *Adding property to trusts*

- Both movable and immovable property (*note: there is a typo in the study guide*) can be added to a trust through an authorized means of conveyance p 514
- Property must be conveyed through specific form, if required. For example, a donation to a trust must be done in an authentic act p 514
- Any person, including the settlor, may add property to the trust p 514
- The trust document may be structured to restrict or deny additions of property p 514
- The trustee must accept donations to the trust p 514 LA RS 9:1931-1932
- Gratuitous donations by written instrument must be accepted in writing p 514
- Gratuitous donations by manual gift need not be in writing p 514
- When the trust instrument is the same one that donates property into the trust initially, the donations formalities must be followed, so that trust document must be an authentic act p 514
- If the trust property is movable (for example, cash), and is made during the donor's lifetime, the donation can be made by either authentic act or by manual gift, but it still must be accepted by the trustee p 515
- Additions to a trust that are by onerous donation do not have to be by authentic act p 515
- Testamentary trust additions must be by notarial or olographic testament p 515

## *Pour Over Trust*

- A revocable trust created during the lifetime of the testator with property added for the benefit of specific people, and at the testator's death assets "pour over" into the trust as a safety net during the probate proceeding p 515
- The difference between a testamentary trust and a pour over trust is that a testamentary trust is created in a testament and won't take effect until the death of the testator; but a pour over trust is created during the lifetime of the donor, and it is a revocable living trust used alongside a testament.

## *Recordation*

- When a trust contains property, the property must be recorded in the name of the trust to be effective against third parties
- The trust document must be recorded (or an extract of it) in each parish where the trust owns property p 515
- The trust will have to file its own tax return

## What you can't do with a trust

- Anything illegal, immoral, or impossible p 517 LA RS 9:2027
    - If there are any illegal, impossible, or immoral conditions in the trust, the trust may be judicially dissolved p 517
- The number of prohibited actions with a trust is far lower than that for testaments in Chapter 24.

## What can you do with a trust?

- Place conditions that are not illegal, impossible, or immoral on property donated to a trust p 517 LA RS 9:1736

### *Separation of principal and income*

- The trust document can provide that the income and principal are owned by different people p 517
- There may be more than 1 income beneficiary p 517 LA RS 9:1801-1807
- There may be successive income beneficiaries p 517
    - When the first beneficiary dies, or at a time expiration, a new beneficiary comes into their place p 518 LA RS 9:1807
- Class trusts do not allow successive beneficiaries
- If there are several *income* beneficiaries and one of them dies, his descendants will represent him if they also have an interest in the principal p 519 LA RS 9:1965
- In the trust instrument, the settlor may allow the trustee (if the trustee is not a beneficiary) the right to allocate income in different amounts among the income beneficiaries or even to allocate income back to principal p 519 LA RS 9:1961
- The settlor may say when income can be distributed and may authorize income to accumulate in the trust for years before it is distributed (with the exception of forced heirs and the forced portion in trust, see below) p 519 LA RS 9:1961-1963
- Principal beneficiaries cannot be successive p 520
- If a testamentary trust designates a principal beneficiary and that principal beneficiary dies, their descendants may represent them as principal beneficiary p 520
- The principal beneficiary receives no benefit until the trust is terminated unless he is also the income beneficiary p 520
- The trustee must administer the trust prudently and equally in the best interest of all beneficiaries p 520 LA RS 9:2082

### *Invasion of the trust principal for income beneficiary*

- If the trust instrument allows, the trustee may invade (take money from) the principal under certain conditions: to provide income for the medical, educational, or other needs of the income beneficiary p 520 LA RS 9:2068
- This invasion cannot happen if it would impinge on the legitime (forced portion) of a forced heir that is being held in trust p 521 LA RS 9:1847

### *Forced portion in trust*

- One of the favored ways to protect the forced portion of a forced heir is to put it in a trust
- When the legitime is in a trust, special rules apply p 521
- The income needs of the forced heir must be examined annually and if they're not being met elsewhere, the forced heir has a right to a distribution as needed for health, education, support, and maintenance after considering all their other income and support for the year p 521 LA RS 9:1841
- It does not mean they are entitled to an annual distribution; it means they are qualified for one if their needs are not being met
- The trust must not exceed the life of the forced heir p 521

## 25 • TRUSTS

- When the trust terminates, the principal must be distributed to the forced heir or his heirs, legatees, or assigns *free from a trust* p 521
- Income from a forced portion in trust may be given to a surviving spouse or can be burdened with a usufruct p 521 LA RS 9:1841-1844

### *Designation of trustee, successive trustees, multiple trustees*

- The settlor may designate an original trustee and an alternate trustee p 522
- The trust instrument can provide methods of choosing trustees p 522
- The trust instrument can allow a trustee to choose his own successor or replacement p 522
- There can be more than 1 trustee. If there are co-trustees, decisions are made by a majority of them p 522
- Co-trustees can each have different and distinct responsibilities and powers p 522
- The settlor may name himself as trustee in an inter vivos trust (often tested)

### *Spendthrift trust*

- A type of trust (which must be specifically and expressly notated in the instrument creating the trust) that protects the beneficiary's interest in the trust from being used as collateral for loans, and seizure by creditors p 523 LA RS 9:2002
- A spendthrift trust is useful for anyone who wants to leave significant wealth to a loved one but has concerns about those funds lasting
- A court may allow seizure of a spendthrift trust in certain instances:
  - Unpaid alimony (called periodic spousal support in Louisiana) or child support;
  - Necessary payments for services rendered to the beneficiary; or
  - The result of negligence or intentional acts of the trust beneficiary (a tort judgment against the beneficiary) p 523 LA RS 9:2002

## Providing for disposition of trust property upon refusal by, or death, of a beneficiary

- A person receiving an interest in a trust may renounce or refuse their interest in a trust p 524
- If all beneficiaries refuse, the trust fails p 524 LA RS 9:1990.1
- If a testamentary trust fails, property that would have gone into the trust devolves:
  - Under the residual clause of the testament; or
  - If there is no residual clause, it devolves by the rules of intestacy p 524
- A person who would have received the property in a trust cannot refuse the trust and hope to take the property free of the trust through a residual clause or intestacy p 525
- If the person refusing the interest in the trust is only either a principal or an income beneficiary (not both), then the trust will not fail p 525 LA RS 9:1990
- There are default rules as to who can step in if a principal or income beneficiary does not want to accept the trust, or the settlor can modify the trust instrument p 525
- Refusal of an inter vivos trust must be by authentic act p 525
- Refusal of a testamentary trust must be by a writing p 525
- A beneficiary may refuse in favor of another (just like a succession), but the refusal is considered an ac-

ceptance and is subject to any restraints on alienation p 525
- The settlor can change the order of successor beneficiaries in the trust document p 525
- The settlor can designate who receives the principal's interest in the event of his death p 525

## Trust for the care and benefit of an animal (pet trust)

- A trust may be created to care for one or more animals p 526
- This is a private trust for specific animals, usually pets of the settlor p 526
- Pets must be in existence and ascertainable at the time of the creation of the trust
- The trust may designate a caretaker for each animal who will have custody of that animal
- Care of animals is liberally construed
- The trust shall terminate upon the death of the last surviving animal named in the trust
- The trust instrument may designate a beneficiary to receive the trust property at the dissolution of the trust p 526

## Class trusts

- Are created for a class of people, not an individual p 528
- The people in the class may or may not be individually identifiable
- Example: a class may be created for all of a settlor's descendants; or all of the people who live on a certain street
- A class trust is limited in existence to no more than 3 generations removed from the settlor p 528
- Only 1 member of the class must be in existence at the time of creation of the trust p 528
- The trust instrument can provide that each individual can have a separate trust when the class closes or dissolves p 528

## Charitable trusts

- Are for charity p 528 LA RS 9:2271-2337
- Unlike other trusts, these may exist in perpetuity

## Limitations on trust terms

- Property may not be tied up longer than the life of a surviving income beneficiary, or 20 years after the death of the settlor, whichever is later p 529 LA RS 9:1831
- A corporate settlor with corporate beneficiaries can exist no longer than 50 years p 529 LA RS 9:1831

# 26

# Public Inventory

## The public inventory of succession property

- A step in the succession proceeding in which the decedent's property is located, identified, inventoried, and appraised p 530
- A court-appointed notary (or 1 in each parish where the decedent has property) conducts the inventory in the presence of at least 2 competent witnesses, assisted by 2 competent appraisers p 530 LA CCP art 3131, 3132
- *A lost art:* Now, most successions use a "sworn detailed descriptive list" of assets and liabilities, and an inheritance tax return p 531

### *Benefit of a public inventory*

- Even though a public inventory can cost some money, it can save the estate money, too p 531
- Intestate estates with high liquidity (a lot of property) and high in contingent liabilities (such as medical bills) may benefit from a public inventory, because a disinterested party swearing to the fair market value before paying taxes and having the heirs accept the succession may be in their best interest p 531
- A formal appraisal managed by an impartial public officer (the notary) is not likely to be attacked by creditors and revenue officials p 531

## The role and duty of the notary

- The notary's role is to plan, manage, and coordinate the process that creates a final report in the form of a *procès verbal* p 531 LA CCP art 3133
- The notary has a duty to act impartially towards both the attorney as well as the heirs p 532

### *Formality*

- The inventory is a formal proceeding under the direction of the court, which the notary supervises and coordinates p 532
- At the end of the inventory, the notary must sign the *procès verbal* p 532

### *Appointment of appraisers*

- Once the notary is appointed, he then appoints appraisers to value movables and immovables p 533
- The notary must inform the appraisers of the nature and scope of the inventory and make sure they determine the *fair market value* as of the *date of death of the decedent* p 533

- Appraisers of immovables must state the purpose of the appraisal in the report, and they should not use mortgage-loan appraisal standards for certifications p 533
- The notary should remind the appraisers that they are under oath p 533

## *Privilege for payment of fees*

- Fees from the estate for a public inventory are payable before other claims from the estate p 533

# Process of public inventory

## *Preparation*

- First, the notary will do a walk-through, to determine what is community and what is separate p 533
- The notary must determine the extent of the property

## *Conducting the inventory*

- The public inventory is a formal proceeding ordered by a court p 533
- First, the notary will "open" the inventory, by administering the oath to appraisers in the presence of witnesses and attendees p 534
- Then, the itemized listing and recording of property begins by the appraisers p 534
- The notary should be present as long as appraisers are present p 534
- When the itemized report is complete, the notary can prepare the *procès verbal* report p 534
- When the *procès verbal* is complete, the appraisers, witnesses, and the others sign in front of each other and the notary
- A draft of the report will be given first to the attorneys and heirs, then submitted to the court p 534

## *Reporting to the court*

- A certified copy of the *procès verbal* must be filed with the collector of revenue in addition to being filed with the court p 534 LA CCP art 3134
- The report is proof of its contents, but it can be challenged (called "traversed") by a motion p 535
- The notary must file the following:
    o Signed oaths of the appraisers
    o Petition authorizing filing of inventory
    o *Procès verbal*
    o Affidavit of notary appointed to inventory
    o Motion and order to pay notary's fee and discharge notary p 535
- See sample forms on p. 536 in the study guide

# Notary as commissioner

- The public inventory is one of a limited number of notary functions that require the notary to report directly to the court p 535

# 27

# Small Succession (Succession by Affidavit)

- A small succession is one that:
  - Has a gross value (the value of all the assets before deducting debts) of $125,000 or less at the time of death; or
  - If a judicial succession has not been opened for more than 20 years after the death of the decedent, regardless of the value of the estate p 542 LA CCP art 3421
- A small succession by affidavit is available (and judicial opening is not necessary) if:
  - The estate qualifies as a small succession; and
  - The decedent either died without a will while domiciled in Louisiana; or
  - The decedent died testate leaving no immovable property, and probating the will would have the same effect as intestacy; or
  - The decedent died with a will while domiciled in another state, if the will was probated in the other state and the decedent's sole heirs are his descendants, ascendants, brothers, or sisters, or descendants of brothers and sisters, surviving spouse, and/or beneficiaries of the decedent's will that was probated in another state p 542 LA CCP art 3431

## Procedure for succession by affidavit

- If the succession meets the definition of a small succession *and* meets the conditions for small succession by affidavit, the heirs can take possession of the assets (subject to any debts) without opening a judicial succession p 543
- The heirs must execute an affidavit in the form provided in LA Code of Civil Procedure art. 3432 p 543
- The affidavit must be executed by the surviving spouse and one or more competent heirs, if any p 543
- If there is no surviving spouse, then two competent major heirs execute it p 543
- If none, then a third person who is unrelated to the deceased but has knowledge of the matters contained in the affidavit executes it p 543
- If there is a surviving spouse or competent heir, but they are absent, a judicial succession must be opened p 543
- If a person is domiciled outside of Louisiana and left property in Louisiana to legatees under a testament, the proper affidavit to use is found in LA Code of Civil Procedure art. 3432.1 p 544
- Small successions that do not meet the conditions of LA C.C.P. art. 3431 are not eligible for succession by affidavit, and a notary who prepares succession documents for ineligible successions is committing the unauthorized practice of law p 546

## *What information must be included in the affidavit?*

- The information is in the statute:
  - decedent's date of death
  - his last residence
  - his spouse and family information
  - the names and last known residences of all the heirs
  - a listing of the decedent's estate
  - along with the values of the property, including the legal description of any immovable property
- The heirs must accept the succession without administration.
- A certified death certificate must be attached to the affidavit LA CCP art 3432

# 28

# Business Entities

- Business entities come into existence when the organizational documents are approved and recorded by the Louisiana Secretary of State p 547
- Any interest in any business entity is an *incorporeal movable* p 547
- The most common types of business entities in Louisiana are: sole proprietorships, partnerships, partnerships in commendam, limited liability partnerships, corporations, LLCs, and associations p 547

## Classification of business entities

### Sole proprietorship

- The simplest form of business entity p 548
- A sole proprietor is an individual who owns a business that is not distinct from the owner p 548
- A married couple in a legal regime (community property relationship) can have a sole proprietorship p 549 art 2346
- The sole proprietorship is the same legal entity as the person who creates the business p 548
- The sole proprietorship can have a business name that distinguishes it from the person who owns it, but that is called an assumed name and it must be registered with the clerk of court where the person intends to do business p 549 LA RS 51:281
    - Assumed names can be in any language but must be expressed in English characters and cannot contain the name of any public park, playground, or other public facility p 549 LA RS 51:281.1
- An individual or a company can also register for a trade name in Louisiana, which must be registered with the Secretary of State. The trade name is a name other than a registered company name (an equivalent of DBA or "doing business as"), but registering them with the Secretary of State ensures that they are not used by any other company p 550
    - Registration of a trade name is good for 10 years but can be renewed for more 10-year periods p 550

### Partnership

- A partnership is a juridical person p 548
- The people in the partnership are called partners, and are distinct from the partnership p 548
- A partnership is created by a contract between two or more people, to combine risk and efforts to collaborate at mutual risk for their common profit or commercial benefit p 548 art 2801
- Trustees and succession representatives, *in their capacities as such*, may be partners (although the trust or succession is not a juridical person) p 548 art 2801

## Ordinary partnership

- Has a single class of partners, called general partners p 551
- General partners manage equally, and share profits, losses, and distribution of assets equally, if there is no agreement otherwise p 551 art 2803
- General partners are equally liable for debts and other liabilities p 551 art 2817
- Contributions are restored to the partners in the ratio contributed unless otherwise agreed
- An ordinary partnership does not have to be in writing, unless the partnership owns immovables p 551

## Partnership in commendam

- This type of partnership has at least 1 general partner and 1 or more partners in commendam (limited partners) p 552 art 2837
- There are 1 or more commendam partners who have limited powers, rights, and liability (they are liable only to the extent of their investment in the partnership) p 552
- Partners in commendam do not participate in the management or administration of the partnership; or conduct business on behalf of the partnership. If they do, then they can become liable as general partners p 553 art 2843, 2844
- The agreement for a partnership in commendam must be in writing and filed with the Secretary of State p 552 art 2841
- The partnership name for a partnership in commendam must clearly reflect that it is a limited or commendam partnership and it must not suggest that any commendam partner is a general partner p 552 art 2838

## Registered limited liability partnership (RLLP)

- Special type of partnership that limits the tort liability for one partner to the amount of the partner's interest in the partnership's assets p 554 LA RS 9:3432
- It does not protect the partnership's assets
- It does not protect a partner personally
- The registered limited liability partnership must register and file with the Secretary of State

# Special rules regarding all partnerships

## Partnership names

- Names may include the names of the partners, but if it does, it must include *all* of their names p 554
- Names for partnerships in commendam:
    - Name must appear in the contract of partnership;
    - Include language that clearly identifies it as a limited partnership or commendam partnership; and
    - Does not imply that a commendam or limited partner is a general partner p 554
- Specific rules for banking, architecture, surveying firms, engineering, law firms, and other professional firm names are covered in their respective chapters in the Civil Code p 554
- A certificate of assumed name must be filed with the Secretary of State if:
    - A person as a sole proprietor is operating under a name other than his own; or

## 28 ▪ BUSINESS ENTITIES

- o A partnership is operating under a name other than the name of the partnership p 554

*Ownership of immovable property*

- A partnership may own property if, at the time of acquisition, there is a written contract of partnership p 554
- If there is no written contract, then the partners own the property as owners in indivision p 554

*Written contracts of partnership*

- Necessary for ownership of immovables p 554
- Necessary for limited partnerships p 552
- Necessary, in an authentic form, when the partners desire to avoid collation to the succession of an ascendant where the ascendant (parent or grandparent) enters into a partnership with a descendant (child or grandchild) p 556 art 1247
- Written contracts of partnership are not required to be in English p 556

*Filing and recording*

- Required for partnership in commendam
- Required for limited liability partnerships
- Required for partnerships that own or will own immovable property that must be recorded
- Recordation puts third parties on notice
- The Secretary of State is where the partnerships are registered p 556 LA RS 9:3401
- An annual report must be filed each year for the partnership for any that has a filing on record p 557

*Termination of a partnership*

- A partnership, other than a partnership in commendam, terminates by any of the following:
  - o Unanimous consent of the partners
  - o Judgment of termination
  - o Chapter 7 bankruptcy
  - o Reduction of the membership to 1 person
  - o Expiration of its term
  - o Attainment of, or the impossibility of attainment of, the object of the partnership
  - o In accordance with the contract of partnership p 558
- A partnership in commendam terminates by:
  - o The retirement from the partnership, or the death, interdiction, or dissolution, of the sole or any general partner; except
  - o The partnership is continued with the consent of the remaining general partners if it is stated in the partnership agreement that they have a right to do so, and all remaining partners agree to do so within 90 days p 558 art 2826

# Corporations

- A corporation is a juridical person p 548

- The people in the corporation are either shareholders or members (depending on the corporation), and are distinct from the corporation p 548
- Generally, neither shareholders nor members of the corporation are liable for debts that the corporation incurs p 548
- Depending on the type of corporation, members or shareholders may share in the profits p 549
- A 1-member corporation is allowable p 549
- Business corporations, other than banks and insurance companies, are governed under Title 12 of the Civil Code p 549
- One of the main benefits of creating a corporation is that members are generally shielded from personal liability. This is a very complex area of the law and it may be in your client's best interest to speak to a lawyer or accountant to determine which entity best suits their needs. Some types of corporations may subject your client to double taxation, so be sure that they speak to their tax representative before entering into a corporation. And please don't offer legal advice, as this could subject you to fines and penalties, and potentially the loss of your commission, for the unauthorized practice of law.

## *Creation of a corporation*

- A corporation is created when 1 or more incorporators file articles of incorporation and a registered agent's consent to appointment with the Secretary of State p 558
- An *incorporator* may be an individual (a natural person) or an entity (a juridical person) p 559
- Who can be members or shareholders? This depends on the type of corporation; please ask a tax adviser
- The corporation must have a legal purpose. Usually, it is "any lawful business or activity." If the business or activity is regulated under any statutes, such as banking or insurance, that must be its stated purpose p 559

## *Articles of Incorporation*

- Must be typewritten or printed
- In the English language
- Signed by an incorporator if the corporation has not been formed
- Contain the corporate name
- Acknowledged by the person who signed the articles, or may instead be executed by authentic act, or filed electronically under the provisions of LA R.S. 12:1701 p 559

## *Corporate name*

- May be foreign but must be written in English letters
- Must contain one of the following words in full or abbreviated: corporation (corp.), incorporated (inc.), limited (ltd.), or company (co.) p 561
- Must be distinguishable from every other previously registered corporation or trade name
- Must not suggest that it is a bank, insurance company, charitable or non-profit entity, or agency of the state or the federal government p 562
- A person may reserve in advance, for 120 non-renewable days, the exclusive right to use a name p 562
- A corporate name that is terminated is reserved for 5 years after the date of termination p 562

## 28 • BUSINESS ENTITIES

### *Office and agent for the corporation*

- A corporation must maintain an office in the state of Louisiana known as its registered office p 562
- The registered office can be a different place from its place of business p 562
- if the registered office, which is where the corporation gets its official mail from the Secretary of State, moves, the corporation must notify the Secretary of State p 562
- The registered agent is the person who will accept service of process for the corporation in the event that the corporation is sued p 562
- The registered agent must reside in this state; it can be a person or an entity, and if it is an entity, must be authorized to do business in this state p 563
- If the registered agent moves, or the corporation changes the registered agent, the corporation must notify the Secretary of State p 563

### *Filing with the Secretary of State*

- If all of the documents for the corporation are prepared correctly and the filing fees are appropriate, the Secretary of State will accept them and record the time and date of filing p 563
- If the Secretary of State refuses them, he must return them to the corporation or its representative within 5 days and briefly state the reason for the refusal p 563
- Articles of Incorporation are effective:
    o Retroactive to the date they were signed, if they are received within 5 days of being signed (by the incorporators); or
    o If received after 5 days of the date of being signed (by the incorporators), then the date they are received for filing; or
    o A later date than the date filed, if requested, not to exceed 90 days from the date of filing p 563 LA RS 12:1-123

### *Certificate of Existence and Good Standing*

- Anyone can ask the Secretary of State to furnish them with a certificate of existence or a certificate of good standing as conclusive evidence of their corporation's compliance with the laws of the state p 564
- Often, this is necessary when applying for certain government jobs

### *Annual report*

- Just like any other time you file anything with the Secretary of State, a corporation also has to file an annual report on or before the anniversary date of the corporation, signed by the chairman of the corporate board, or filed electronically p 564

### *Corporate ownership and management*

- A corporation is owned by its shareholders, represented by shares of stock p 564
- Voting rights are proportional to the amount of stock each shareholder owns p 564
- Stocks may be issued in different classes, so be careful if someone asks for help in setting up a corporation; it is very complex and subtle
- Shareholders elect a board of directors who vote the stock shares and make the decisions p 564
- The board of directors has a fiduciary duty to the stockholders and to the corporation p 564

- Bylaws are the operating rules that the corporation has for the selection of directors and officers, and conducting meetings, among other things p 564
- This is a very basic version of the role of the board of directors and its rights and duties

# Limited Liability Company

- An LLC is a juridical person p 549
- The people in the LLC are "members" and are distinct from the corporation p 549
- Ownership is represented by membership p 549
- LLCs have the same powers, rights, and privileges as corporations p 549

## *Creation of an LLC*

- The LLC comes into existence with the filing of the Articles of Organization p 568
- One or more persons who have capacity to contract may form an LLC p 565
- The organizer does not need to be a member or manager p 565
- The organizer can be an individual (a natural person) or another entity (a juridical person) p 565
- Just like a corporation, the LLC must have a purpose, and the stated purpose is usually "any lawful purpose" p 565

## *Articles of Organization*

- Similar to Articles of Incorporation, the LLC has Articles of Organization p 565
- The Articles of Organization must be:
    - Written in English (even if they contain foreign words)
    - Signed by the organizer
    - Acknowledged by the person or 1 of the persons who signed the Articles of Organization, or may be executed by authentic act, or filed electronically
- The Articles of Organization *must* contain:
    - The name of the LLC
    - The purpose of the LLC p 566
- The Articles of Organization *may* contain 1 or more of the following:
    - If there are limitations on the members to bind the LLC
    - A statement whether the LLC will be managed by members
    - Restrictions of members
    - Dissolution date (if any) of the LLC
    - If persons dealing with the LLC can rely on a certificate of members stating that certain people have authority p 566

## *LLC name*

- Must include the words Limited Liability Company, or LLC, or LC
- Must be distinguishable from every other corporate name registered with the Secretary of State

# 28 ▪ BUSINESS ENTITIES

- Cannot imply that it is an engineering or surveying firm, or one regulated by the Office of Financial Institutions, or a branch of the state or federal government p 567
- LLC name must be registered under the assumed name registration requirement p 567 LA RS 51:281

## *Registered Office and Agent*

- An LLC must maintain a registered office in this state, which is included in the initial report, and which must be changed with the Secretary of State if there are any changes made to that office p 567
- Much like a corporation, an LLC must also maintain a registered agent in the state of Louisiana who can accept service of process in the event that that is necessary p 568

## *Filing articles with the Secretary of State*

### Initial report

- An Initial Report is filed along with the Articles of Organization, which is signed by each person (or his agent) who signed the Articles of Organization p 568
- The Initial Report must contain:
    - Name and municipal address (not a P.O. box) of the LLC's registered office
    - Full name and municipal address (not a P.O. box) of the LLC's registered agent
    - An affidavit of acknowledgment and acceptance of appointment by the registered agent
    - The name and municipal addresses of the first managers if they have been selected (if not, then a supplement must be filed later) p 568
- After the proper paperwork has been submitted, the Secretary of State will send back a Certificate of Organization showing the date of the filing p 569 LA RS 12:1304
- An LLC is effective from:
    - The issuance of the Certificate of Organization from the Secretary of State; or
    - Retroactive to the date of the notarization if the Articles were executed by authentic act and were filed within 5 days of the date of notarization p 569 LA RS 12:1304 c

### Annual report

- Just like any other time you file anything with the Secretary of State, an LLC also has to file an annual report on or before the anniversary date of the organization p 569

## *Limited Liability Company powers*

- All LLCs have the powers, rights, and privileges similar to a corporation and a partnership p 569
- All LLCs are in perpetual existence unless limited in their Articles of Organization p 569

## *Company ownership and management*

- The ownership of an LLC is vested in members (equity owners) who share in the profits and losses and have a right to receive distributions of assets and to vote, unless limited by the Articles of Organization p 569
- Membership may be assigned (granted to another person), but the assignee is not entitled to become or to exercise the rights of that member (nor has any liability) until other members approve in writing p 569

- A member's ownership interest is established through an Operating Agreement. This is a document which is not filed with the Secretary of State, but is a contract that lays out the rights and duties of the members, how they act between each other, and how the members' rights may distribute at death p 570
- Management of the company may be vested in one or more managers if the members themselves don't want to manage p 570
- Management will usually be spelled out in the Articles of Organization or the Operating Agreement p 570

### *Representation before state entities*

- If the LLC has 5 or fewer members, then to go before any state agency or board, the LLC must have a representative, chosen by the majority, and evidenced *by an authentic act* p 571 LA RS 12:1317.1
- No similar provision exists for corporations, partnerships, or unincorporated associations

### *Dissolution of an LLC*

- An event specified in the Articles of Organization; or
- By consent of a majority of the members; or
- By judicial decree

## Unincorporated Associations

- A legal entity formed for nonprofit purposes by its members to work towards a common purpose p 549 LA 12:501
- The association may not be otherwise legally incorporated, unless it was created by a trust
- No organizational document requirements exist, and no declaration of its existence need be registered p 549
    - But because unincorporated associations can own immovable property, rules regarding the ownership of property may require organizational documents;
    - And a Statement of Authority (in an authentic act) is required for the purchase, alienation, or encumbrance of immovables (see Chapter 21)
- Unincorporated associations also have the capacity to receive donations, the right to assert injuries in tort, and may assert claims germane to its purpose before any governmental body p 571

# 29

# Miscellaneous Acts and Forms

## Acknowledgment of Paternity

- Most acknowledgments of paternity are forms provided by the Office of Vital Records p 572
- The notary does have a duty, however, to inform the party or parties of their rights and responsibilities p 572
- LA R.S. 9:392 requires that prior to the execution of an acknowledgment of paternity, that notary shall inform the mother and the alleged father of certain rights, including:
- Rights to genetic testing
- Rights to consult attorneys
- Rights to file paternity suits
- Rights of visitation
- Child support issues
- Inheritance issues
- Time frames for revocation of an act of acknowledgment by the father without cause p 572-573

Even though there is no statute that requires that this rights and responsibilities disclosure be signed, it would be the best practice to have a form and get it signed p 573

If the putative father voluntarily wants to filiate a child but does not have a form, the notary can prepare one in an authentic act. The act should include:

- Full and complete appearance clauses for all parties (including social security numbers)
- Sufficient information to identify the child being acknowledged, including date and place of birth
- Clear declaration by the father of his acknowledgment
- A concurrence by the mother if she is available and willing

The form for the *three-party acknowledgment* (see Chapter 12) is set forth in LA R.S. 40:34.5.1.

## Act of Adult Adoption

After the person to be adopted has reached the age of majority, he can be adopted by notarial act in certain circumstances p 575

- He can be adopted immediately, without the need for judicial authorization, if the adoptive parent is the spouse or surviving spouse of a parent of the person to be adopted p 575
    - Any other act of adult adoption must be done with judicial authority p 575

- The form for adult adoption must be an authentic act, executed by the parties *and* the spouses (for concurrence only) of the parties p 575
- The act of adult adoption cannot be done by a procuration nor by a mandate p 575 art 213
- A person may change their name in the act of adult adoption form p 576 LA RS 9:465
- The act of adult adoption (or judgment, if it is done judicially) must be recorded with the Clerk of Court in *any* parish in the conveyance records p 576 art 214, LA RS 9:463

## Act of Correction by Notary

- If a clerical error is made affecting movable or immovable property or any right affecting movable or immovable property, either the notary who prepared the act or the notary before whom the act was passed may correct the error by an act of correction p 576
- The correction is usually retroactive to the date of filing of the original property record p 576
- This is intended to correct minor typographical errors, not to make substantive changes p 576
- This act of correction is made before 2 witnesses and another notary p 576 LA RS 35:2.1
- This version of act of correction (unlike the one by parties, below), is always an *authentic act* (even if stated in the form of an affidavit by the original notary)
- Form and content of act, will contain, at a minimum:
    - An appearance clause
    - A description of the original instrument being corrected
    - A description of the error being corrected
    - The correct information being substituted for the erroneous information
    - The notary's authorization and request for the Clerk of Court to correct the original record

### *Act of Correction by Parties*

- An error in a notarial act affecting property or any other rights may be corrected by the act of all the parties to the original act p 577
- This act of correction by the parties can correct both minor typographical errors *and* make substantive changes to the agreement, such as reforming a contract p 577
- The form of the act of correction by the parties should comply with the form of the original act (i.e., if the original act was an authentic act, the correction should be an authentic act) p 578
- The act of correction by the parties should contain:
    - An appearance clause
    - A description of the original instrument being corrected
    - A description of the original language in the instrument
    - The new information being substituted
    - The parties' authorization and parties' request for the Clerk of Court to correct the information p 578

## Affidavit of Distinction

- When a person with a similar name to a judgment debtor finds himself with a judicial mortgage in error, he may need to file an Affidavit of Distinction p 578 LA RS 9:5501

- This affidavit is similar to an Affidavit of Identity p 578 LA RS 9:5503
- There is a sample form for the Affidavit of Distinction in the study guide p 579

## Building Contract (Private Works Act) Liens

- The Private Works Act establishes a privilege on an immovable to secure obligations of the owner for construction or repairs made by laborers, contractors, professional consultants, lessors, sellers of materials, equipment, and machinery used in construction p 581
- There are specific time limits that contractors, etc. have to file these liens p 581
- They must file within 60 days after notice of completion or abandonment of the work, or 70 days if the person filing is a seller of materials p 581 LA RS 9:4804
- Certain other notifications are required to the owner if the claimant is a professional consultant or a lessor of movables p 582 9:4823
- A statement of claim must be filed for a lien, even though the privilege arises by operation of law. The statement of claim must be filed in the proper time limits and must:
  - Be in writing
  - Be signed by the person asserting the claim
  - Contain a reasonable identification of the immovable
  - Describe the amount and nature of the obligation
  - Identify the owner who is liable p 583 LA RS 9:4831
- The statement of a claim or privilege must be filed with the recorder of mortgages in the parish where the work was performed and must contain a sufficient property description p 583 LA RS 9:4831
- This is a very complex and nuanced area of the law. Please proceed with caution.

## Certified Copy of Original Act by Notary

- A notary can make a certified true copy of an act executed by him p 584 art 1840
- A notary can execute the original act and make several certified true copies at the same time p 584 (This is particularly helpful for the client when executing a power of attorney.)
- A notarial act filed in the registry of the court may be copied and certified as true by the Clerk of Court p 585 art 1841 (Especially used for immovables in 2 or more parishes.)

### *Certified Copy of Lost Original Act*

- A notary public may issue a conforming copy of any act passed before him when the original has been lost p 585 LA RS 9:2758

### *Certified Copy for Executory Process*

- For the fast-track foreclosure process called the executory process, a certified true copy of any of the originals from the notary are sufficient for the process. A sample of the form for this submission is in the study guide p 585 LA RS 9:13:4102

### *Certified Copy of Original Document*

- Notaries cannot make certified copies of certain documents. But, we are asked to all the time. So, we can make a copy of the document and certify that the copy we made is a true copy of it. A form for this can be found in the study guide p 586

- A birth certificate cannot be certified by anyone other than the custodian of that record p 586

## Certificate of Custodian of Private Documents

- During discovery (a process involving evidence pre-trial in lawsuits), notaries may be asked to certify that documents maintained by private custodians, like medical records from a medical records clerk, are true copies from them, by making an affidavit in a form similar to the one in the study guide p 587

## Declaration of Intent to Change Domicile

- In addition to actually moving to a new place, a person may wish to file a Declaration of Intent to Change Domicile as a way to further cement their new domicile p 588

## Designation of Tutorship (Tutorship by Will)

- When 2 parents are alive and married, the child is under parental authority. When a parent dies, the remaining parent becomes the tutor (see Chapter 12 for a thorough discussion) p 588
- By notarial (authentic) act or by testament, the surviving parent may designate the tutor of any minor children upon their death p 588 art 257

## Jurat

- A jurat is a certification before an officer, placed at the end of an affidavit, stating someone appeared before you and swears that they made a statement under oath p 589
- It is also commonly the stamp we refer to with those words on it: "Sworn to and subscribed…"

## Limited Emancipation by Authentic Act

- Confers upon the minor the ability to make certain kinds of juridical acts, e.g. contracts p 589
- Effective on the date the authentic act is executed, without a need for filing p 589
- Limited emancipation does not relieve the parents from damages caused by their minor child (e.g., for torts) p 590 art 2318
- The parties to the limited emancipation, or a court for good cause, can modify or terminate it by a subsequent authentic act, but any act undertaken before modification or termination is still effective p 590
- The limited emancipation is effective when executed. But a modification or termination of it must be filed:
  o when movables are involved, in the conveyance records of the minor's domicile to be effective against third persons
  o when immovables are involved, in the conveyance records of the parish where the property is located to be effective against third persons p 590

## Matrimonial Agreement

- Must include:
  o Full appearance clause for each party
  o Declaration of the intent to marry, with dates, etc.
  o Declaration that they intend to alter the legal regime

## 29 ▪ MISCELLANEOUS ACTS

- o Recitation that they wish to enter a separate property regime
- o Signatures conforming to all statutory requirements (authentic act, or act under private signature duly acknowledged) p 590 art 2331
- Matrimonial agreement is effective between the spouses when signed, but effective toward third parties when recorded in the conveyance records:
  - o In the parish where immovables are situated, for immovables; or
  - o In the parish where the spouses are domiciled, for movables p 591 art 2332
- A matrimonial agreement may be entered into without court approval *before* a marriage; or within 1 year after moving domicile into the state of Louisiana from another state; or with judicial approval at any other time p 592 art 2329

## Non-Legal Custodian's Agreement

- A consent agreement for a "non-legal custodian" to give consent for a minor to receive medical or educational services p 592 LA RS 9:975
- This is valid for 1 year p 592
- There is a detailed sample in the study guide p 593

## Paraph

- The notary's instrument placed on the front of a document to connect and identify it with another instrument passed before the notary p 595
- Usually, this is done with a mortgage and the note is paraphed p 595
- A sample of paraph language is in the study guide p 595 (and in Chapter 21)

## Partition

- The division of property into physical shares p 595
- Partition may be voluntary or judicial, in which case the judge will appoint a notary p 596
- Content of the act of partition is the same as the act of exchange (see Chapter 21). The partitioners are called *exchangers* p 596
- The act of partition is a conveyance, and *must* include:
  - o Partitioners' declaration that they are owners in indivision of specifically described property
  - o The legal description of the property
  - o A declaration that the partitioners no longer wish to remain co-owners and wish to partition
  - o The recitation that each party accepts full and complete ownership of their portion
  - o The receiving party transfers all rights to all other portions
  - o The receiving party no longer has any interest in the land as a whole p 597
- The act of partition *may* include:
  - o Assumption of liabilities
  - o Discharges or waivers to end disputes
  - o Special agreements to change record of ownership p 597

- Note: if the land is not subdivided, it may be required to be subdivided by a municipality or other entity before it can be partitioned; check with local authorities.

## Protest

- A protest is a certificate of dishonor made by a notary that a check or other commercial paper was dishonored (rejected) when presented for payment p 597
- This is most commonly used on drafts drawn outside the United States

# 30

# Caveat Notarius (Cautionary Tales)

## Personal appearance of parties

- The parties signing must appear before you. It is the law and your duty to ensure their presence.
- If the parties do not appear before you, and you notarize a document, you are committing a false declaration on your part, and can be guilty of the crimes of misfeasance, fraud, forgery, or malfeasance p 608
- You may be required to testify, in court, that you witnessed a person sign a document p 608

### *Appearance alternatives*

- Affidavits and testaments must be executed in person by the person named, but some acts may allow an alternative appearance, such as a witness or party (personal) acknowledgment p 609
- But when an acknowledgement is duly acknowledged by a party to the act, it is considered self-proving only as to that party p 609
- Examples of appearance alternatives:
  - Witness acknowledgment: witnesses could have witnessed a sale and later acknowledged by one of the witnesses before a notary
  - Appearance by representation: procuration
  - Appearance by representative: under a specific power of attorney in a real estate sale
  - Appearances before multiple notaries: an act may circulate between notaries for multiple signatures
  - "Counterparts": multiple copies of the same act are executed for different people to execute (before one notary or multiple ones) and combine into one document p 610

## Strict adherence to requirements of form

- The form, *especially the authentic act*, must be enacted with the formality specified by the Civil Code or it can fail as a notarial act – and the notary can be liable for damages p 611

## Cash sales and disguised donations

- In any cash sale, the true intent of the parties must be expressed, or it can be considered lesionary and the sale can fail because it is a donation in disguise. The notary must be cognizant of his role and duty to the parties and the public, or he can be held accountable if someone challenges the execution of this transaction p 621
- Remember, we do not have "consideration" in Louisiana p 621 (as discussed in Chapter 11 on Contracts)

## Waiver of warranty – "as is" language

- Waiver of redhibition must conform to Civil Code art. 2548: be written in clear and unambiguous language, be contained in the sale document, and be brought to the attention of the buyer or explained to them p 623
- Prudent practice may be to include a paragraph at the end of the disclosure stating that the waiver of warranty has been included, read, and explained; and have the client initial that paragraph p 624

## Blank spaces in contracts

- Make sure all blank lines in contracts are filled out, or marked through, or blank pages marked as saying "This Page Intentionally Left Blank," so that unscrupulous persons don't insert pages that don't belong and alter the content of the contract (it happens) p 624

## Authenticating documents for your family or business

- There is no provision against acting as a notary for family, unless the notary is:
  - A legatee in a testament of a family member; or
  - The notary is a party to the transaction at hand p 625
- The prudent notary should not execute any instrument where he has any personal or pecuniary interest in the transaction (other than collecting his fee) p 626

## Attesting to signature only

- This is a complex area of the law. Attesting to signatures of complex documents is often unnerving, but of very little risk to the notary. In many such cases, the job of the non-attorney notary is to attest to the signature only, and not concern themselves with the contents of most documents (other than testaments, which must be read aloud).
- The issue with out-of-state mortgages (or in-state mortgages that are executed in multiple parts) which render a duty to the notary to record, is resolved by having the parties absolve the notary of the statutory recording duty, in writing p 627
- Disclaimers stating that the notary did not prepare any title examination, etc. should be placed in the body of the act itself, according to the study guide, although then the notary would have to re-prepare the documents. It may be easier to have the affiants execute an affidavit that absolves the notary of any liability for form or substance in the act p 628

## Acts in foreign language

- The language of the act is immaterial as long as it is in a language understood by all, *including the notary* – except for the formation of Articles of Incorporation, LLCs, and certain other documents presented to the Secretary of State, which must be in English p 630

# About the Author

MICHELE CHILDRESS is an attorney licensed in Louisiana, since 2002. She received her notary commission that same year. She earned her B.A. from Loyola University–New Orleans and her Juris Doctor degree from Loyola as well. She is a member of the Louisiana Bar Association with twenty years of experience in law and legal research. She has edited and produced modern editions of Joseph Story's *Commentaries on the Constitution of the United States* and Woodrow Wilson's *Constitutional Government in the United States*.

Michele is a commissioned Louisiana notary who, with her husband Alan, has owned a notary/shipping service in Jefferson Parish. She has performed thousands of notarial acts covering a wide range of subjects and formats. They offer remote prep seminars for the notary exam, live and recorded, through the website *www.notarysidepiece.com*.

If you have suggestions for improving this outline, please email *quidprolaw@gmail.com*.

Visit us at *www.quidprobooks.com*.

www.ingramcontent.com/pod-product-compliance
Lightning Source LLC
Chambersburg PA
CBHW080432230426
43662CB00015B/2257